ROUTLEDGE · E

GENERAL EDITOR

D0129766

WILLIAM WORDSWORTH

Selected Poetry and Prose

ROUTLEDGE · ENGLISH · TEXTS
GENERAL EDITOR · JOHN DRAKAKIS

WILLIAM WORDSWORTH

Selected Poetry and Prose

Edited by
Philip Hobsbaum

LONDON AND NEW YORK

First published in 1989 by
Routledge
11 New Fetter Lane, London EC4P 4EE
29 West 35th Street, New York NY 10001

Reprinted 1991

Introduction, Critical commentary, and Notes
© 1989 Philip Hobsbaum

Printed in Great Britain
by T.J. Press (Padstow) Ltd, Cornwall

British Library Cataloguing in
Publication Data

Wordsworth, William, 1770–1850–
    [Selections]. William Wordsworth:
    selected poetry and prose.
    I. Title   II. Hobsbaum, Philip, 1932–
    828'.709

    ISBN 0–415–01605–3

Library of Congress Caataloging in
Publication Data

Wordsworth, William, 1770–1850.
    [Selections, 1988]
    Selected poetry and prose/William
    Wordsworth; edited by Philip Hobsbaum.
    p.   cm. –(Routledge English texts)
    Bibliography: p.
    ISBN 0–415–01605–3
    I. Hobsbaum, Philip,   II. Title.
    III. Series.
PR5853.H57   1988
821'.7–dc19   88–23663

For Patrick and Rose Reilly

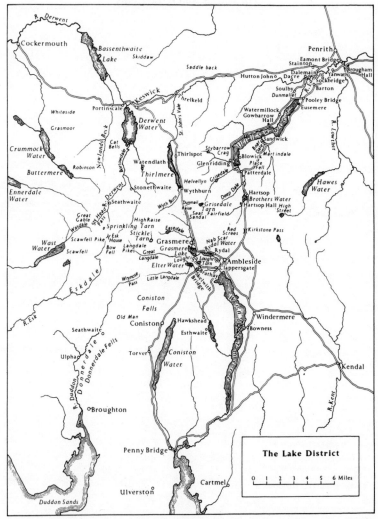

MAP 1

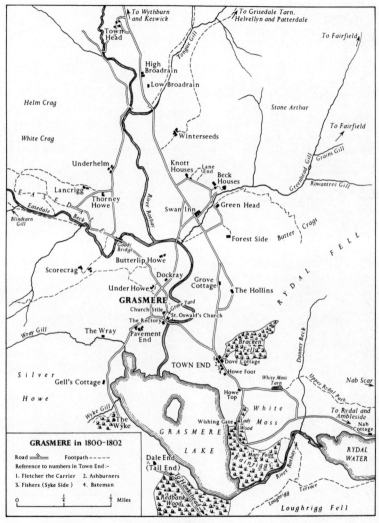

To Wythburn and Keswick
To Grisedale Tarn, Helvellyn and Patterdale
To Fairfield

Town Head
High Broadrain
Low Broadrain
Tongue Gill

Helm Crag
Stone Arthur
To Fairfield

White Crag
Winterseeds

Underhelm
Knott Houses
Lane End
Beck Houses
Grains Gill
Greenhead Gill
Rowantrec Gill

Lancrigg
Thorney Howe
Swan Inn
Green Head

E—A—E—D
Easedale Beck
Blindtarn Gill
Forest Side
Butter Crags

RYDAL FELL

Goody Bridge
Butterlip Howe
Scorecrag
Dockray
Grove Cottage
The Hollins

Under Howe
GRASMERE
Grave Yard
Church Stile
St. Oswald's Church
Dunney Beck

Wray Gill
The Rectory
The Wray
Pavement End
Bracken Fella

Silver
Howe
Gell's Cottage
TOWN END
Dove Cottage
Howe Foot
White Moss Tarn
Nab Scar
Upper Rydal Path

Wyke Gill
The Wyke
GRASMERE LAKE
Howe Top
White Moss
Wishing Gate
Lady Wood
To Rydal and Ambleside
Nab Cottage

RYDAL WATER

Dale End (Tail End)
Fairfield
Mary Point
River Rothay

GRASMERE in 1800-1802

Road ⚌⚌ Footpath - - - -
Reference to numbers in Town End :-
1. Fletcher the Carrier   2. Ashburners
3. Fishers (Syke Side)   4. Bateman

0   ¼   ½   Miles

Redbank Wood
Loughrigg Terrace
Loughrigg Fell

MAP 2

Contents

Preface

This is a book by Wordsworth; it is also a book about Wordsworth. The good intentions of editors and critics have, for the most part, tended to obscure the achievement of one of England's greatest poets. As F. R. Leavis put it, 'you can't tell a student to look through his copy of the Wordsworth in the Oxford Standard Authors and mark the poems that in his opinion are worth going back to. There are nine hundred small-print double-column pages'. That was the edition, by Thomas Hutchinson, on which the present editor was brought up, and it would be churlish not to acknowledge it. Yet, for all its inclusiveness, it prints an inferior version of *The Prelude*, it conceals 'The ruined cottage' in Book First of *The Excursion*, and it leaves out poems such as 'Home at Grasmere' and 'St Paul's' that many a discerning reader would prefer to (say) the bulk of *Lyrical Ballads* (1798). Nobody said that the second volume, *Lyrical Ballads* (1800, *sc.* 1801), was a genuinely separate collection, containing as it did masterpieces such as 'Nutting', 'Poems on the naming of places', and 'Michael'.

Here, then, is a selection of the poems which the editor takes to be the best of Wordsworth, in (what is not true of previous selections) the best versions. It will not prevent the reader from frequenting other editions. Indeed, at the time of writing, the Cornell Wordsworth is still in progress, providing the *aficionado* with variant readings of even the most recondite texts. But one has to start somewhere, and the present edition is designed to supply an answer to the question, 'What makes Wordsworth a great poet?', with a text backed up by a biographical introduction and a critical commentary, as well as by explanatory notes.

The editor is conscious of debts to past colleagues, notably that great Wordsworthian, W. J. Harvey, whose untimely death prevented the completion of what would have been a major study; also the late Diane Macdonell who, 'before her summer faded', produced a remarkable post-structuralist reading of Wordsworth. But the crucial debts are to the living: to Paddy Lyons, who suggested that I undertake the present edition; to John Drakakis, who commissioned it; Ingrid Swanson, whose help with other responsibilities expedited this one; Janice Mackay, who typed the final manuscript with insight and efficiency; my wife, Rosemary, for her patience and forbearance; and Patrick and Rose Reilly, to whom the edition is dedicated, for encouragement over the years with this and many other projects.

Introduction

William Wordsworth was born at Cockermouth in the county of
Cumberland, north-west England, on 7 April 1770. His father, John
Wordsworth, was an attorney who became business manager to Sir
James Lowther, a principal landlord in this area; the Lake District, as
it is called. Wordsworth's mother, Ann, was the daughter of
William Cookson, a linen-draper who had married into the family of
a long line of squires. The poet himself was the second of five
children. Richard, the eldest, became a lawyer like his father, and
practised as a solicitor in London. Dorothy, third eldest, was the close
companion of the poet through most of his adult life. John, also close
to William, went to sea and rose to become a merchant captain in the
service of the East India Company. The youngest, Christopher,
found distinguished patronage while serving as a clergyman, and
ended his career as Master of Trinity College, Cambridge.

The family lived in the largest house in Cockermouth and were
reasonably well-to-do. They would have been even better off had the
father obtained a regular salary from his employer. Instead, he accu-
mulated against Sir James Lowther's estate a claim which eventually
became the subject of legal dispute. It may seem strange that this
practical man of affairs should have a dreamy side to his nature, but it
was so. In the leisure time left over from rent-collecting and
foreclosure, John Wordsworth encouraged his son William to read
and learn by heart portions of the English poets that were his own
favourites, such as Spenser, Shakespeare, and Milton. He could not
have foreseen that his son would grow up to be their peer.

From his earliest years, the young Wordsworth loved to wander 'in the high places, on the lonesome peaks, / Among the mountains and the winds'. This turning to the natural forms of landscape was intensified by the sudden death of his mother in 1778 and the resultant breaking up of the family home at Cockermouth. Dorothy was sent to her mother's cousin in Halifax, across the Pennines; and the brothers went to live with their grandparents at Penrith, and were all sent, as soon as they were old enough, to be boarders at Archbishop Sandys's School in Hawkshead, some 25 precipitous miles away in the neighbouring county of Westmorland. Pupils came there from as far afield as Carlisle and Lancaster, and many of Wordsworth's contemporaries were to distinguish themselves as scholars and clergymen. The headmaster was a Fellow of Emmanuel College, Cambridge, William Taylor, of whom Wordsworth was to write, 'He loved the poets'. Taylor died prematurely in 1786, and his successor, Thomas Bowman, directed the young Wordsworth's attention to the latest tendencies in the poetry of the time. These were in strong contrast to Dryden, Pope, and Johnson, who had ruled the literary world, so to speak, from the metropolis. Wordsworth responded, rather, to James Thomson, forerunner of Romanticism; his disciple, Mark Akenside, who in turn influenced William Cowper, pioneer of what was to be Wordsworth's own meditative-descriptive mode; and the early Romantic, Helen Maria Williams. This last was the subject of Wordsworth's first published poem, a sonnet which appeared in the *European Magazine* for March 1787 when he was 17: 'She wept. – Life's purple tide began to flow / In languid streams through every thrilling vein'.

Already the young radical had allied himself to a novel concept of the artist as figure of authority. He was to declare 'poetry is the spontaneous overflow of powerful feelings; it takes its origin from emotion recollected in tranquillity'. This is one of the crucial definitions of Romanticism. Luckily for Wordsworth, he was able to build upon it.

Wordsworth's father had died in 1783, and his uncles, Christopher Crackanthorpe Cookson and Richard Wordsworth, became his guardians. He never got on with the former, but Richard, his father's elder brother, helped him to go to Cambridge with a loan that, however, was not paid off for almost twenty years. Wordsworth entered St John's College in 1787, and it was expected that he would work for a Fellowship and end up as some superior kind of clergyman. But he neglected the mathematics necessary for this, and eventually gave up any pretence of pursuing an academic career: 'The poet's soul was with me at that time, / Sweet meditations'. Part of his first summer vacation was spent at Hawkshead, revisiting the old peasant woman with whom he had boarded as a schoolboy. He also went over to Penrith, where his mother had lived before she had married. There, on only the second or third occasion since they were small children, he saw his sister Dorothy who, as an economy measure, had been removed from her adopted home in Halifax and had come to live with their grandparents. He found her a tiny creature, and later was to write of the 'shooting lights' of her 'wild eyes'. Wordsworth also met, as a grown woman, Dorothy's friend Mary Hutchinson, whom he may have remembered from their time together in nursery school.

Wordsworth's feelings as a result of this return to his early environment gave rise to a nostalgic poem, *An Evening Walk*, addressed to Dorothy: 'Where peace to Grasmere's lonely island leads, / To willowy hedgerows and to emerald meads'. He wrote this at Cambridge instead of taking his examinations, but he kept the university terms in order to obtain a pass degree. In his third summer vacation he decided to go on a pedestrian tour through France and the Swiss Alps.

Wordsworth had a companion on this venture, a college friend intending to be a clergyman. Though not dissimilar in background, and certainly short of cash, the Welshman, Robert Jones, was a contrast physically. He was plump and rosy, while Wordsworth had already acquired the tough, bony, awkward figure of his middle years. They reached Calais in July 1790 and went due south, walking on average 20 miles a day. Wordsworth thrilled to the first flush of enthusiasm over the French Revolution: 'France standing on the top of golden hours, / And human nature seeming born again'. By September they had crossed the Alps and from Basle they travelled by boat down the Rhine, returning to England via Belgium. The aspiring poet took his degree in January 1791; spending the earlier months of that year in London, the summer with Robert Jones in Wales. He found himself facing difficulties with his uncles Crackanthorpe and Wordsworth, who could not understand why he did not choose a profession. However, he managed to persuade his elder brother,

Richard, to intercede with the uncle of the same name for a further loan in support of a sojourn in France, so that his knowledge of the language might be improved.

Wordsworth went to Orléans and, in the three months he stayed there, became involved with Annette Vallon, the daughter of a surgeon whose widow had remarried. Wordsworth continued his relationship with this young lady in her home town of Blois, where she discovered she was pregnant. There is a reference to the wrath of her family in a poem written ten years after the event, 'Vaudracour and Julia': 'To conceal / The threatened shame the parents of the maid / Found means to hurry her away by night'. Annette bore their illegitimate child, Caroline, in Orléans on 15 December 1792. By that time Wordsworth had been in Paris which, in the aftermath of the September Massacres, 'seemed a place of fear. . . . Defenceless as a wood where tigers roam'. He had hastened to London and was apparently unable to maintain contact with Annette Vallon after France declared war against Britain in February 1793. Fear of mob rule forced him from the radical stand of his youth to follow a political path which led him eventually into an entrenched conservatism.

The annoyance of Wordsworth's uncles at his unaccountable behaviour was exacerbated to breaking-point when the news about Annette came to light. *An Evening Walk* and *Descriptive Sketches*, the latter poem written during this second French sojourn, came out from a London publisher as two small separate volumes in 1793, and attracted little attention. Wordsworth was glad enough in June to tour to the Isle of Wight and to Salisbury as the paid companion of a former school-friend, William Calvert. But their travelling-carriage broke down, and Wordsworth, in a state of depression, went on by himself, traversing Salisbury Plain and ending up with Robert Jones at his father's house in North Wales. He later stayed with William Calvert and his brother, Raisley, back in Cumberland. Indeed, in May they put their house at his disposal, and he installed Dorothy there to keep him company. For the first time since childhood, brother and sister were living *en famille*. Dorothy was able to inaugurate her vocation as amanuensis to her brother by transcribing into legible script a poem he had been writing about his adventures after he parted with Calvert on Salisbury Plain. In June, however, she was left with friends near Barrow-in-Furness so that Wordsworth could nurse Raisley Calvert through what was to be a terminal illness.

Raisley died in January 1795, in gratitude making Wordsworth a bequest to advance him a step on his way towards independence. A further step was taken in February when Wordsworth went on to London. He met a Cambridge contemporary, Basil Montagu, who had been recently widowed and was finding difficulty in combining his law practice with bringing up his small son. He proposed that Wordsworth and Dorothy should take up residence, rent free, in a vacant house called Racedown Lodge, about 10 miles from the Dorset coast, which belonged to the father of some friends of his. There the Wordsworths could make a home for the boy in return for an annual payment from himself. The consequence was that William and Dorothy Wordsworth, and the small Basil, moved to Racedown in September 1795. Through economy in housekeeping, ever afterwards their habit, they managed to subsist.

The Pinneys, in whose father's house this new family now lived, introduced Wordsworth to Joseph Cottle, a publisher in Bristol, and to Samuel Taylor Coleridge, also at the time resident in the city. Coleridge, who was to become the greatest critic of that and perhaps of any other age, with an eye that (as Dorothy wrote) spoke every emotion of his animated mind, must have seemed even at this stage a visionary. He had not completed his degree at Cambridge, where he had come into residence the year Wordsworth went down. Instead, he intended to start an egalitarian community in Pennsylvania, USA, together with another young poet, Robert Southey, whose sister-in-law, Sara Fricker, he had recently married. Coleridge had already been impressed by *The Evening Walk* and *Descriptive Sketches*, and his friendship with Wordsworth, who hungered for recognition as a writer, was to intensify as the American scheme lapsed.

Dorothy's friend, Mary Hutchinson, came to stay at Racedown in November 1796, remaining till June the following year. Coleridge, with whom Wordsworth had been in correspondence, followed her as house guest. He listened, enraptured, to Wordsworth's reading of 'The ruined cottage', a poem related to the adventures on Salisbury Plain, and declared to all who would hear him that his new friend was the greatest poet since Milton; a proposition which looks more discussible now than it must have seemed then.

That year, 1797–8, was for Wordsworth the *annus mirabilis*: from that period emanate some of his finest poems. He wrote himself that Dorothy 'preserved me still a poet' and that Coleridge lent a 'living

5

help / To regulate my soul'. This friendship filled a vacancy in Coleridge's life, too, for his marriage to the wholly unintellectual Sara Fricker was not turning out well. He was determined to bring the Wordsworths closer to him, and negotiated through his patron, Thomas Poole, their renting of Alfoxden House which was adjacent to his own current residence at Nether Stowey, in the lee of the Quantock Hills. Wordsworth moved his little family up to Somerset in July 1797. Proximity to Coleridge brought about plans for the production of their respective tragedies, *The Borderers* and *Osorio*; for a huge philosophical poem to be written by Wordsworth and to be called *The Recluse*; for a joint publication to be called *Lyrical Ballads*. This last was the only one of these plans to reach fruition. It proved to be a collection of poems concerned with rustic life written by Wordsworth, together with Coleridge's sophisticated rehandling of ballad form, a tale of the supernatural called 'The rime of the ancyent marinere'.

The new home at Alfoxden brought many visitors, and their readings and ramblings attracted unsympathetic notice from the neighbours. It was a time when English people feared either a revolution, similar to that which had already taken place across the Channel, or an outright invasion. Talk of spies was heard everywhere, so the Alfoxden tenancy was not allowed to continue beyond midsummer 1798. Young Basil Montagu, whose keep for some time had not been forthcoming from his father, was deposited with an aunt. The Wordsworths solved the problem of their homelessness by going off on a walking tour. First they went to the Wye Valley, where Wordsworth composed 'Tintern Abbey', then, with Coleridge, to Wales. Coleridge produced a further solution to their troubles by proposing that they all go to Germany for several years, partly to learn the language, partly so that he could promote his philosophical interests. It took until September to organize finances, and this was done mainly by borrowing money from anyone willing to lend it to them. Coleridge had actually landed an annuity, from the Wedgewoods of pottery fame.

William and Dorothy Wordsworth, together with Coleridge and his young neighbour, John Chester, reached Hamburg in September 1798. After a fortnight, Coleridge and Chester went to the island resort of Ratzeburg, 'all in high life among Barons, counts and countesses', said Dorothy later, 'we should have been ruined'.

Instead the Wordsworths took the more modest course of going to Goslar 'whose melancholy walls . . . once imperial' stood conveniently near to the Harz mountains which were rumoured to be spectacular. In fact, however, the winter set in so bitterly as to prevent even these hardy specimens venturing from their lodgings, and such inhabitants as they met proved to be petty tradespeople, 'a low and selfish race', wrote Dorothy. Thrown back on his memories, and frightened by a severe influenza which Dorothy had contracted, Wordsworth wrote three of the 'Lucy' poems commemorating the death of an imaginary girl, and also the earliest and most inspired version of the autobiographical poem which came to be known much later as *The Prelude*.

The thaw of February 1799 found Wordsworth and Dorothy walking through the Harz Mountains, making their way ultimately to England. From May onwards they spent seven months working on a farm in Sockburn-on-Tees, County Durham, leased by their friends, the Hutchinsons. Here Wordsworth renewed his acquaintance with Mary of that ilk. He found that in his absence Cottle had published *Lyrical Ballads* and that, although adversely reviewed, the collection had sold out. Wordsworth wanted to secure a larger London market for a new edition by transferring the copyright from Cottle to the publishers who had produced *An Evening Walk* and *Descriptive Sketches*. He invited the Bristol man up to Sockburn for a northern tour. Cottle duly arrived, accompanied by Coleridge who perceived the advantage of a free trip. This was how Coleridge first met not only Mary Hutchinson but her younger sister, Sara. Slight, girlish and enthusiastic, this other Sara seemed to the great critic far more congenial than his wife. But he did not have long in which to cultivate the acquaintance. Only two days after the arrival of the gentlemen from the south, Wordsworth took them off to admire the glories of his own terrain, the Lake District. It was now October, and the rheumaticky Cottle got no further than Greta Bridge, in the foothills of the Pennines. But the remaining travellers encountered further on their route Wordsworth's seafaring brother, John, and continued with him along the lake of Haweswater, making a southward detour around the highest of the mist-hung mountains until they got to Bowness, going across Windermere by ferry, and so to Hawkshead. Wordsworth, it is plain, was on a homing voyage and, when the party reached Grasmere, he knew this to be the place where he had to live. Coleridge, deeply impressed by a world of scenery absolutely new to him, toured for a fortnight but returned to Sockburn where he improved his acquaintance with Sara Hutchinson. Wordsworth, however, took a tiny house in Grasmere, one of a group called Town-End, now singled out as 'Dove Cottage'. He and Dorothy moved there in December 1799.

This was to be the Wordsworths' residence for eight and a half years. A series of rambles to familiarize themselves with the contiguous sectors of Westmorland resulted in, among other works, the evocative 'Poems on the naming of places'. These walks were described with preternatural powers of observation in Dorothy Wordsworth's *Grasmere Journals*, not published in her lifetime; there had been a precedent journal, only in parts surviving, at Alfoxden. At the end of June Coleridge, who had decided to join this community in the Lakes, arrived with his unenthusiastic wife, Sara, and his 4-year-old son, Hartley; another child had died while he was in Germany. Coleridge rented Greta Hall, a comfortable house in Keswick. It was some 13 miles away from the Wordsworths; but this proved to be no distance at all for such experienced walkers. On the contrary, it had the advantage of keeping Sara Coleridge outside the immediate circle. Wordsworth showed Coleridge the lyric poems he had been writing; his critical friend, however, was interested only in *The Recluse*. In self-defence, so to speak, Wordsworth began a series of 'songs' prelusive to the still unwritten work, but only two were finished. 'The brothers' was a dialogue showing John Wordsworth returning from sea to his native mountains at long last only to find the poet dead. 'Michael' was a narrative of silent suffering; the story of a shepherd and his son. Only one piece of writing can reasonably be considered part of *The Recluse*, and that is a descriptive poem called 'Home at Grasmere', which recounts the Wordsworths' pleasure at settling in their native Lake District. This, however, did not amount to the work Coleridge had in contemplation.

What did transpire was the new edition of *Lyrical Ballads* with additional poems, published in London early in 1801. It includes a preface from Wordsworth outlining his approach to literature. The polemical tone he adopted created a false dichotomy between art and nature, and gave many of his readers the impression that he was trying to write poetry in the language of peasants. Coleridge was later to make the necessary distinctions between theory and practice

8

in his book *Biographia Literaria*. At present, however, he felt the Lake District weather was beyond his capacity of endurance, and went off to London before the winter of 1801 set in. He left behind at Greta Hall his wife and two children, one born as recently as September. He did, it must be said, return in March.

Wordsworth laboured over a revision of 'The ruined cottage' and wrote some of what in future years were to be his anthology pieces: 'I wandered lonely as a cloud', 'To the cuckoo', 'My heart leaps up', and the first four stanzas of the 'Ode: intimations of immortality'. A third edition of *Lyrical Ballads* appeared in 1802; but Wordsworth made no attempt to put the more recent poems into a companion volume.

Mary Hutchinson, now Wordsworth's friend as much as Dorothy's, had been a constant visitor at 'Dove Cottage' between 1800 and 1801, and she and Wordsworth had decided to get married as soon as the financial horizon brightened. But before their union could take place, there were certain other matters to be settled. In August 1802, Wordsworth and Dorothy were enabled by the Peace of Amiens to make a visit to Calais to see Annette Vallon and her 9-year-old daughter, Caroline. The Wordsworths stayed for a month; presumably some financial transactions took place. Though Annette called herself Madame Williams, the name Wordsworth being hard to pronounce in a French intonation, as far as the poet was concerned she belonged to a past context. No doubt war had put diffi-culties in the way of Wordsworth's either joining her in France or bringing her to England, and during that lapse of time the attraction, such it was, faded.

For Wordsworth, at any rate, the way was clear. The long-standing debt due to the family from their late father's employer had been settled by that magnate's heir; and a distribution of funds among the siblings took place. Dorothy's little independence ensured that she was promoted to the position of paying guest without losing her function as secretary and housekeeper. The burden, however, was about to be shared. Wordsworth's marriage to Mary Hutchinson took place on 4 October 1802, at Brompton Church near Gallow Hill Farm, North Yorkshire, where Mary had been keeping house for her brother Tom, who had moved from Sockburn a couple of years previously. She seems to have been a tall dark-haired woman, benevo-lent but scant of speech, whose stately looks were intriguingly variegated by what, in one of her unaffected letters, she termed her 'squinty eye'. She gave birth to a son, John, in June 1803, and was by August deemed well enough to be left behind while Wordsworth, Dorothy and Coleridge set off for a tour of Scotland.

The trio had a jaunting-car, Irish style, drawn by an old horse. Coleridge complained a good deal about this, and also about his health, until Wordsworth suggested that he split off and make his way direct to Edinburgh, which was their destination. Instead, however, he took an eccentric itinerary through the rainbeaten Highlands, covering on foot by his own account 260 miles in eight days. The Wordsworths, lightened of their incubus, got as far north as Glencoe, then back by the Trossachs, Falkirk, and Edinburgh, to Lasswade, where they met the then poet and future novelist, Walter Scott, who remained a firm friend. Once returned to Grasmere in the autumn, Dorothy began an evocation of the scenery in her *Recollections of a Tour Made in Scotland*, while Wordsworth wrote some resonant poems on the subject.

Coleridge reappeared at 'Dove Cottage' in December 1803, ill from incessant laudanum-drinking and determined to go to a warmer climate. A useful contact procured him a government post in Malta. His imminent departure impelled Wordsworth to produce a collection of poems for Coleridge to take abroad. The collection was to include a further revision of 'The ruined cottage' and what we now recognize to have been the first five books of the 1805 *Prelude*; of course, this autobiographical poem had not yet acquired that name. The effort was not that of Wordsworth alone: making fair copies of his tumultuous manuscripts, and further copies for home consumption, kept Mary and Dorothy busy. Coleridge left the Lake District in January 1804, before the copying was completed, but he was able to receive a packet posted to him at Dunmow, Essex, where he was staying with his wealthy friends, the Beaumonts. He did not actually reach Malta till April.

The Wordsworth circle, nevertheless, expanded. Robert Southey had brought his wife up to Greta Hall in the autumn of 1803 to join her sister and her eminent brother-in-law for a holiday. As it turned out, Southey was to be domiciled there for the rest of his life; Coleridge's children, by the dereliction of their father, being raised alongside Southey's own. An even more distinguished writer, William Hazlitt, spent that same autumn in Keswick; and a young aspirant, Thomas De Quincey, began writing to Wordsworth in praise of his work, and was to become his close acquaintance from the autumn of 1807, and subsequent neighbour. Hazlitt in *The Spirit of the Age* and De Quincey in his *Recollections of the Lakes and the Lake Poets* have left us their impressions of Wordsworth at that time. Both comment upon his extraordinary depth of character, as instanced in his power of eye and the rugged harmony of his voice. However slighting the attitudes of Wordsworth's reviewers, he was in process of gathering together a remarkable band of advocates.

There was, however, an untimely bereavement. John, after Dorothy the dearest to Wordsworth of all his siblings, was lost together with his ship off Portland Bill, a promontory jutting out from the south coast of England. He was commemorated in the year that he died, 1805, by the formal but moving 'Elegaic stanzas': 'Not without hope we suffer and we mourn'. There were, with the passing of time, additions to the family: Wordsworth's second child, Dora, had been born in 1804, the year of Coleridge's departure; Thomas in 1806; Catharine in 1808; William in 1810. Mary's sister, Sara Hutchinson, lived with the Wordsworths from 1805, and as early as 1806 they were thinking of a move from 'Dove Cottage' to a larger place. They had arranged to spend the winter of that year at the hall farm attached to the estate of Coleorton, the Leicestershire seat of Sir George and Lady Beaumont, Coleridge's friends. But just as arrangements had been made, they heard that Coleridge had returned from Malta and was about to reappear in the Lake District. Months passed, but there was no further communication. The Wordsworths were at last setting off south when a note came to announce that their friend was at hand. They all managed to meet at Kendal to find Coleridge very much altered for the worse, a seemingly hopeless addict to opium. The once speaking eyes, Dorothy wrote, were now lost in flesh like those of a person in dropsy. Since he declared himself definitively separated from his wife, the Wordsworths invited him down to Coleorton, and he spent the winter with them there. His continued obsession with Sara Hutchinson, who was present as one of the family, made life difficult. In spite of this, Wordsworth was able to gather the shorter poems he had written since *Lyrical Ballads* and bring them out as *Poems, in Two Volumes* in April 1807.

Posterity has favoured these pieces; but, at the time, they were attacked. Most notable among the adverse voices was that of Francis

Jeffrey, writing in the *Edinburgh Review*, who found the poems 'low, silly and uninteresting'. The volume failed to achieve a substantial sale, and Wordsworth withdrew from a potential publisher his latest narrative poem, finished in 1808, *The White Doe of Rylstone*. He had hoped to make some money from this imitation of the then fabulously popular Walter Scott; nevertheless, he still took on the tenancy of a larger house in Grasmere, Allan Bank. The rooms were draughty and the chimneys smoked, but this did not deter Coleridge, who was in residence from September 1808 to May 1810. For most of that period Sara Hutchinson acted as his amanuensis, helping especially with a magazine he had started called *The Friend*. But his increasingly anti-social behaviour, the result of drug addiction, eventually drove her out to the farm in mid-Wales which her brother Tom now worked. After a few weeks Coleridge also left, to stay with his estranged wife and their in-laws, the Southeys, at Greta Hall. A further visitor to Allan Bank was Basil Montagu, whose son Wordsworth and Dorothy had looked after in their Racedown and Alfoxden days. Confident in his third marriage and a successful law practice, Montagu decided to take Coleridge back with him to London, instal him in his house, and see what his own doctor could do for him. Wordsworth, perhaps injudiciously, gave Montagu a warning as to the intemperate habits of his proposed guest. When down in London, Montagu – very injudiciously – repeated Wordsworth's warning to Coleridge. This caused a tremendous quarrel, and Coleridge, already separated from his wife, now estranged himself from his closest friend.

In February 1812 Coleridge was in Wordsworth's vicinity – the family had the previous year moved to the old Grasmere Rectory – but he did not call. Wordsworth felt this rudeness keenly enough to go to London in April and attempt some kind of reconciliation. An ancillary outcome was that Wordsworth, staying at the great town house of Sir George Beaumont, found himself to be a literary lion. While he was away, however, his 4-year-old daughter, Catharine, died from a seizure, the aftermath of an illness, possibly encephalitis, contracted a few months previously. She is the figure invoked in one of Wordsworth's most poignant sonnets, 'Surprized by joy'. Six months later, in December, his son Thomas died of pneumonia following an attack of measles. But even this second loss did not bring Coleridge to his side. Wordsworth resumed work on *The Excursion* which for many years had been building up from the clear-cut narrative

12

of 'The ruined cottage' to an immense dialogue taking place between a Wanderer, a Solitary, a Pastor, and the poet himself. The work was completed in 1814, and came out that year to a reception even more hostile than that directed at the *Poems* of 1807. Predictably to the fore was Francis Jeffrey who began his *Edinburgh Review* critique with the admonitory words, 'This will never do', though he did allow that there were single lines that sparkled like gems in a desert.

By now the family had moved once more. In May 1813 they went from the Rectory, which had proved damp, to a gentrified farm-house, 2 miles from Grasmere along the road to Ambleside. The house had been renamed Rydal Mount, and it was to be Wordsworth's home for the remainder of his life. That life had stabilized in other respects as his political sympathies aligned themselves to the right. Lord Lonsdale, heir to the magnate who had employed Wordsworth's father, in this year secured for Wordsworth the post of Distributor of Stamps for Westmorland and Penrith. The work was concerned with the collection of Inland Revenue duties on wills, licences, and legal documents of a kindred nature. It brought in enough income for a clerk to be employed in the commission of basic tasks; in his spare time he copied out Wordsworth's manuscripts. Thus the household was kept going and the children educated. One son went to Sedbergh, the other for a time to the Charterhouse; a demonstration, if one were needed, that their father had become a firm Tory. In 1818 John Keats, who had met Wordsworth in London, called at Rydal Mount. But the master of the house was out campaigning in favour of his patron's sons, both parliamentary candidates in adjacent pocket boroughs.

A further Scottish tour took place in 1814, with Mary, Sara, and young John. They met James Hogg, poet and folklorist, popularly called the Ettrick Shepherd; he visited Rydal Mount shortly afterwards. A collected edition of Wordsworth's poems came out in 1815, and the previously withheld *White Doe of Rylstone* was published the same year. Richard Wordsworth, the elder brother, died in 1816, leaving Dorothy what would have been called in that era a modest competence. Coleridge, in the same year, had put himself into the hands of a doctor under whose care, at a house in Highgate, north of London, he managed to finish his critical work, *Biographia Literaria*. This came out in 1817 and included a sustained account of Wordsworth's poetry in relation to its author's theories.

In February 1816, Wordsworth's illegitimate daughter, Caroline, had been married to Jean-Baptiste Baudouin, a junior civil servant. She signed her name at the ceremony as 'A. C. Wordsworth', but her father did not go to Paris to give her away. A proxy stood in for him as godfather to her daughter, Louise Marie Caroline Dorothée, born in December of the same year. The previous month an illegitimate son had been born to De Quincey, resident at Dove Cottage since 1809, by a farm-girl whom he subsequently married. Wordsworth found his conduct inexcusable, and he was henceforth excluded from the Circle.

Wordsworth had been revising his narrative, *Peter Bell*, begun in 1798, and it came out in 1819 to a chorus of not undeserved ridicule. The poem would have made more sense if published when first written, in the context of *Lyrical Ballads*. Wordsworth's itinerary as Stamp Distributor gave rise to work that did him more credit: a sonnet sequence on the River Duddon appeared in 1820. In the same year there was a tour of the Continent with Mary and Dorothy, in part retracing the path of his early excursion with Robert Jones. This was worked into a sonnet cycle, together with a further sequence called *Ecclesiastical Sonnets*. There were other tours, and other sonnets, but most of Wordsworth's literary effort was expended in putting together a five-volume collected edition of his work and attempting a final version of the still unnamed *Prelude*. This poem had appeared only in extracts and was now meant to be published posthumously.

Sara Hutchinson, who had made her home with her brother-in-law and sister for thirty years, died in 1835, and Dorothy, who had been severely ill some six years previously, collapsed under a form of senile dementia now called Alzheimer's disease. Wordsworth's old friends dropped away: Scott and Crabbe had died in 1832, Coleridge and Lamb in 1834, Felicia Hemans, one of the first professional women poets, in 1835. These, and the ostensible subject of Wordsworth's final masterpiece, 'Extempore effusion upon the death of James Hogg', were vigorously eulogized in a metre the aging poet had never previously attempted. A worse blow even than any of these was the death of his daughter Dora in 1847. She had been the last of his long line of female helpers, more necessary to him than ever as his eyesight deteriorated. He had witnessed with reluctance her marriage some six years previously to a former soldier, one of his most ardent admirers, the widowed Edward Quillinan. In spite of these bereavements, Wordsworth appeared to continue in his normal courses, and certainly over the years he was visited by admirers such as the Wilberforces, the Arnolds, F. W. Faber together with various students, and John Stuart Mill. Wordsworth died of pneumonia on 23 April 1850, at the last mistaking a young visitor to his sickroom for Dora.

The enfeebled Dorothy, who was nursed for twenty years with the solicitude she had in earlier life extended to others, died in 1855, and that silent monitor, Mary Wordsworth, who had been blind for some time, followed her in 1859 when almost 90. It was Mary who had given *The Prelude* the title which now seems so inevitable. As Wordsworth intended, the poem came out posthumously; remaining, however, a puzzle to many of the poet's admirers. *The Prelude* was omitted from several editions of the poetical works on grounds of inferiority. Much could be said against the '1850' version of the poem – in fact finalized in 1839 – but it remains a distinguished work. The '1805' version, developed into a thirteen-book poem from the five-book version of 1804, is more lively and familiar; this, however, was not published until 1926. The 1798–9 *Prelude*, preferable to either of the other versions, appeared in print only in the 1970s. At the present time of writing, the Cornell edition of Wordsworth is in progress, treating even his slightest drafts with care, publishing photocopies and transcripts of many variants. The interpretation of Wordsworth has, even now, not come to a close.

The selection that follows is unusual to this extent, that it does not seek to represent all phases of Wordsworth's work. Rather it is an attempt to show the achievement of the poet at its very best. This has led to the exclusion of several Lyrical Ballads, of *The Excursion* and the '1850' *Prelude*, and such poems as *The White Doe of Rylstone* and *Peter Bell*. Included, however, is the little-known 'Home at Grasmere' which is the basis for *The Excursion* and in many respects preferable as a poem. Many readers will expect to find certain pieces which, in the present editor's view, do not rank in the first file of Wordsworth's output. As a concession, some of these are included in an appendix. Nevertheless, it is 'The ruined cottage' of 1797, the *Prelude* of 1798–9, 'Michael', and some other poems of that calibre that form the essential Wordsworth. Works such as these place him, along with Chaucer, Shakespeare, and Milton, as one of the cornerstones of English poetry.

The text is based on the earliest versions of the poems, as of the Preface to *Lyrical Ballads*. Wordsworth was notoriously bad as a reviser and it seemed better to represent him by his first thoughts, which are his best. Wordsworth's own spelling and punctuation is adhered to except in instances where this is obsolescent or in other ways distracting. Spellings such as 'chearful' for 'cheerful', 'sate' for 'sat' and 'shew' for 'show' have been given their modern equivalents. Wordsworth's preference for the z-form in spellings such as 'surprized' has been followed except in the Preface to *Lyrical Ballads* and its appendix, where Wordsworth adopted s-forms. Capitals, which in Wordsworth are not used consistently, have been reduced to lower case except, of course, for proper nouns and for special usages such as 'Nature'. In the prose, Wordsworth's heavy punctuation, involving many redundant commas, has been lightened somewhat. In poems based on Wordsworth's own manuscripts, such as 'The ruined cottage', the author's own, very light, punctuation has been followed except in such instances as would make for unhelpful ambiguity. Since Wordsworth preferred dictating to penmanship, most of the poems exist in copies made by Dorothy Wordsworth, Mary Wordsworth, and other amanuenses. It is impossible to determine how far they imposed their own punctuation on Wordsworth's texts. In the end, the editor's criterion has been that which would result in the presentation of a clear text to a modern audience.

WILLIAM WORDSWORTH
Selected Poetry and Prose

WILLIAM
WORDSWORTH

Selected Poetry and Prose

THE RUINED COTTAGE

Give me a spark of nature's fire,
'Tis the best learning I desire.

. . .

My Muse though homely in attire
May touch the heart.
                                    Burns. –

First Part

'Twas summer; and the sun was mounted high.
Along the south the uplands feebly glared
Through a pale steam and all the northern downs
In clearer air ascending showed their brown
And dappled surfaces distinct with shades
Of deep embattled clouds that lay in spots
Determined and unmoved; with steady beams
Of clear and pleasant sunshine interposed,
Pleasant to him who on the soft cool grass
Extends his careless limbs beside the root   10

---

* Numbers in square brackets refer to pages on which notes may be found.

Of some huge oak whose aged branches make
A twilight of their own, a dewy shade
Where the wren warbles, while the dreaming man
Half conscious of that soothing melody
With sidelong eye looks out upon the scene
By those impending branches made
More soft and distant. Other lot was mine,
Across a bare wide common I had toiled
With languid feet which by the slippery ground
Were baffled still; my limbs from very heat   20
Could find no rest nor my weak arm disperse
The insect host which gathered round my face
And joined their murmurs to the tedious noise
Of seeds of bursting gorse which crackled round.
I turned my steps towards a group of trees
Which midway in the level stood alone
And thither come at length beneath a shade
Of clustering elms that sprang from the same root
I found a ruined cottage, four clay walls
That stared upon each other. 'Twas a spot   30
The wandering gypsy in a stormy night
Would pass it with his moveables to house
On the open plain beneath the imperfect arch
Of a cold lime-kiln. As I looked around
Beside the door I saw an aged man
Stretched on a bench whose edge with short bright moss
Was green and studded o'er with fungus flowers,
An iron-pointed staff lay at his side,
Him had I seen the day before alone
And in the middle of the public way   40
Standing to rest himself. His eyes were turned
Towards the setting sun while with that staff
Behind him fixed he propped a long white pack
Which crossed his shoulders: wares for maids who live
In lonely villages or straggling huts.
      Now on the bench he lay
Stretched at his length, and with that weary load
Pillowed his head – I guess he had no thought
Of his way-wandering life. His eyes were shut,

The shadows of the breezy elms above   50
Dappled his face. With thirsty heat oppressed
At length I hailed him, glad to see his hat
Bedewed with water-drops, as if the brim
Had newly scooped a running stream. He rose
And, pointing to a sun-flower, bade me climb
The wall where that same gaudy flower
Looked out upon the road. It was a plot
Of garden-ground, now wild, its matted weeds
Marked with the steps of them who as they pass
The gooseberry trees that shot in long lank slips   60
Or currants showing on a leafless stem
In scanty strings had tempted to o'erleap
The broken wall. Within that cheerless spot
Where two tall hedgerows of thick willow boughs
Joined in a damp cold nook I found a well
Half choked with weeds and grass – across its mouth
A spider's web hung to the water's edge
And on its wet and slimy footstone lay
The useless fragment of a wooden bowl
– I slaked my thirst and to the shady bench   70
Returned, and while I stood unbonnetted
To catch the current of the breezy air
The old man said, 'Oh! Master time has been
When I could never pass this way, but she
Who lived within these walls, when I appeared
A daughter's welcome gave me, and I loved her
As my own child. Oh! Sir the good die first
And they whose hearts are dry as summer dust
Burn to the socket. – Many a passenger
Has blessed poor Margaret for her gentle looks   80
When she upheld the cool refreshment drawn
From that forsaken well, and no one came
But he was welcome, no one went away
But that it seemed she loved him. She is dead
And nettles rot and adders sun themselves
Upon the floor where I have seen her sit
And rock her baby in its cradle. She
Is dead and in her grave. And this poor hut

Stripped of its outward garb of household flower,
Of rose and jasmine offers to the wind   90
A cold bare wall whose top you see is tricked
With weeds and the rank spear grass – from this casement
You see the swallow's nest has dropped away.
The poor man's horse
That feeds upon the lanes, from cold night showers
Finds shelter now within the chimney wall
Where I have seen her evening's hearth-stone blaze
And through the window spread upon the road
Its cheerful light. You see the wall
Though open to the sky yet stained with smoke,   100
A wretched covert 'tis for man or beast.
Poor Margaret
She had a husband once, a sober man,
I knew him, often I have heard her say
That he was up and busy at his loom
In summer ere the mower's scythe had swept
The dewy grass and in the early spring
Ere the last star had vanished. They who passed
At evening, from behind the garden fence
Might hear his busy spade which he would ply   110
After his daily work till the daylight
Was gone, and every leaf and every flower
Were lost in the dark hedges. So they lived
In peace and comfort and two pretty babes
Were their best hope next to the God in Heaven.
– You may remember, now some ten years gone
Two blighting seasons when the fields were left
With half a harvest. – It pleased Heaven to add
A worse affliction in the plague of war,
A happy land was stricken to the heart.   120
A dearth was in the land. They were hard times,
A wanderer among the cottages
I with my pack of winter raiment, saw
What the poor suffered – Many of the rich
Sunk down as in a dream among the poor
And of the poor did many cease to be
And their place knew them not. 'Twas at this time

22

As Margaret told me on this very bench
A fever seized her husband. In disease
He lingered long and when his strength returned   130
He found the little he had stored to meet
The hour of accident or crippling age
Was all consumed. A dearth was in the land,
A time of trouble – shoals of artisans
Were from the merchants turned away
To hang for bread on parish charity
They and their wives and children, happier far
Could they have lived as do the little birds
That peck along the hedges, or the kite
That makes her dwelling in the mountain rocks.   140
Ill fared it now with Robert, at his door he stood
And whistled many a snatch of merry tunes
That had no mirth in them, or with his knife
Carved uncouth figures on the heads of sticks
Then idly sought about through every nook
Of house or garden any casual task
Of use or ornament and with a strange
Amusing but uneasy novelty
He blended where he might the various tasks
Of summer, autumn, winter and of spring,   150
The passenger might see him at the door
With his small hammer on the threshold stone
Pointing lame buckle-tongues and rusty nails
The treasured store of an old household box
Or braiding cords or weaving bells and caps
Of rushes, play-things for his babes,
But this endured not, his good-humour soon
Became a weight in which no pleasure was
And poverty brought on a petted mood
And a sore temper, day by day he drooped   160
And he would leave his home and to the town
Without an errand would he turn his steps
Or wander here and there among the fields,
One while he would speak lightly of his babes
And with a cruel tongue, at other times
He played with them wild freaks of merriment

23

And 'twas a piteous thing to see the looks
Of the poor innocent children. "Every smile"
Said Margaret to me here beneath these trees
"Made my heart bleed".' At this the old man paused   170
And looking up to those enormous elms
He said "tis now the hour of deepest noon
At this still season of repose and peace
This hour when all things which are not at rest
Are cheerful, while this multitude of flies
Fills all the air with happy melody,
Why should a tear be in an old man's eye?
Why should we thus with an untoward mind
And in the weakness of humanity
From natural wisdom turn our hearts away,   180
To natural comfort shut our eyes and ears
And feeding on disquiet thus disturb
The tone of Nature with our restless thoughts?'

Second Part

He spake with somewhat of a solemn tone
But when he ended there was in his face
Such easy cheerfulness, a look so mild
That for a little time it stole away
All recollection and that simple tale
Passed from my mind like a forgotten sound.
A while on trivial things we held discourse   190
To me soon tasteless. In my own despite
I thought of that poor woman as of one
Whom I had known and loved. He had rehearsed
Her homely tale with such familiar power
With such a countenance of love, an eye
So busy, that the things of which he spake
Seemed present and, attention now relaxed,
I felt a creeping chillness in my veins.
I rose, and turning from that breezy shade
Went out into the open air, and stood   200
To drink the comfort of the summer sun,
Long time I had not stayed ere looking round

24

Upon that tranquil ruin, and impelled
By a mild force of curious pensiveness
I begged of the old man that for my sake
He would resume his story. He replied
'It were a wantonness, and would demand
Severe reproof, if we were men whose hearts
Could hold vain dalliance with the misery
Even of the dead and idly thence extract   210
A passing pleasure felt but never marked
By reason, barren of all future good.
We know that there is often found
In mournful thoughts and always might be found
A power to virtue friendly – were't not so
I am a dreamer among men – indeed
An idle dreamer. 'Tis a common tale
By moving accidents uncharactered,
A tale of silent suffering hardly clothed
In bodily form and to the grosser sense   220
But ill adapted, scarcely palpable
To him who does not think. At your request
I will proceed.

       While thus it fared with those
To whom this cottage till that hapless year
Had been a blessed home, it was my chance
To travel in a country far remote
And glad I was when halting by yon gate
Which leads from the green lane again I saw
These lofty elm-trees. Long I did not rest,
With many pleasant thoughts I cheered my way   230
O'er the flat common. At the door arrived
I knocked, and when I entered with the hope
Of usual greeting Margaret looked at me
A little while, then turned her head away
Speechless, and sitting down upon a chair
Wept bitterly. I wist not what to do
Or how to speak to her. Poor wretch! at last
She rose from off her seat – and then – Oh Sir
I cannot *tell* how she pronounced my name,
With fervent love and with a face of grief   240

Unutterably helpless and a look
That seemed to cling upon me she inquired
If I had seen her husband. As she spake
A strange surprize and fear came o'er my heart
And I could make no answer – then she told
That he had disappeared; just two months gone
He left his house, two wretched days had passed
And on the third by the first break of light
Within her casement full in view she saw
A purse of gold. "I trembled at the sight"   250
Said Margaret "for I knew it was his hand
That placed it there, and on that very day
By one, a stranger, from my husband sent,
The tidings came that he had joined a troop
Of soldiers going to a distant land,
He left me thus – Poor man! he had not heart
To take a farewell of me and he feared
That I should follow with my babes and sink
Beneath the misery of a soldier's life".
This tale did Margaret tell with many tears   260
And when she ended I had little power
To give her comfort and was glad to take
Such words of hope from her own mouth as served
To cheer us both – but long we had not talked
Ere we built up a pile of better thoughts
And with a brighter eye she looked around
As if she had been shedding tears of joy,
We parted. 'Twas the early spring,
I left her busy with her garden tools
And well remember o'er the fence she looked   270
And while I paced along the foot-way path
Called out, and sent a blessing after me
With tender cheerfulness and with a voice
That seemed the very sound of happy thoughts.

    I roved o'er many a hill and many a dale
With this my weary load, in heat and cold
Through many a wood, and many an open plain
In sunshine or in shade, in wet or fair

Now blithe, now drooping – as it might befall,
My best companions now the driving winds   280
And now the music of my own sad steps
With many short-lived thoughts that passed between
And disappeared. I came this way
Towards the wane of summer when the wheat
Was yellow and the soft and bladed grass
Sprung up afresh and o'er the hay-field spread
Its tender green. When I had reached the door
I found that she was absent. In the shade
Where now we sit I waited her return,
Her cottage in its outward look appeared   290
As cheerful as before; in any show
Of neatness little changed, but that I thought
The honeysuckle crowded round the door
And from the wall hung down in heavier tufts
And knots of worthless stone-crop started out
Along the window's edge and grew like weeds
Against the lower panes. I turned aside
And strolled into her garden. It was changed,
The unprofitable bindweed spread his bells
From side to side, and with unwieldy wreaths   300
Had dragged the rose from its sustaining wall
And bowed it down to earth, the border tufts
Daisy, and thrift and lowly camomile
And thyme had straggled out into the paths
Which they were used to deck. Ere this an hour
Was wasted, back I turned my restless steps
And as I walked before the door it chanced
A stranger passed, and guessing whom I sought
He said that she was used to ramble far.
The sun was sinking in the west and now   310
I sat with sad impatience. From within
Her solitary infant cried aloud,
The spot though fair seemed very desolate,
The longer I remained more desolate
And looking round I saw the corner stones,
Till then unmarked, on either side the door
With dull red stains discoloured and stuck o'er

27

With tufts and hairs of wool as if the sheep
That feed upon the commons thither came
As to a couching-place and rubbed their sides   320
Even at her threshold. The church-clock struck eight,
I turned and saw her distant a few steps,
Her face was pale and thin, her figure too
Was changed. As she unlocked the door she said
"It grieves me you have waited here so long
But in good truth I've wandered much of late
And sometimes, to my shame I speak, have need
Of my best prayers to bring me back again".
While on the board she spread our evening meal
She told me she had lost her elder child,   330
That he for months had been a serving boy
Apprenticed by the parish. "I am changed
And to myself have done much wrong
And to this helpless infant. I have slept
Weeping and weeping I have waked, my tears
Have flowed as if my body were not such
As others are, and I could never die
But I am now in mind and heart
More easy, and I hope" said she "that heaven
Will give me patience to endure the things   340
Which I behold at home". It would have grieved
Your very soul to see her. Evermore
Her eyelids drooped, her eyes were downward cast,
She did not look at me. In every act
Pertaining to her house affairs appeared
The careless stillness which a thinking mind
Gives to an idle matter – still she sighed
But yet no motion of her breast was seen,
No heaving of the heart. While by the fire
We sat together, sighs came on my ear   350
I knew not how and hardly whence they came.
I took my staff and when I kissed her babe
The tears were in her eyes. I left her then
With the best hope and comfort I could give,
She thanked me for my will, for my hope
It seemed she did not thank me.

                    I returned
And took my rounds along this road again
Ere on its sunny bank the primrose flower
Had chronicled the earliest day of spring.
I found her sad and drooping, she had learned   360
No tidings of her husband, if he lived
She knew not that he lived, if he were dead
She knew not he was dead, she seemed not changed
In person or appearance, but her house
Bespoke a sleepy hand of negligence,
The windows they were dim and her few books
Which one upon the other heretofore
Had been piled up against the corner panes
In seemly order, now with straggling leaves
Lay scattered here and there, open or shut   370
As they had chanced to fall. Her infant babe
Had from its mother caught the trick of grief
And sighed among its playthings; once again
I turned towards the garden gate and saw
More plainly still that poverty and grief
Were now come nearer to her, all was hard
With weeds defaced and knots of withered grass,
No ridges there appeared of clear black mould,
No winter greenness; of her herbs and flowers
The better part were gnawed away   380
Or trampled on the earth; a chain of straw
Which had been twisted round the tender stem
Of a young apple-tree lay at its root,
The bark was nibbled round by truant sheep.
Margaret stood near, her infant in her arms
And seeing that my eye was on the tree
She said "I fear it will be dead and gone
Ere Robert come again". Towards the house
Together we returned and she inquired
If I had any hope. But for her babe   390
And for her little friendless boy she said
She had no wish to live, that she must die
Of sorrow – yet I saw the idle loom
Still in its place, his Sunday garments hung

Upon the self-same nail, his very staff
Stood undisturbed behind the door. And when
I passed this way, beaten by autumn winds
She told me that her little babe was dead
And she was left alone. That very time
I yet remember, through the miry lane   400
She went with me a mile when the bare trees
Trickled with foggy damps, and in such sort
That any heart had ached to hear her, begged
That wheresoe'er I went I still would ask
For him whom she had lost. Five tedious years
She lingered in unquiet widowhood
A wife, and widow. Needs must it have been
A sore heart-wasting. Master! I have heard
That in that broken arbour she would sit
The idle length of half a sabbath day   410
There – where you see the toadstool's lazy head –
And when a dog passed by she still would quit
The shade and look abroad. On this old bench
For hours she sat, and evermore, her eye
Was busy in the distance, shaping things
That made her heart beat quick. See'st thou that path?
The greensward now has broken its grey line;
There, to and fro she paced through many a day
Of the warm summer, from a belt of flax
That girt her waist spinning the long-drawn thread   420
With backward steps – yet ever as there passed
A man whose garments showed the soldier's red
Or crippled mendicant in sailor's garb
The little child who sat to turn the wheel
Ceased from his toil, and she with faltering voice
Expecting still to learn her husband's fate
Made many a fond inquiry and when they
Whose presence gave no comfort were gone by
Her heart was still more sad. And by yon gate
That bars the traveller's road she often sat   430
And if a stranger-horseman came the latch
Would lift, and in his face look wistfully
Most happy if from aught discovered there

Of tender feeling she might dare repeat
The same sad question – Meanwhile her poor hut
Sunk to decay, for he was gone whose hand
At the first nippings of October frost,
Closed up each chink and with fresh bands of straw
Chequered the green-grown thatch. And so she sat
Through the long winter, reckless and alone   440
'Till this reft house by frost and thaw and rain
Was sapped, and when she slept the nightly damps
Did chill her breast and in the stormy day
Her tattered clothes were ruffled by the wind
Even by the side of her own fire – Yet still
She loved the wretched spot, nor would for worlds
Have parted hence, and still that length of road
And this rude bench one torturing hope endeared,
Fast-rooted at her heart and Stranger! here
In sickness she remained, and here she died   450
Last human tenant of these ruined walls.'

1797   rev. text, *The Excursion* (1814)

MICHAEL

A pastoral poem

If from the public way you turn your steps
Up the tumultuous brook of Green-head Gill,
You will suppose that with an upright path
Your feet must struggle; in such bold ascent
The pastoral mountains front you, face to face.
But, courage! for beside that boisterous brook
The mountains have all opened out themselves,
And made a hidden valley of their own.
No habitation there is seen; but such
As journey thither find themselves alone   10
With a few sheep, with rocks and stones, and kites
That overhead are sailing in the sky.

It is in truth an utter solitude,
Nor should I have made mention of this dell

31

But for one object which you might pass by,
Might see and notice not. Beside the brook
There is a straggling heap of unhewn stones!
And to that place a story appertains,
Which, though it be ungarnished with events,
Is not unfit, I deem, for the fire-side,   20
Or for the summer shade. It was the first,
The earliest of those tales that spake to me
Of shepherds, dwellers in the valleys, men
Whom I already loved, not verily
For their own sakes, but for the fields and hills
Where was their occupation and abode.
And hence this tale, while I was yet a boy
Careless of books, yet having felt the power
Of Nature, by the gentle agency
Of natural objects led me on to feel   30
For passions that were not my own, and think
At random and imperfectly indeed
On man; the heart of man and human life.
Therefore, although it be a history
Homely and rude, I will relate the same
For the delight of a few natural hearts,
And with yet fonder feeling, for the sake
Of youthful poets, who among these hills
Will be my second self when I am gone.

Upon the forest-side in Grasmere Vale   40
There dwelt a shepherd, Michael was his name,
An old man, stout of heart, and strong of limb.
His bodily frame had been from youth to age
Of an unusual strength: his mind was keen
Intense and frugal, apt for all affairs,
And in his shepherd's calling he was prompt
And watchful more than ordinary men.
Hence he had learned the meaning of all winds,
Of blasts of every tone, and often-times
When others heeded not, he heard the south   50
Make subterraneous music, like the noise
Of bagpipers on distant Highland hills;

The shepherd, at such warning, of his flock
Bethought him, and he to himself would say
The winds are now devising work for me!
And truly at all times the storm, that drives
The traveller to a shelter, summoned him
Up to the mountains: he had been alone
Amid the heart of many thousand mists
That came to him and left him on the heights.   60
So lived he till his eightieth year was passed.

And grossly that man errs, who should suppose
That the green valleys, and the streams and rocks
Were things indifferent to the shepherd's thoughts.
Fields, where with cheerful spirits he had breathed
The common air; the hills, which he so oft
Had climbed with vigorous steps: which had impressed
So many incidents upon his mind
Of hardship, skill or courage, joy or fear;
Which like a book preserved the memory   70
Of the dumb animals, whom he had saved,
Had fed or sheltered, linking to such acts,
So grateful in themselves, the certainty
Of honourable gains; these fields, these hills
Which were his living being, even more
Than his own blood – what could they less? had laid
Strong hold on his affections, were to him
A pleasurable feeling of blind love,
The pleasure which there is in life itself.

He had not passed his days in singleness.   80
He had a wife, a comely matron, old
Though younger than himself full twenty years.
She was a woman of a stirring life
Whose heart was in her house: two wheels she had
Of antique form, this large for spinning wool,
That small for flax, and if one wheel had rest,
It was because the other was at work.
The pair had but one inmate in their house,
An only child, who had been born to them

When Michael telling o'er his years began 90
To deem that he was old, in shepherd's phrase,
With one foot in the grave. This only son,
With two brave sheep dogs tried in many a storm,
The one of an inestimable worth,
Made all their household. I may truly say,
That they were as a proverb in the vale
For endless industry. When day was gone,
And from their occupations out of doors
The son and father were come home, even then
Their labour did not cease, unless when all 100
Turned to their cleanly supper-board, and there
Each with a mess of pottage and skimmed milk,
Sat round their basket piled with oaten cakes,
And their plain home-made cheese. Yet when their meal
Was ended, Luke (for so the son was named)
And his old father, both betook themselves
To such convenient work, as might employ
Their hands by the fire-side; perhaps to card
Wool for the housewife's spindle, or repair
Some injury done to sickle, flail, or scythe, 110
Or other implement of house or field.

Down from the ceiling by the chimney's edge,
Which in our ancient uncouth country style
Did with a huge projection overbrow
Large space beneath, as duly as the light
Of day grew dim, the housewife hung a lamp;
An aged utensil, which had performed
Service beyond all others of its kind.
Early at evening did it burn and late,
Surviving comrade of uncounted hours 120
Which going by from year to year had found
And left the couple neither gay perhaps
Nor cheerful, yet with objects and with hopes
Living a life of eager industry.
And now, when Luke was in his eighteenth year,
There by the light of this old lamp they sat,
Father and son, while late into the night

The housewife plied her own peculiar work,
Making the cottage through the silent hours
Murmur as with the sound of summer flies.   130
Not with a waste of words, but for the sake
Of pleasure, which I know that I shall give
To many living now, I of this lamp
Speak thus minutely: for there are no few
Whose memories will bear witness to my tale.
The light was famous in its neighbourhood,
And was a public symbol of the life
The thrifty pair had lived. For, as it chanced,
Their cottage on a plot or rising ground
Stood single, with large prospect north and south,   140
High into Easedale, up to Dunmal-Raise,
And westward to the village near the lake.
And from this constant light so regular
And so far seen, the house itself by all
Who dwelt within the limits of the vale,
Both old and young, was named The Evening Star.

Thus living on through such a length of years,
The shepherd, if he loved himself, must needs
Have loved his help-mate; but to Michael's heart
This son of his old age was yet more dear –   150
Effect which might perhaps have been produced
By that instinctive tenderness, the same
Blind spirit, which is in the blood of all,
Or that a child, more than all other gifts,
Brings hope with it, and forward-looking thoughts,
And stirrings of inquietude, when they
By tendency of nature needs must fail.
From such, and other causes, to the thoughts
Of the old man his only son was now
The dearest object that he knew on earth.   160
Exceeding was the love he bare to him,
His heart and his heart's joy! For oftentimes
Old Michael, while he was a babe in arms,
Had done him female service, not alone
For dalliance and delight, as is the use

Of fathers, but with patient mind enforced
To acts of tenderness; and he had rocked
His cradle with a woman's gentle hand.

And in a later time, ere yet the boy
Had put on boy's attire, did Michael love,   170
Albeit of a stern unbending mind,
To have the young one in his sight, when he
Had work by his own door, or when he sat
With sheep before him on his shepherd's stool,
Beneath that large old oak, which near their door
Stood, and from its enormous breadth of shade
Chosen for the shearer's covert from the sun,
Thence in our rustic dialect was called
The Clipping Tree, a name which yet it bears.
There, while they two were sitting in the shade,   180
With others round them, earnest all and blithe,
Would Michael exercise his heart with looks
Of fond correction and reproof bestowed
Upon the child, if he disturbed the sheep
By catching at their legs, or with his shouts
Scared them, while they lay still beneath the shears.

And when by Heaven's good grace the boy grew up
A healthy lad, and carried in his cheek
Two steady roses that were five years old,
Then Michael from a winter coppice cut   190
With his own hand a sapling, which he hooped
With iron, making it throughout in all
Due requisites a perfect shepherd's staff,
And gave it to the boy; wherewith equipped
He as a watchman oftentimes was placed
At gate or gap, to stem or turn the flock,
And to his office prematurely called
There stood the urchin, as you will divine,
Something between a hindrance and a help,
And for this cause not always, I believe,   200
Receiving from his father hire of praise.
Though nought was left undone, which staff or voice,

36

Or looks, or threatening gestures could perform.
But soon as Luke, full ten years old, could stand
Against the mountain blasts, and to the heights,
Not fearing toil, nor length of weary ways,
He with his father daily went, and they
Were as companions, why should I relate
That objects which the shepherd loved before
Were dearer now? that from the boy there came   210
Feelings and emanations, things which were
Light to the sun and music to the wind;
And that the old man's heart seemed born again.
Thus in his father's sight the boy grew up:
And now when he had reached his eighteenth year,
He was his comfort and his daily hope.

While this good household thus were living on
From day to day, to Michael's ear there came
Distressful tidings. Long before the time
Of which I speak, the shepherd had been bound   220
In surety for his brother's son, a man
Of an industrious life, and ample means,
But unforeseen misfortunes suddenly
Had pressed upon him, and old Michael now
Was summoned to discharge the forfeiture,
A grievous penalty, but little less
Than half his substance. This unlooked-for claim
At the first hearing, for a moment took
More hope out of his life than he supposed
That any old man ever could have lost.   230
As soon as he had gathered so much strength
That he could look his trouble in the face,
It seemed that his sole refuge was to sell
A portion of his patrimonial fields.
Such was his first resolve; he thought again,
And his heart failed him. 'Isabel,' said he,
Two evenings after he had heard the news,
'I have been toiling more than seventy years,
And in the open sunshine of God's love
Have we all lived, yet if these fields of ours   240

37

Should pass into a stranger's hand, I think
That I could not lie quiet in my grave.
Our lot is a hard lot; the sun itself
Has scarcely been more diligent than I,
And I have lived to be a fool at last
To my own family. An evil man
That was, and made an evil choice, if he
Were false to us; and if he were not false,
There are ten thousand to whom loss like this
Had been no sorrow. I forgive him – but   250
'Twere better to be dumb than to talk thus.
When I began, my purpose was to speak
Of remedies and of a cheerful hope.
Our Luke shall leave us, Isabel; the land
Shall not go from us, and it shall be free,
He shall possess it, free as is the wind
That passes over it. We have, thou knowest,
Another kinsman, he will be our friend
In this distress. He is a prosperous man,
Thriving in trade, and Luke to him shall go,   260
And with his kinsman's help and his own thrift,
He quickly will repair this loss, and then
May come again to us. If here he stay,
What can be done? Where every one is poor
What can be gained?' At this, the old man paused,
And Isabel sat silent, for her mind
Was busy, looking back into past times.
There's Richard Bateman, thought she to herself,
He was a parish-boy – at the church-door
They made a gathering for him, shillings, pence,   270
And halfpennies, wherewith the neighbours bought
A basket, which they filled with pedlar's wares,
And with this basket on his arm, the lad
Went up to London, found a master there,
Who out of many chose the trusty boy
To go and overlook his merchandise
Beyond the seas, where he grew wond'rous rich,
And left estates and monies to the poor,
And at his birth-place built a chapel, floored

38

With marble, which he sent from foreign lands.   280
These thoughts, and many others of like sort,
Passed quickly through the mind of Isabel,
And her face brightened. The old man was glad,
And thus resumed. 'Well! Isabel, this scheme
These two days has been meat and drink to me.
Far more than we have lost is left us yet.
– We have enough – I wish indeed that I
Were younger, but this hope is a good hope.
– Make ready Luke's best garments, of the best
Buy for him more, and let us send him forth   290
Tomorrow, or the next day, or tonight:
– If he could go, the boy should go tonight.'

Here Michael ceased, and to the fields went forth
With a light heart. The housewife for five days
Was restless morn and night, and all day long
Wrought on with her best fingers to prepare
Things needful for the journey of her son.
But Isabel was glad when Sunday came
To stop her in her work; for, when she lay
By Michael's side, she for the two last nights   300
Heard him, how he was troubled in his sleep:
And when they rose at morning she could see
That all his hopes were gone. That day at noon
She said to Luke, while they two by themselves
Were sitting at the door, 'Thou must not go,
We have no other child but thee to lose,
None to remember – do not go away,
For if thou leave thy father he will die.'
The lad made answer with a jocund voice,
And Isabel, when she had told her fears,   310
Recovered heart. That evening her best fare
Did she bring forth, and all together sat
Like happy people round a Christmas fire.

Next morning Isabel resumed her work,
And all the ensuing week the house appeared
As cheerful as a grove in spring: at length

The expected letter from their kinsman came,
With kind assurances that he would do
His utmost for the welfare of the boy,
To which requests were added that forthwith   320
He might be sent to him. Ten times or more
The letter was read over; Isabel
Went forth to show it to the neighbours round:
Nor was there at that time on English land
A prouder heart than Luke's. When Isabel
Had to her house returned, the old man said
'He shall depart tomorrow.' To this word
The housewife answered, talking much of things
Which, if at such short notice he should go,
Would surely be forgotten. But at length   330
She gave consent, and Michael was at ease.

Near the tumultuous brook of Green-head Gill,
In that deep valley, Michael had designed
To build a sheep-fold, and, before he heard
The tidings of his melancholy loss,
For this same purpose he had gathered up
A heap of stones, which close to the brook side
Lay thrown together, ready for the work.
With Luke that evening thitherward he walked;
And soon as they had reached the place he stopped   340
And thus the old man spake to him. 'My son,
Tomorrow thou wilt leave me; with full heart
I look upon thee, for thou art the same
That wert a promise to me ere thy birth,
And all thy life hast been my daily joy.
I will relate to thee some little part
Of our two histories; 'twill do thee good
When thou art from me, even if I should speak
Of things thou canst not know of. – After thou
First cam'st into the world, as it befalls   350
To new-born infants, thou didst sleep away
Two days, and blessings from thy father's tongue
Then fell upon thee. Day by day passed on,
And still I loved thee with increasing love.

40

Never to living ear came sweeter sounds
Than when I heard thee by our own fire-side
First uttering without words a natural tune,
When thou, a feeding babe, didst in thy joy
Sing at thy mother's breast. Month followed month,
And in the open fields my life was passed   360
And in the mountains, else I think that thou
Hadst been brought up upon thy father's knees.
– But we were playmates, Luke; among these hills,
As well thou know'st, in us the old and young
Have played together, nor with me didst thou
Lack any pleasure which a boy can know.'

Luke had a manly heart; but at these words
He sobbed aloud; the old man grasped his hand,
And said, 'Nay do not take it so – I see
That these are things of which I need not speak.   370
– Even to the utmost I have been to thee
A kind and a good father: and herein
I but repay a gift which I myself
Received at others' hands, for, though now old
Beyond the common life of man, I still
Remember them who loved me in my youth.
Both of them sleep together: here they lived
As all their forefathers had done, and when
At length their time was come, they were not loth
To give their bodies to the family mould.   380
I wished that thou should'st live the life they lived.
But 'tis a long time to look back, my son,
And see so little gain from sixty years.
These fields were burthened when they came to me;
'Till I was forty years of age, not more
Than half of my inheritance was mine.
I toiled and toiled; God blessed me in my work,
And 'till these three weeks past the land was free.
– It looks as if it never could endure
Another master. Heaven forgive me, Luke,   390
If I judge ill for thee, but it seems good
That thou should'st go.' At this the old man paused,

Then, pointing to the stones near which they stood,
Thus, after a short silence, he resumed:
'This was a work for us, and now, my son,
It is a work for me. But, lay one stone –
Here, lay it for me, Luke, with thine own hands.
I for the purpose brought thee to this place.
Nay, boy, be of good hope: – we both may live
To see a better day. At eighty-four   400
I still am strong and stout; – do thou thy part,
I will do mine. – I will begin again
With many tasks that were resigned to thee;
Up to the heights, and in among the storms,
Will I without thee go again, and do
All works which I was wont to do alone,
Before I knew thy face. – Heaven bless thee, boy!
Thy heart these two weeks has been beating fast
With many hopes – it should be so – yes – yes –
I knew that thou could'st never have a wish   410
To leave me, Luke, thou hast been bound to me
Only by links of love, when thou art gone
What will be left to us! – But, I forget
My purposes. Lay now the corner-stone,
As I requested, and hereafter, Luke,
When thou art gone away, should evil men
Be thy companions, let this sheep-fold be
Thy anchor and thy shield; amid all fear
And all temptation, let it be to thee
An emblem of the life thy fathers lived,   420
Who, being innocent, did for that cause
Bestir them in good deeds. Now, fare thee well –
When thou return'st, thou in this place wilt see
A work which is not here, a covenant
'Twill be between us – but whatever fate
Befall thee, I shall love thee to the last,
And bear thy memory with me to the grave.'

The shepherd ended here; and Luke stooped down,
And as his father had requested, laid
The first stone of the sheep-fold; at the sight   430

The old man's grief broke from him, to his heart
He pressed his son, he kisséd him and wept;
And to the house together they returned.

Next morning, as had been resolved, the boy
Began his journey, and when he had reached
The public way, he put on a bold face;
And all the neighbours as he passed their doors
Came forth, with wishes and with farewell prayers,
That followed him 'till he was out of sight.

A good report did from their kinsman come,   440
Of Luke and his well-doing; and the boy
Wrote loving letters, full of wond'rous news,
Which, as the housewife phrased it, were throughout
The prettiest letters that were ever seen.
Both parents read them with rejoicing hearts.
So, many months passed on: and once again
The shepherd went about his daily work
With confidence and cheerful thoughts; and now
Sometimes when he could find a leisure hour
He to that valley took his way, and there   450
Wrought at the sheep-fold. Meantime Luke began
To slacken in his duty, and at length
He in the dissolute city gave himself
To evil courses: ignominy and shame
Fell on him, so that he was driven at last
To seek a hiding-place beyond the seas.

There is a comfort in the strength of love;
'Twill make a thing endurable, which else
Would break the heart: – Old Michael found it so.
I have conversed with more than one who well   460
Remember the old man, and what he was
Years after he had heard this heavy news.
His bodily frame had been from youth to age
Of an unusual strength. Among the rocks
He went, and still looked up upon the sun,

And listened to the wind; and as before
Performed all kinds of labour for his sheep,
And for the land his small inheritance.
And to that hollow dell from time to time
Did he repair, to build the fold of which   470
His flock had need. 'Tis not forgotten yet
The pity which was then in every heart
For the old man – and 'tis believed by all
That many and many a day he thither went,
And never lifted up a single stone.

There, by the sheep-fold, sometimes was he seen
Sitting alone, with that his faithful dog,
Then old, beside him, lying at his feet.
The length of full seven years from time to time
He at the building of this sheep-fold wrought,   480
And left the work unfinished when he died.

Three years, or little more, did Isabel,
Survive her husband: at her death the estate
Was sold, and went into a stranger's hand.
The cottage which was named The Evening Star
Is gone, the ploughshare has been through the ground
On which it stood; great changes have been wrought
In all the neighbourhood, yet the oak is left
That grew beside their door; and the remains
Of the unfinished sheep-fold may be seen   490
Beside the boisterous brook of Green-head Gill.

1800   *Lyrical Ballads*, 2nd edn (1801)

'IN SOFT WARM WINTER MORNINGS'

In soft warm winter mornings when the snow
Had fallen through the whole night and up they went
Into the heights, at such a busy time
The dear beloved boy would sometimes win
Forgetfulnesses through the father's thought,
And he would stand beside him like a man

44

Robbed of all purpose – when the boy by chance
Or wilfully had on some steep descent
Unsettled with his foot a tuft of snow
Small as a sparrow's egg which, sliding down   10
Inch after inch before a yard were gone,
Had gathered up a small round mass that split
With its own weight and made a hundred tufts
Which branching each his several way did each
Collect his separate mass which one and all
Went bounding on till in its turn each broke
Into a thousand fragments which branched off
Splitting and gathering till the mountain seemed
Raced over by a thousand living things,
Ten thousand snow-white rabbits of the cliffs,   20
At sight whereof the lad would whoop for joy;
And when the race was ended he would point
Down to the fork of that gigantic tree
Which far beneath them, by the devious track
Left by the runners in that elfin race,
Had been impressed upon the snow and lay
With track beginning at the lad's own feet
And branches covering half the mountain side.
There, with a mingled sentiment of love,
Authority and sympathy and blame,   30
The old man stood spectator of the sight;
Meanwhile that princely dog of which I spake
Eagerly following his peculiar work
While every echo slept among the snow,
As if defrauded of his voice unheard
Barked restlessly among the sullen rocks.

1800

LINES WRITTEN A FEW MILES ABOVE TINTERN ABBEY
ON REVISITING THE BANKS OF THE WYE DURING A TOUR,
JULY 13, 1798

Five years have passed; five summers, with the length
Of five long winters! and again I hear

These waters, rolling from their mountain-springs
With a sweet inland murmur. – Once again
Do I behold these steep and lofty cliffs,
Which on a wild secluded scene impress
Thoughts of more deep seclusion; and connect
The landscape with the quiet of the sky.
The day is come when I again repose
Here, under this dark sycamore, and view   10
These plots of cottage-ground, these orchard-tufts,
Which, at this season, with their unripe fruits,
Among the woods and copses lose themselves,
Nor, with their green and simple hue, disturb
The wild green landscape. Once again I see
These hedgerows, hardly hedgerows, little lines
Of sportive wood run wild; these pastoral farms
Green to the very door; and wreaths of smoke
Sent up, in silence, from among the trees,
With some uncertain notice, as might seem,   20
Of vagrant dwellers in the houseless woods,
Or of some hermit's cave, where by his fire
The hermit sits alone.

                    Though absent long,
These forms of beauty have not been to me,
As is a landscape to a blind man's eye:
But oft, in lonely rooms, and mid the din
Of towns and cities, I have owed to them,
In hours of weariness, sensations sweet,
Felt in the blood, and felt along the heart,
And passing even into my purer mind   30
With tranquil restoration: – feelings too
Of unremembered pleasure; such, perhaps,
As may have had no trivial influence
On that best portion of a good man's life;
His little, nameless, unremembered acts
Of kindness and of love. Nor less, I trust,
To them I may have owed another gift,
Of aspect more sublime; that blessed mood,
In which the burthen of the mystery,

In which the heavy and the weary weight   40
Of all this unintelligible world
Is lightened: – that serene and blessed mood,
In which the affections gently lead us on,
Until, the breath of this corporeal frame,
And even the motion of our human blood
Almost suspended, we are laid asleep
In body, and become a living soul:
While with an eye made quiet by the power
Of harmony, and the deep power of joy,
We see into the life of things.   50

                    If this
Be but a vain belief, yet, oh! how oft,
In darkness, and amid the many shapes
Of joyless daylight; when the fretful stir
Unprofitable, and the fever of the world,
Have hung upon the beatings of my heart,
How oft, in spirit, have I turned to thee
O sylvan Wye! Thou wanderer through the woods,
How often has my spirit turned to thee!
And now, with gleams of half-extinguished thought,
With many recognitions dim and faint,   60
And somewhat of a sad perplexity,
The picture of the mind revives again:
While here I stand, not only with the sense
Of present pleasure, but with pleasing thoughts
That in this moment there is life and food
For future years. And so I dare to hope
Though changed, no doubt, from what I was, when first
I came among these hills; when like a roe
I bounded o'er the mountains, by the sides
Of the deep rivers, and the lonely streams,   70
Wherever nature led; more like a man
Flying from something that he dreads, than one
Who sought the thing he loved. For nature then
(The coarser pleasures of my boyish days,
And their glad animal movements all gone by,)
To me was all in all – I cannot paint

What then I was. The sounding cataract
Haunted me like a passion: the tall rock,
The mountain, and the deep and gloomy wood,
Their colours and their forms, were then to me   80
An appetite: a feeling and a love,
That had no need of a remoter charm,
By thought supplied, or any interest
Unborrowed from the eye. – That time is past,
And all its aching joys are now no more,
And all its dizzy raptures. Not for this
Faint I, nor mourn nor murmur: other gifts
Have followed, for such loss, I would believe,
Abundant recompense. For I have learned
To look on nature, not as in the hour   90
Of thoughtless youth, but hearing oftentimes
The still, sad music of humanity,
Not harsh nor grating, though of ample power
To chasten and subdue. And I have felt
A presence that disturbs me with the joy
Of elevated thoughts; a sense sublime
Of something far more deeply interfused,
Whose dwelling is the light of setting suns,
And the round ocean, and the living air,
And the blue sky, and in the mind of man,   100
A motion and a spirit, that impels
All thinking things, all objects of all thought,
And rolls through all things. Therefore am I still
A lover of the meadows and the woods,
And mountains; and of all that we behold
From this green earth; of all the mighty world
Of eye and ear, both what they half-create,
And what perceive; well pleased to recognize
In nature and the language of the sense,
The anchor of my purest thoughts, the nurse,   110
The guide, the guardian of my heart, and soul
Of all my moral being.

                    Nor, perchance,
If I were not thus taught, should I the more

Suffer my genial spirits to decay:
For thou art with me, here, upon the banks
Of this fair river; thou, my dearest friend,
My dear, dear friend, and in thy voice I catch
The language of my former heart, and read
My former pleasures in the shooting lights
Of thy wild eyes. Oh! yet a little while   120
May I behold in thee what I was once,
My dear, dear sister! And this prayer I make,
Knowing that Nature never did betray
The heart that loved her; 'tis her privilege,
Through all the years of this our life, to lead
From joy to joy: for she can so inform
The mind that is within us, so impress
With quietness and beauty, and so feed
With lofty thoughts, that neither evil tongues,
Rash judgments, nor the sneers of selfish men,   130
Nor greetings where no kindness is, nor all
The dreary intercourse of daily life,
Shall e'er prevail against us, or disturb
Our cheerful faith that all which we behold
Is full of blessings. Therefore let the moon
Shine on thee in thy solitary walk;
And let the misty mountain winds be free
To blow against thee: and in after years,
When these wild ecstasies shall be matured
Into a sober pleasure, when thy mind   140
Shall be a mansion for all lovely forms,
Thy memory be as a dwelling-place
For all sweet sounds and harmonies; Oh! then,
If solitude, or fear, or pain, or grief,
Should be thy portion, with what healing thoughts
Of tender joy wilt thou remember me,
And these my exhortations! Nor, perchance,
If I should be, where I no more can hear
Thy voice, nor catch from thy wild eyes these gleams
Of past existence, wilt thou then forget   150
That on the banks of this delighted stream
We stood together; and that I, so long

A worshipper of Nature, hither came,
Unwearied in that service: rather say
With warmer love, oh! with far deeper zeal
Of holier love. Nor wilt thou then forget,
That after many wanderings, many years
Of absence, these steep woods and lofty cliffs,
And this green pastoral landscape, were to me
More dear, both for themselves, and for thy sake.   160

1798   *Lyrical Ballads* (1798)

NUTTING

———————— It seems a day,
One of those heavenly days which cannot die,
When forth I sallied from our cottage-door,
And with a wallet o'er my shoulder slung,
A nutting crook in hand, I turned my steps
Towards the distant woods, a figure quaint,
Tricked out in proud disguise of beggar's weeds
Put on for the occasion, by advice
And exhortation of my frugal dame.
Motley accoutrements! of power to smile   10
At thorns, and brakes, and brambles, and, in truth,
More ragged than need was. Among the woods,
And o'er the pathless rocks, I forced my way
Until, at length, I came to one dear nook
Unvisited, where not a broken bough
Drooped with its withered leaves, ungracious sign
Of devastation, but the hazels rose
Tall and erect, with milk-white clusters hung,
A virgin scene! – A little while I stood,
Breathing with such suppression of the heart   20
As joy delights in; and with wise restraint
Voluptuous, fearless of a rival, eyed
The banquet, or beneath the trees I sat
Among the flowers, and with the flowers I played;
A temper known to those, who, after long
And weary expectation, have been blessed

With sudden happiness beyond all hope. –
– Perhaps it was a bower beneath whose leaves
The violets of five seasons re-appear
And fade, unseen by any human eye, 30
Where fairy water-breaks do murmur on
For ever, and I saw the sparkling foam,
And with my cheek on one of those green stones
That, fleeced with moss, beneath the shady trees,
Lay round me scattered like a flock of sheep,
I heard the murmur and the murmuring sound,
In that sweet mood when pleasure loves to pay
Tribute to ease, and, of its joy secure
The heart luxuriates with indifferent things,
Wasting its kindliness on stocks and stones, 40
And on the vacant air. Then up I rose,
And dragged to earth both branch and bough, with crash
And merciless ravage; and the shady nook
Of hazels, and the green and mossy bower,
Deformed and sullied, patiently gave up
Their quiet being: and unless I now
Confound my present feelings with the past,
Even then, when from the bower I turned away,
Exulting, rich beyond the wealth of kings
I felt a sense of pain when I beheld 50
The silent trees and the intruding sky. –

    Then, dearest Maiden! move along these shades
In gentleness of heart; with gentle hand
Touch, – for there is a spirit in the woods.

1798   *Lyrical Ballads*, 2nd edn (1801)

The 'Lucy' poems

'STRANGE FITS OF PASSION I HAVE KNOWN'

Strange fits of passion I have known,
And I will dare to tell,
But in the lover's ear alone,
What once to me befell.

When she I loved was strong and gay   5
And like a rose in June,
I to her cottage bent my way,
Beneath the evening moon.

Upon the moon I fixed my eye
All over the wide lea;   10
My horse trudged on, and we drew nigh
Those paths so dear to me.

And now we reached the orchard plot,
And, as we climbed the hill,
Towards the roof of Lucy's cot   15
The moon descended still.

In one of those sweet dreams I slept,
Kind Nature's gentlest boon!
And, all the while, my eyes I kept
On the descending moon.   20

My horse moved on; hoof after hoof
He raised and never stopped:
When down behind the cottage roof
At once the planet dropped.

What fond and wayward, thoughts will slide   25
Into a lover's head –
'O mercy!' to myself I cried,
'If Lucy should be dead!'

1798   *Lyrical Ballads*, 2nd edn (1801)

'A SLUMBER DID MY SPIRIT SEAL'

A slumber did my spirit seal;
    I had no human fears:
She seemed a thing that could not feel
    The touch of earthly years.

No motion has she now, no force;   5
    She neither hears nor sees,
Rolled round in earth's diurnal course
    With rocks and stones and trees.

1798   *Lyrical Ballads*, 2nd edn (1801)

SONG

She dwelt among th' untrodden ways
    Beside the springs of Dove,
A maid whom there were none to praise
    And very few to love.

A violet by a mossy stone   5
    Half-hidden from the eye!
– Fair, as a star when only one
    Is shining in the sky!

She *lived* unknown, and few could know
    When Lucy ceased to be;   10

But she is in her grave, and Oh!
　　The difference to me.

1798　　　　　　　　　　　*Lyrical Ballads*, 2nd edn (1801)

'I TRAVELLED AMONG UNKNOWN MEN'

I travelled among unknown men,
　　In lands beyond the sea;
Nor England! did I know till then
　　What love I bore to thee.

'Tis past, that melancholy dream!　　　　　　　　　　5
　　Nor will I quit thy shore
A second time; for still I seem
　　To love thee more and more.

Among thy mountains did I feel
　　The joy of my desire;　　　　　　　　　　　　　　10
And she I cherished turned her wheel
　　Beside an English fire.

Thy mornings showed – thy nights concealed
　　The bowers where Lucy played;
And thine is, too, the last green field　　　　　　　　15
　　Which Lucy's eyes surveyed!

1801　　　　　　　　　　*Poems, in Two Volumes* (1807)

'THREE YEARS SHE GREW IN SUN AND SHOWER'

Three years she grew in sun and shower,
Then Nature said, 'A lovelier flower
On earth was never sown;
This child I to myself will take,
She shall be mine, and I will make　　　　　　　　　5
A lady of my own.

Myself will to my darling be
Both law and impulse, and with me
The girl in rock and plain,

54

In earth and heaven, in glade and bower,   10
Shall feel an overseeing power
To kindle or restrain.

She shall be sportive as the fawn
That wild with glee across the lawn
Or up the mountain springs,   15
And hers shall be the breathing balm,
And hers the silence and the calm
Of mute insensate things.

The floating clouds their state shall lend
To her, for her the willow bend,   20
Nor shall she fail to see
Even in the motions of the storm
A beauty that shall mould her form
By silent sympathy.

The stars of midnight shall be dear   25
To her, and she shall lean her ear
In many a secret place
Where rivulets dance their wayward round,
And beauty born of murmuring sound
Shall pass into her face.   30

And vital feelings of delight
Shall rear her form to stately height,
Her virgin bosom swell,
Such thoughts to Lucy I will give
While she and I together live   35
Here in this happy dell.'

Thus Nature spake – The work was done –
How soon my Lucy's race was run!
She died and left to me
This heath, this calm and quiet scene,   40
The memory of what has been,
And never more will be.

1798–9   *Lyrical Ballads*, 2nd edn (1801)

Poems on the naming of places

I

'IT WAS AN APRIL MORNING: FRESH AND CLEAR'

It was an April morning: fresh and clear
The rivulet, delighting in its strength,
Ran with a young man's speed, and yet the voice
Of waters which the winter had supplied
Was softened down into a vernal tone,
The spirit of enjoyment and desire,
And hopes and wishes, from all living things
Went circling, like a multitude of sounds.
The budding groves appeared as if in haste
To spur the steps of June; as if their shades   10
Of *various* green were hindrances that stood
Between them and their object: yet, meanwhile,
There was such deep contentment in the air
That every naked ash, and tardy tree
Yet leafless, seemed as though the countenance
With which it looked on this delightful day
Were native to the summer. – Up the brook
I roamed in the confusion of my heart,
Alive to all things and forgetting all.
At length I to a sudden turning came   20
In this continuous glen, where down a rock
The stream, so ardent in its course before,

Sent forth such sallies of glad sound, that all
Which I till then had heard, appeared the voice
Of common pleasure: beast and bird, the lamb,
The shepherd's dog, the linnet and the thrush
Vied with this waterfall, and made a song
Which, while I listened, seemed like the wild growth
Or like some natural produce of the air
That could not cease to be. Green leaves were here,   30
But 'twas the foliage of the rocks, the birch,
The yew, the holly, and the bright green thorn,
With hanging islands of resplendent furze:
And on a summit, distant a short space,
By any who should look beyond the dell,
A single mountain cottage might be seen.
I gazed and gazed, and to myself I said,
'Our thoughts at least are ours; and this wild nook,
My Emma, I will dedicate to thee.'
—— Soon did the spot become my other home,   40
My dwelling, and my out-of-doors abode.
And, of the shepherds who have seen me there,
To whom I sometimes in our idle talk
Have told this fancy, two or three, perhaps,
Years after we are gone and in our graves,
When they have cause to speak of this wild place,
May call it by the name of Emma's Dell.

II

TO JOANNA

Amid the smoke of cities did you pass
Your time of early youth, and there you learned,
From years of quiet industry, to love
The living beings by your own fire-side,
With such a strong devotion, that your heart
Is slow towards the sympathies of them
Who look upon the hills with tenderness,
And make dear friendships with the streams and groves.
Yet we who are transgressors in this kind,
Dwelling retired in our simplicity   10

Among the woods and fields, we love you well,
Joanna! and I guess, since you have been
So distant from us now for two long years,
That you will gladly listen to discourse
However trivial, if you thence are taught
That they, with whom you once were happy, talk
Familiarly of you and of old times.
While I was seated, now some ten days past,
Beneath those lofty firs, that overtop
Their ancient neighbour, the old steeple tower,   20
The vicar from his gloomy house hard by
Came forth to greet me, and when he had asked,
'How fares Joanna, that wild-hearted maid!
And when will she return to us?' he paused,
And after short exchange of village news,
He with grave looks demanded, for what cause,
Reviving obsolete idolatry,
I like a runic priest, in characters
Of formidable size, had chiselled out
Some uncouth name upon the native rock,   30
Above the Rotha, by the forest side.
– Now, by those dear immunities of heart
Engendered betwixt malice and true love,
I was not loth to be so catechized,
And this was my reply. – 'As it befell,
One summer morning we had walked abroad
At break of day, Joanna and myself.
– 'Twas that delightful season, when the broom,
Full flowered and visible on every steep,
Along the copses runs in veins of gold.   40
Our pathway led us on to Rotha's banks,
And when we came in front of that tall rock
Which looks towards the east, I there stopped short,
And traced the lofty barrier with my eye
From base to summit; such delight I found
To note in shrub and tree, in stone and flower,
That intermixture of delicious hues,
Along so vast a surface, all at once,
In one impression, by connecting force

58

Of their own beauty, imaged in the heart.   50
– When I had gazed perhaps two minutes' space,
Joanna, looking in my eyes, beheld
That ravishment of mine, and laughed aloud.
The rock, like something starting from a sleep,
Took up the lady's voice, and laughed again:
That ancient woman seated on Helm-crag
Was ready with her cavern; Hammar-Scar,
And the tall steep of Silver-How sent forth
A noise of laughter; southern Loughrigg heard,
And Fairfield answered with a mountain tone: 60
Helvellyn far into the clear blue sky
Carried the lady's voice, – old Skiddaw blew
His speaking trumpet; – back out of the clouds
Of Glaramara southward came the voice;
And Kirkstone tossed it from his misty head.
Now whether, (said I to our cordial friend
Who in the hey-day of astonishment
Smiled in my face) this were in simple truth
A work accomplished by the brotherhood
Of ancient mountains, or my ear was touched   70
With dreams and visionary impulses,
Is not for me to tell; but sure I am
That there was a loud uproar in the hills.
And, while we both were listening, to my side
The fair Joanna drew, as if she wished
To shelter from some object of her fear.
– And hence, long afterwards, when eighteen moons
Were wasted, as I chanced to walk alone
Beneath this rock, at sun-rise, on a calm
And silent morning, I sat down, and there,   80
In memory of affections old and true,
I chiselled out in those rude characters
Joanna's name upon the living stone.
And I, and all who dwell by my fire-side
Have called the lovely rock, Joanna's Rock.'

III

'THERE IS AN EMINENCE, – OF THESE OUR HILLS'

There is an eminence, – of these our hills
The last that parleys with the setting sun.
We can behold it from our orchard seat,
And, when at evening we pursue our walk
Along the public way, this cliff, so high
Above us, and so distant in its height,
Is visible, and often seems to send
Its own deep quiet to restore our hearts.
The meteors make of it a favourite haunt:
The star of Jove, so beautiful and large   10
In the mid heav'ns, is never half so fair
As when he shines above it. 'Tis in truth
The loneliest place we have among the clouds.
And she who dwells with me, whom I have loved
With such communion, that no place on earth
Can ever be a solitude to me,
Hath said, this lonesome peak shall bear my name.

IV

'A NARROW GIRDLE OF ROUGH STONES AND CRAGS'

A narrow girdle of rough stones and crags,
A rude and natural causeway, interposed
Between the water and a winding slope
Of copse and thicket, leaves the eastern shore
Of Grasmere safe in its own privacy.
And there, myself and two beloved friends,
One calm September morning, ere the mist
Had altogether yielded to the sun,
Sauntered on this retired and difficult way.
—— Ill suits the road with one in haste, but we   10
Played with our time; and as we strolled along,
It was our occupation to observe
Such objects as the waves had tossed ashore,
Feather, or leaf, or weed, or withered bough,
Each on the other heaped along the line

Of the dry wreck. And in our vacant mood,
Not seldom did we stop to watch some tuft
Of dandelion seed or thistle's beard,
Which, seeming lifeless half, and half impelled
By some internal feeling, skimmed along   20
Close to the surface of the lake that lay
Asleep in a dead calm, ran closely on
Along the dead calm lake, now here, now there,
In all its sportive wanderings all the while
Making report of an invisible breeze
That was its wings, its chariot, and its horse,
Its very playmate, and its moving soul.
—— And often, trifling with a privilege
Alike indulged to all, we paused, one now,
And now the other, to point out, perchance   30
To pluck, some flower or water-weed, too fair
Either to be divided from the place
On which it grew, or to be left alone
To its own beauty. Many such there are,
Fair ferns and flowers, and chiefly that tall plant
So stately, of the Queen Osmunda named,
Plant lovelier in its own retired abode
On Grasmere's beach, than naiad by the side
Of Grecian brook, or lady of the mere
Sole-sitting by the shores of old romance.   40
—— So fared we that sweet morning: from the fields
Meanwhile, a noise was heard, the busy mirth
Of reapers, men and women, boys and girls.
Delighted much to listen to those sounds,
And in the fashion which I have described,
Feeding unthinking fancies, we advanced
Along the indented shore; when suddenly,
Through a thin veil of glittering haze, we saw
Before us on a point of jutting land
The tall and upright figure of a man   50
Attired in peasant's garb, who stood alone
Angling beside the margin of the lake.
That way we turned our steps; nor was it long,
Ere making ready comments on the sight

61

Which then we saw, with one and the same voice
We all cried out, that he must be indeed
An idle man, who thus could lose a day
Of the mid harvest, when the labourer's hire
Is ample, and some little might be stored
Wherewith to cheer him in the winter time.   60
Thus talking of that peasant we approached
Close to the spot where with his rod and line
He stood alone; whereat he turned his head
To greet us – and we saw a man worn down
By sickness, gaunt and lean, with sunken cheeks
And wasted limbs, his legs so long and lean
That for my single self I looked at them,
Forgetful of the body they sustained. –
Too weak to labour in the harvest field,
The man was using his best skill to gain   70
A pittance from the dead unfeeling lake
That knew not of his wants. I will not say
What thoughts immediately were ours, nor how
The happy idleness of that sweet morn,
With all its lovely images, was changed
To serious musing and to self-reproach.
Nor did we fail to see within ourselves
What need there is to be reserved in speech,
And temper all our thoughts with charity.
– Therefore, unwilling to forget that day,   80
My friend, myself, and she who then received
The same admonishment, have called the place
By a memorial name, uncouth indeed
As e'er by mariner was giv'n to bay
Or foreland on a new-discovered coast,
And, Point Rash-Judgment is the name it bears.

V

TO M. H.

Our walk was far among the ancient trees:
There was no road, nor any woodman's path,
But the thick umbrage, checking the wild growth

Of weed and sapling, on the soft green turf
Beneath the branches of itself had made
A track which brought us to a slip of lawn,
And a small bed of water in the woods.
All round this pool both flocks and herds might drink
On its firm margin, even as from a well
Or some stone-basin which the herdsman's hand   10
Had shaped for their refreshment, nor did sun
Or wind from any quarter ever come
But as a blessing to this calm recess,
This glade of water and this one green field.
The spot was made by Nature for herself:
The travellers know it not, and 'twill remain
Unknown to them; but it is beautiful,
And if a man should plant his cottage near,
Should sleep beneath the shelter of its trees,
And blend its waters with his daily meal,   20
He would so love it that in his death-hour
Its image would survive among his thoughts,
And, therefore, my sweet Mary, this still nook
With all its beeches we have named from you.

1799–1800   *Lyrical Ballads*, 2nd edn (1801)

Home at Grasmere

Once on the brow of yonder hill I stopped,
While I was yet a schoolboy (of what age
I cannot well remember, but the hour
I well remember though the year be gone),
And with a sudden influx overcome
At sight of this seclusion, I forgot
My haste – for hasty had my footsteps been,
As boyish my pursuits – and sighing said,
'What happy fortune were it here to live!
And if I thought of dying, if a thought   10
Of mortal separation could come in
With paradise before me, here to die.'
I was no prophet, nor had even a hope,
Scarcely a wish, but one bright pleasing thought,
A fancy in the heart of what might be
The lot of others, never could be mine.
   The place from which I looked was soft and green,
Not giddy yet aerial, with a depth
Of vale below, a height of hills above.
Long did I halt; I could have made it even   20
My business and my errand so to halt.
For rest of body 'twas a perfect place;
All that luxurious nature could desire,
But tempting to the spirit. Who could look
And not feel motions there? I thought of clouds

That sail on winds; of breezes that delight
To play on water, or in endless chase
Pursue each other through the liquid depths
Of grass or corn, over and through and through,
In billow after billow evermore;   30
Of sunbeams, shadows, butterflies, and birds,
Angels, and winged creatures that are lords
Without restraint of all which they behold.
I sat, and stirred in spirit as I looked,
I seemed to feel such liberty was mine,
Such power and joy; but only for this end:
To flit from field to rock, from rock to field,
From shore to island, and from isle to shore,
From open place to covert, from a bed
Of meadow-flowers into a tuft of wood,   40
From high to low, from low to high, yet still
Within the bounds of this huge concave; here
Should be my home, this valley be my world.

   From that time forward was the place to me
As beautiful in thought as it had been
When present to my bodily eyes; a haunt
Of my affections, oftentimes in joy
A brighter joy, in sorrow (but of that
I have known little), in such gloom, at least,
Such damp of the gay mind as stood to me   50
In place of sorrow, 'twas a gleam of light.
And now 'tis mine for life: dear vale,
One of thy lowly dwellings is my home!

   Yes, the realities of life – so cold,
So cowardly, so ready to betray,
So stinted in the measure of their grace,
As we report them, doing them much wrong –
Have been to me more bountiful than hope,
Less timid than desire. Oh bold indeed
They have been! Bold and bounteous unto me,   60
Who have myself been bold, not wanting trust,
Nor resolution, nor at last the hope
Which is of wisdom, for I feel it is.

And did it cost so much, and did it ask
Such length of discipline, and could it seem
An act of courage, and the thing itself
A conquest? Shame that this was ever so,
Not to the boy or youth, but shame to thee,
Sage man, thou sun in its meridian strength,
Thou flower in its full blow, thou king and crown   70
Of human nature; shame to thee, sage man.
Thy prudence, thy experience, thy desires,
Thy apprehensions – blush thou for them all.
But I am safe; yes, one at least is safe;
What once was deemed so difficult is now
Smooth, easy, without obstacle; what once
Did to my blindness seem a sacrifice,
The same is now a choice of the whole heart.
If e'er the acceptance of such dower was deemed
A condensation or a weak indulgence   80
To a sick fancy, it is now an act
Of reason that exultingly aspires.
This solitude is mine; the distant thought
Is fetched out of the heaven in which it was.
The unappropriated bliss hath found
An owner, and that owner I am he.
The lord of this enjoyment is on earth
And in my breast. What wonder if I speak
With fervour, am exalted with the thought
Of my possessions, of my genuine wealth   90
Inward and outward? What I keep, have gained,
Shall gain, must gain, if sound be my belief
From past and present rightly understood,
That in my day of childhood I was less
The mind of Nature, less, take all in all,
Whatever may be lost, than I am now.
For proof behold this valley and behold
Yon cottage, where with me my Emma dwells.
Aye, think on that, my heart, and cease to stir;
Pause upon that, and let the breathing frame   100
No longer breathe, but all be satisfied.
Oh, if such silence be not thanks to God

For what hath been bestowed, then where, where then
Shall gratitude find rest? Mine eyes did ne'er
Rest on a lovely object, nor my mind
Take pleasure in the midst of happy thoughts,
But either she whom now I have, who now
Divides with me this loved abode, was there
Or not far off. Where'er my footsteps turned,
Her voice was like a hidden bird that sang;   110
The thought of her was like a flash of light
Or an unseen companionship, a breath
Or fragrance independent of the wind;
In all my goings, in the new and old
Of all my meditations, and in this
Favourite of all, in this the most of all.
What being, therefore, since the birth of man
Had ever more abundant cause to speak
Thanks, and if music and the power of song
Make him more thankful, then to call on these   120
To aid him and with these resound his joy?
The boon is absolute; surpassing grace
To me hath been vouchsafed; among the bowers
Of blissful Eden this was neither given
Nor could be given – possession of the good
Which had been sighed for, ancient thought fulfilled,
And dear imaginations realized
Up to their highest measure, yea, and more.
  Embrace me then, ye hills, and close me in;
Now in the clear and open day I feel   130
Your guardianship; I take it to my heart;
'Tis like the solemn shelter of the night.
But I would call thee beautiful, for mild
And soft and gay and beautiful thou art,
Dear valley, having in thy face a smile
Though peaceful, full of gladness. Thou art pleased,
Pleased with thy crags and woody steeps, thy lake,
Its one green island and its winding shores,
The multitude of little rocky hills,
Thy church and cottages of mountain stone –   140
Clustered like stars, some few, but single most,

And lurking dimly in their shy retreats,
Or glancing at each other cheerful looks,
Like separated stars with clouds between.
What want we? Have we not perpetual streams,
Warm woods and sunny hills, and fresh green fields,
And mountains not less green, and flocks and herds,
And thickets full of songsters, and the voice
Of lordly birds – an unexpected sound
Heard now and then from morn to latest eve   150
Admonishing the man who walks below
Of solitude and silence in the sky?
These have we, and a thousand nooks of earth
Have also these; but nowhere else is found –
No where (or is it fancy?) can be found –
The one sensation that is here; 'tis here,
Here as it found its way into my heart
In childhood, here as it abides by day,
By night, here only; or in chosen minds
That take it with them hence, where'er they go.   160
'Tis (but I cannot name it), 'tis the sense
Of majesty and beauty and repose,
A blended holiness of earth and sky,
Something that makes this individual spot,
This small abiding-place of many men,
A termination and a last retreat,
A centre, come from wheresoe'er you will,
A whole without dependence or defect,
Made for itself and happy in itself,
Perfect contentment, unity entire.   170

   Long is it since we met to part no more,
Since I and Emma heard each other's call
And were companions once again, like birds
Which by the intruding fowler had been scared,
Two of a scattered brood that could not bear
To live in loneliness; 'tis long since we,
Remembering much and hoping more, found means
To walk abreast, though in a narrow path,
With undivided steps. Our home was sweet;
Could it be less? If we were forced to change,   180

Our home again was sweet; but still, for youth,
Strong as it seems and bold, is inly weak
And diffident, the destiny of life
Remained unfixed, and therefore we were still

[. . .]

We will be free, and, as we mean to live
In culture of divinity and truth,
Will choose the noblest temple that we know.
Not in mistrust or ignorance of the mind
And of the power she has within herself
To ennoble all things made we this resolve;
Far less from any momentary fit
Of inconsiderate fancy, light and vain;
But that we deemed it wise to take the help   200
Which lay within our reach; and here, we knew,
Help could be found of no mean sort; the spirit
Of singleness and unity and peace.
In this majestic, self-sufficing world,
This all in all of Nature, it will suit,
We said, no other spot on earth so well,
Simplicity of purpose, love intense,
Ambition not aspiring to the prize
Of outward things, but for the prize within –
Highest ambition. In the daily walks   210
Of business 'twill be harmony and grace
For the perpetual pleasure of the sense,
And for the soul – I do not say too much,
Though much be said – an image for the soul,
A habit of Eternity and God.
   Nor have we been deceived; thus far the effect
Falls not below the loftiest of our hopes.
Bleak season was it, turbulent and bleak,
When hitherward we journeyed, and on foot,
Through bursts of sunshine and through flying snows,   220
Paced the long vales – how long they were, and yet
How fast that length of way was left behind,
Wensley's long vale and Sedbergh's naked heights.

69

The frosty wind, as if to make amends
For its keen breath, was aiding to our course
And drove us onward like two ships at sea.
Stern was the face of nature; we rejoiced
In that stern countenance, for our souls had there
A feeling of their strength. The naked trees,
The icy brooks, as on we passed, appeared   230
To question us: 'Whence come ye? To what end?'
They seemed to say. 'What would ye?' said the shower,
'Wild wanderers, whither through my dark domain?'
The sunbeam said, 'Be happy.' They were moved,
All things were moved; they round us as we went,
We in the midst of them. And when the trance
Came to us, as we stood by Hart-leap Well –
The intimation of the milder day
Which is to come, the fairer world than this –
And raised us up, dejected as we were   240
Among the records of that doleful place
By sorrow for the hunted beast who there
Had yielded up his breath, the awful trance –
The vision of humanity and of God
The Mourner, God the Sufferer, when the heart
Of his poor creatures suffers wrongfully –
Both in the sadness and the joy we found
A promise and an earnest that we twain,
A pair seceding from the common world,
Might in that hallowed spot to which our steps   250
Were tending, in that individual nook,
Might even thus early for ourselves secure,
And in the midst of these unhappy times,
A portion of the blessedness which love
And knowledge will, we trust, hereafter give
To all the vales of earth and all mankind.
    Thrice hath the winter moon been filled with light
Since that dear day when Grasmere, our dear vale,
Received us. Bright and solemn was the sky
That faced us with a passionate welcoming   260
And led us to our threshold, to a home
Within a home, what was to be, and soon,

Our love within a love. Then darkness came,
Composing darkness, with its quiet load
Of full contentment, in a little shed
Disturbed, uneasy in itself, as seemed,
And wondering at its new inhabitants.
It loves us now, this vale so beautiful
Begins to love us! By a sullen storm,
Two months unwearied of severest storm,   270
It put the temper of our minds to proof,
And found us faithful through the gloom, and heard
The poet mutter his prelusive songs
With cheerful heart, an unknown voice of joy
Among the silence of the woods and hills,
Silent to any gladsomeness of sound
With all their shepherds.
              But the gates of spring
Are opened; churlish winter hath given leave
That she should entertain for this one day,
Perhaps for many genial days to come,   280
His guests and make them happy. They are pleased,
But most of all, the birds that haunt the flood,
With the mild summons, inmates though they be
Of winter's household. They are jubilant
This day, who drooped or seemed to droop so long;
They show their pleasure, and shall I do less?
Happier of happy though I be, like them
I cannot take possession of the sky,
Mount with a thoughtless impulse, and wheel there,
One of a mighty multitude whose way   290
And motion is a harmony and dance
Magnificent. Behold them, how they shape,
Orb after orb, their course, still round and round,
Above the area of the lake, their own
Adopted region, girding it about
In wanton repetition, yet therewith –
With that large circle evermore renewed –
Hundreds of curves and circlets, high and low,
Backwards and forwards, progress intricate,
As if one spirit was in all and swayed   300

Their indefatigable flight. 'Tis done,
Ten times, or more, I fancied it had ceased,
And lo! the vanished company again
Ascending – list again! I hear their wings:
Faint, faint at first, and then an eager sound,
Passed in a moment, and as faint again!
They tempt the sun to sport among their plumes;
They tempt the water and the gleaming ice
To show them a fair image. 'Tis themselves,
Their own fair forms upon the glimmering plain,   310
Painted more soft and fair as they descend,
Almost to touch, then up again aloft,
Up with a sally and a flash of speed,
As if they scorned both resting-place and rest.
Spring! for this day belongs to thee, rejoice!
Not upon me alone hath been bestowed –
Me, blessed with many onward-looking thoughts –
The sunshine and mild air. Oh, surely these
Are grateful; not the happy choirs of love,
Thine own peculiar family, sweet spring,   320
That sport among green leaves so blithe a train.

   But two are missing – two, a lonely pair
Of milk-white swans. Ah, why are they not here?
These above all, ah, why are they not here
To share in this day's pleasure? From afar
They came, like Emma and myself, to live
Together here in peace and solitude,
Choosing this valley, they who had the choice
Of the whole world. We saw them day by day,
Through those two months of unrelenting storm,   330
Conspicuous in the centre of the lake,
Their safe retreat. We knew them well – I guess
That the whole valley knew them – but to us
They were more dear than may be well believed,
Not only for their beauty and their still
And placid way of life and faithful love
Inseparable, not for these alone,
But that their state so much resembled ours;
They also having chosen this abode;

72

They strangers, and we strangers; they a pair,   340
And we a solitary pair like them.
They should not have departed; many days
I've looked for them in vain, nor on the wing
Have seen them, nor in that small open space
Of blue unfrozen water, where they lodged
And lived so long in quiet, side by side.
Companions, brethren, consecrated friends,
Shall we behold them yet another year
Surviving, they for us and we for them,
And neither pair be broken? Nay, perchance   350
It is too late already for such hope;
The shepherd may have seized the deadly tube
And parted them, incited by a prize
Which, for the sake of those he loves at home
And for the lamb upon the mountain tops,
He should have spared; or haply both are gone,
One death, and that were mercy given to both.

    I cannot look upon this favoured vale
But that I seem, by harbouring this thought,
To wrong it, such unworthy recompence   360
Imagining, of confidence so pure.
Ah! if I wished to follow where the sight
Of all that is before my eyes, the voice
Which is as a presiding spirit here
Would lead me, I should say unto myself,
They who are dwellers in this holy place
Must needs themselves be hallowed. They require
No benediction from the stranger's lips,
For they are blessed already. None would give
The greeting 'peace be with you' unto them,   370
For peace they have; it cannot but be theirs.
And mercy and forbearance – nay, not these;
There is no call for these; that office love
Performs and charity beyond the bounds
Of charity – an overflowing love,
Not for the creature only, but for all
Which is around them, love for every thing
Which in this happy valley we behold!

Thus do we soothe ourselves, and when the thought
Is past we blame it not for having come.   380
What if I floated down a pleasant stream
And now am landed and the motion gone –
Shall I reprove myself? Ah no, the stream
Is flowing and will never cease to flow,
And I shall float upon that stream again.
By such forgetfulness the soul becomes –
Words cannot say how beautiful. Then hail!
Hail to the visible Presence! Hail to thee,
Delightful valley, habitation fair!
And to whatever else of outward form   390
Can give us inward help, can purify
And elevate and harmonize and soothe,
And steal away and for a while deceive
And lap in pleasing rest, and bear us on
Without desire in full complacency,
Contemplating perfection absolute
And entertained as in a placid sleep.
   But not betrayed by tenderness of mind
That feared or wholly overlooked the truth
Did we come hither, with romantic hope   400
To find in midst of so much loveliness
Love, perfect love, of so much majesty
A like majestic frame of mind in those
Who here abide, the persons like the place.
Nor from such hope or aught of such belief
Hath issued any portion of the joy
Which I have felt this day. An awful voice,
'Tis true, I in my walks have often heard,
Sent from the mountains or the sheltered fields,
Shout after shout – reiterated whoop   410
In manner of a bird that takes delight
In answering to itself, or like a hound
Single at chase among the lonely woods –
A human voice, how awful in the gloom
Of coming night, when sky is dark, and earth
Not dark, not yet enlightened, but by snow
Made visible, amid the noise of winds

74

And bleatings manifold of sheep that know
That summons and are gathering round for food –
That voice, the same, the very same, that breath $\qquad$ 420
Which was an utterance awful as the wind,
Or any sound the mountains ever heard.
   That shepherd's voice, it may have reached mine ear
Debased and under profanation, made
An organ for the sounds articulate
Of ribaldry and blasphemy and wrath,
Where drunkenness hath kindled senseless frays.
I came not dreaming of unruffled life,
Untainted manners; born among the hills,
Bred also there, I wanted not a scale $\qquad$ 430
To regulate my hopes; pleased with the good,
I shrink not from the evil in disgust
Or with immoderate pain. I look for man,
The common creature of the brotherhood,
But little differing from the man elsewhere
For selfishness and envy and revenge,
Ill neighbourhood – folly that this should be –
Flattery and double-dealing, strife and wrong.
   Yet is it something gained – it is in truth
A mighty gain – that labour here preserves $\qquad$ 440
His rosy face, a servant only here
Of the fireside or of the open field,
A freeman, therefore sound and unenslaved;
That extreme penury is here unknown,
And cold and hunger's abject wretchedness,
Mortal to body and the heaven-born mind;
That they who want are not too great a weight
For those who can relieve. Here may the heart
Breathe in the air of fellow-suffering
Dreadless, as in a kind of fresher breeze $\qquad$ 450
Of her own native element; the hand
Be ready and unwearied without plea
From task too frequent and beyond its powers,
For languor or indifference or despair.
And as these lofty barriers break the force
Of winds – this deep vale as it doth in part

Conceal us from the storm – so here there is
A Power and a protection for the mind,
Dispensed indeed to other solitudes
Favoured by noble privilege like this, 460
Where kindred independence of estate
Is prevalent, where he who tills the field,
He, happy man! is master of the field
And treads the mountain which his father trod.
Hence, and from other local circumstance,
In this enclosure many of the old
Substantial virtues have a firmer tone
Than in the base and ordinary world.
  Yon cottage, would that it could tell a part
Of its own story. Thousands might give ear, 470
Might hear it and blush deep. There few years past
In this native valley dwelt a man,
The master of a little lot of ground,
A man of mild deportment and discourse,
A scholar also (as the phrase is here),
For he drew much delight from those few books
That lay within his reach, and for this cause
Was by his fellow-dalesmen honoured more.
A shepherd and a tiller of the ground,
Studious withal, and healthy in his frame 480
Of body, and of just and placid mind,
He with his consort and his children saw
Days that were seldom touched by petty strife,
Years safe from large misfortune, long maintained
That course which men the wisest and most pure
Might look on with entire complacency.
Yet in himself and near him were there faults
At work to undermine his happiness
By little and by little. Active, prompt,
And lively was the housewife, in the vale 490
None more industrious; but her industry
Was of that kind, 'tis said, which tended more
To splendid neatness, to a showy trim,
And overlaboured purity of house
Than to substantial thrift. He, on his part

76

Generous and easy-minded, was not free
From carelessness, and thus in course of time
These joint infirmities, combined perchance
With other cause less obvious, brought decay
Of worldly substance and distress of mind,   500
Which to a thoughtful man was hard to shun
And which he could not cure. A blooming girl
Served them, an inmate of the house. Alas!
Poor now in tranquil pleasure, he gave way
To thoughts of troubled pleasure; he became
A lawless suitor of the maid, and she
Yielded unworthily. Unhappy man!
That which he had been weak enough to do
Was misery in remembrance; he was stung,
Stung by his inward thoughts, and by the smiles   510
Of wife and children stung to agony.
His temper urged him not to seek relief
Amid the noise of revellers nor from draught
Of lonely stupefaction; he himself
A rational and suffering man, himself
Was his own world, without a resting-place.
Wretched at home, he had no peace abroad,
Ranged through the mountains, slept upon the earth,
Asked comfort of the open air, and found
No quiet in the darkness of the night,   520
No pleasure in the beauty of the day.
His flock he slighted; his paternal fields
Were as a clog to him, whose spirit wished
To fly, but whither? And yon gracious church,
That has a look so full of peace and hope
And love – benignant mother of the vale,
How fair amid her brood of cottages! –
She was to him a sickness and reproach.
I speak conjecturing from the little known,
The much that to the last remained unknown;   530
But this is sure: he died of his own grief,
He could not bear the weight of his own shame.

  That ridge, which elbowing from the mountain-side
Carries into the plain its rocks and woods,

Conceals a cottage where a father dwells
In widowhood, whose life's co-partner died
Long since, and left him solitary prop
Of many helpless children. I begin
With words which might be prelude to a tale
Of sorrow and dejection, but I feel –   540
Though in the midst of sadness, as might seem –
No sadness, when I think of what mine eyes
Have seen in that delightful family.
Bright garland make they for their father's brows,
Those six fair daughters budding yet, not one,
Not one of all the band a full-blown flower.
Go to the dwelling: There thou shalt have proof
That He who takes away, yet takes not half
Of what he seems to take, or gives it back
Not to our prayer, but far beyond our prayer,   550
He gives it the boon-produce of a soil
Which hope hath never watered. Thou shalt see
A house, which at small distance will appear
In no distinction to have passed beyond
Its fellows, will appear, like them, to have grown
Out of the native rock; but nearer view
Will show it not so grave in outward mien
And soberly arrayed as for the most
Are these rude mountain-dwellings – Nature's care,
Mere friendless Nature's – but a studious work   560
Of many fancies and of many hands,
A play thing and a pride; for such the air
And aspect which the little spot maintains
In spite of lonely winter's nakedness.
They have their jasmine resting on the porch,
Their rose-trees, strong in health, that will be soon
Roof-high; and here and there the garden wall
Is topped with single stones, a showy file
Curious for shape or hue – some round, like balls,
Worn smooth and round by fretting of the brook   570
From which they have been gathered, others bright
And sparry, the rough scatterings of the hills.
These ornaments the cottage chiefly owes

To one, a hardy girl, who mounts the rocks;
Such is her choice; she fears not the bleak wind;
Companion of her father, does for him
Where'er he wanders in his pastoral course
The service of a boy, and with delight
More keen and prouder daring. Yet hath she
Within the garden, like the rest, a bed   580
For her own flowers, or favourite herbs, a space
Holden by sacred charter; and I guess
She also helped to frame that tiny plot
Of garden ground which one day 'twas my chance
To find among the woody rocks that rise
Above the house, a slip of smoother earth
Planted with gooseberry bushes, and in one,
Right in the centre of the prickly shrub,
A mimic bird's-nest, fashioned by the hand,
Was stuck, a staring thing of twisted hay,   590
And one quaint fir-tree towered above the whole.
But in the darkness of the night, then most
This dwelling charms me; covered by the gloom
Then, heedless of good manners, I stop short
And (who could help it?) feed by stealth my sight
With prospect of the company within,
Laid open through the blazing window. There
I see the eldest daughter at her wheel,
Spinning amain, as if to overtake
She knows not what, or teaching in her turn   600
Some little novice of the sisterhood
That skill in this or other household work
Which from her father's honoured hands, herself,
While she was yet a little one, had learned.
Mild man! He is not gay, but they are gay,
And the whole house is filled with gaiety.

From yonder grey stone that stands alone
Close to the foaming stream, look up and see,
Not less than half way up the mountain-side,
A dusky spot, a little grove of firs   610
And seems still smaller than it is. The dame
Who dwells below, she told me that this grove,

Just six weeks younger than her eldest boy,
Was planted by her husband and herself
For a convenient shelter, which in storm
Their sheep might draw to. 'And they know it well,'
Said she, 'for thither do we bear them food
In time of heavy snow.' She then began
In fond obedience to her private thoughts
To speak of her dead husband. Is there not   620
An art, a music, and a stream of words
That shalt be life, the acknowledged voice of life?
Shall speak of what is done among the fields,
Done truly there, or felt, of solid good
And real evil, yet be sweet withal,
More grateful, more harmonious than the breath,
The idle breath of sweetest pipe attuned
To pastoral fancies? Is there such a stream,
Pure and unsullied, flowing from the heart
With motions of true dignity and grace,   630
Or must we seek these things where man is not?
Methinks I could repeat in tuneful verse
Delicious as the gentlest breeze that sounds
Through the aerial fir-grove, could preserve
Some portion of its human history
As gathered from that matron's lips and tell
Of tears that have been shed at sight of it
And moving dialogues between this pair,
Who in the prime of wedlock with joint hands
Did plant this grove, now flourishing while they   640
No longer flourish; he entirely gone,
She withering in her loneliness. Be this
A task above my skill; the silent mind
Has its own treasures, and I think of these,
Love what I see, and honour humankind.

No, we are not alone; we do not stand,
My Emma, here misplaced and desolate,
Loving what no one cares for but ourselves.
We shall not scatter through the plains and rocks
Of this fair vale and o'er its spacious heights   650
Unprofitable kindliness, bestowed

On objects unaccustomed to the gifts
Of feeling, that were cheerless and forlorn
But few weeks past, and would be so again
If we were not. We do not tend a lamp
Whose lustre we alone participate,
Which is dependent upon us alone,
Mortal though bright, a dying, dying flame.
Look where we will, some human heart has been
Before us with its offering; not a tree   660
Sprinkles these little pastures, but the same
Hath furnished matter for a thought, perchance
To some one is as a familiar friend.
Joy spreads and sorrow spreads; and this whole vale,
Home of untutored shepherds as it is,
Swarms with sensation, as with gleams of sunshine,
Shadows or breezes, scents or sounds. Nor deem
These feelings – though subservient more than ours
To every day's demand for daily bread,
And borrowing more their spirit and their shape   670
From self-respecting interests – deem them not
Unworthy therefore and unhallowed. No,
They lift the animal being, do themselves
By nature's kind and ever present aid
Refine the selfishness from which they spring,
Redeem by love the individual sense
Of anxiousness with which they are combined.
Many are pure, the best of them are pure;
The best, and these, remember, most abound,
Are fit associates of the worthiest joy,   680
Joy of the highest and the purest minds;
They blend with it congenially; meanwhile,
Calmly they breathe their own undying life,
Lowly and unassuming as it is,
Through this, their mountain sanctuary (long,
Oh long may it remain inviolate!),
Diffusing health and sober cheerfulness,
And giving to the moments as they pass
Their little boons of animating thought,
That sweeten labour, make it seem and feel   690

To be no arbitrary weight imposed,
But a glad function natural to man.

Fair proof of this, newcomer though I be,
Already have I seen; the inward frame,
Though slowly opening, opens every day.
Nor am I less delighted with the show
As it unfolds itself, now here, now there,
Than is the passing traveller, when his way
Lies through some region then first trod by him
(Say this fair valley's self), when low-hung mists   700
Break up and are beginning to recede.
How pleased he is to hear the murmuring stream,
The many voices, from he knows not where,
To have about him, which way e'er he goes,
Something on every side concealed from view,
In every quarter some thing visible,
Half seen or wholly, lost and found again –
Alternate progress and impediment,
And yet a growing prospect in the main.

Such pleasure now is mine, and what if I –   710
Herein less happy than the traveller –
Am sometimes forced to cast a painful look
Upon unwelcome things, which unawares
Reveal themselves? Not therefore is my mind
Depressed, nor do I fear what is to come;
But confident, enriched at every glance,
The more I see the more is my delight.
Truth justifies herself; and as she dwells
With Hope, who would not follow where she leads?

Nor let me overlook those other loves   720
Where no fear is, those humbler sympathies
That have to me endeared the quietness
Of this sublime retirement. I begin
Already to inscribe upon my heart
A liking for the small grey horse that bears
The paralytic man; I know the ass
On which the cripple in the quarry maimed
Rides to and fro: I know them and their ways.
The famous sheep dog, first in all the vale,

82

Though yet to me a stranger, will not be   730
A stranger long; nor will the blind man's guide,
Meek and neglected thing, of no renown.
Whoever lived a winter in one place,
Beneath the shelter of one cottage-roof,
And has not had his red-breast or his wren?
I have them both; and I shall have my thrush
In spring time, and a hundred warblers more;
And if the banished eagle pair return,
Helvellyn's eagles, to their ancient hold,
Then shall I see, shall claim with those two birds   740
Acquaintance, as they soar amid the heavens.
The owl that gives the name to Owlet Crag
Have I heard shouting, and he soon will be
A chosen one of my regards. See there,
The heifer in yon little croft belongs
To one who holds it dear; with duteous care
She reared it, and in speaking of her charge
I heard her scatter once a word or two,
A term domestic, yea, and motherly,
She being herself a mother. Happy beast,   750
If the caresses of a human voice
Can make it so, and care of human hands.

    And ye as happy under Nature's care,
Strangers to me and all men, or at least
Strangers to all particular amity,
All intercourse of knowledge or of love
That parts the individual from the kind;
Whether in large communities ye dwell
From year to year, not shunning man's abode,
A settled residence, or be from far,   760
Wild creatures, and of many homes, that come
The gift of winds, and whom the winds again
Take from us at your pleasure – yet shall ye
Not want for this, your own subordinate place,
According to your claim, an underplace
In my affections. Witness the delight
With which ere while I saw that multitude
Wheel through the sky and see them now at rest,

Yet not at rest, upon the glassy lake.
They cannot rest; they gambol like young whelps,   770
Active as lambs and overcome with joy;
They try all frolic motions, flutter, plunge,
And beat the passive water with their wings.
Too distant are they for plain view, but lo!
Those little fountains, sparkling in the sun,
Which tell what they are doing, which rise up,
First one and then another silver spout,
As one or other takes the fit of glee –
Fountains and spouts, yet rather in the guise
Of plaything fire-works, which on festal nights   780
Hiss hiss about the feet of wanton boys.
How vast the compass of this theatre,
Yet nothing to be seen but lovely pomp
And silent majesty. The birch tree woods
Are hung with thousand thousand diamond drops
Of melted hoar-frost, every tiny knot
In the bare twigs, each little budding-place
Cased with its several bead; what myriads there
Upon one tree, while all the distant grove
That rises to the summit of the steep   790
Is like a mountain built of silver light!
See yonder the same pageant, and again
Behold the universal imagery
At what a depth, deep in the lake below.
Admonished of the days of love to come,
The raven croaks and fills the sunny air
With a strange sound of genial harmony;
And in and all about that playful band,
Incapable although they be of rest,
And in their fashion very rioters,   800
There is a stillness, and they seem to make
Calm revelry in that their calm abode.
I leave them to their pleasure, and I pass,
Pass with a thought the life of the whole year
That is to come – the throngs of mountain flowers
And lilies that will dance upon the lake.
    Then boldly say that solitude is not

Where these things are: he truly is alone,
He of the multitude, whose eyes are doomed
To hold a vacant commerce day by day   810
With that which he can neither know nor love –
Dead things, to him thrice dead – or worse than this,
With swarms of life, and worse than all, of men,
His fellow men, that are to him no more
Than to the forest hermit are the leaves
That hang aloft in myriads – nay, far less,
Far less for aught that comforts or defends
Or lulls or cheers. Society is here:
The true community, the noblest frame
Of many into one incorporate;   820
That must be looked for here; paternal sway,
One household under God for high and low,
One family and one mansion; to themselves
Appropriate and divided from the world
As if it were a cave, a multitude
Human and brute, possessors undisturbed
Of this recess, their legislative hall,
Their temple, and their glorious dwelling-place.
   Dismissing therefore all Arcadian dreams,
All golden fancies of the golden age,   830
The bright array of shadowy thoughts from times
That were before all time, or are to be
When time is not, the pageantry that stirs
And will be stirring when our eyes are fixed
On lovely objects and we wish to part
With all remembrance of a jarring world –
Give entrance to the sober truth; avow
That Nature to this favourite spot of ours
Yields no exemption, but her awful rights,
Enforces to the utmost and exacts   840
Her tribute of inevitable pain,
And that the sting is added, man himself
For ever busy to afflict himself.
Yet temper this with one sufficient hope
(What need of more?): that we shall neither droop
Nor pine for want of pleasure in the life

Which is about us, nor through dearth of aught
That keeps in health the insatiable mind;
That we shall have for knowledge and for love
Abundance; and that, feeling as we do,   850
How goodly, how exceeding fair, how pure
From all reproach is the ethereal frame
And this deep vale, its earthly counterpart,
By which and under which we are enclosed
To breathe in peace; we shall moreover find
(If sound, and what we ought to be ourselves,
If rightly we observe and justly weigh)
The inmates not unworthy of their home,
The dwellers of the dwelling.
                                   And if this
Were not, we have enough within ourselves,   860
Enough to fill the present day with joy
And overspread the future years with hope –
Our beautiful and quiet home, enriched
Already with a stranger whom we love
Deeply, a stranger of our father's house,
A never-resting pilgrim of the sea,
Who finds at last an hour to his content
Beneath our roof; and others whom we love
Will seek us also, sisters of our hearts,
And one, like them, a brother of our hearts,   870
Philosopher and poet, in whose sight
These mountains will rejoice with open joy.
Such is our wealth: O vale of peace, we are
And must be, with God's will, a happy band!
   But 'tis not to enjoy, for this alone
That we exist; no, something must be done.
I must not walk in unreproved delight
These narrow bounds and think of nothing more,
No duty that looks further and no care.
Each being has his office, lowly some   880
And common, yet all worthy if fulfilled
With zeal, acknowledgement that with the gift
Keeps pace a harvest answering to the seed.
Of ill advised ambition and of pride

I would stand clear, yet unto me I feel
That an internal brightness is vouchsafed
That must not die, that must not pass away.
Why does this inward lustre fondly seek
And gladly blend with outward fellowship?
Why shine they round me thus, whom thus I love?   890
Why do they teach me, whom I thus revere?
Strange question, yet it answers not itself.
That humble roof, embowered among the trees,
That calm fireside – it is not even in them,
Blessed as they are, to furnish a reply
That satisfies and ends in perfect rest.
Possessions have I, wholly, solely mine,
Something within, which yet is shared by none –
Not even the nearest to me and most dear –
Something which power and effort may impart.   900
I would impart it; I would spread it wide,
Immortal in the world which is to come.
I would not wholly perish even in this,
Lie down and be forgotten in the dust,
I and the modest partners of my days,
Making a silent company in death.
It must not be, if I divinely taught
Am privileged to speak as I have felt
Of what in man is human or divine.
   While yet an innocent little one, a heart   910
That doubtless wanted not its tender moods,
I breathed (for this I better recollect)
Among wild appetites and blind desires,
Motions of savage instinct, my delight
And exaltation. Nothing at that time
So welcome, no temptation half so dear
As that which urged me to a daring feat.
Deep pools, tall trees, black chasms, and dizzy crags –
I loved to look in them, to stand and read
Their looks forbidding, read and disobey,   920
Sometimes in act, and evermore in thought.
With impulses which only were by these
Surpassed in strength, I heard of danger met

87

Or sought with courage, enterprize forlorn,
By one, sole keeper of his own intent,
Or by a resolute few, who for the sake
Of glory fronted multitudes in arms.
Yea, to this day I swell with like desire;
I cannot at this moment read a tale
Of two brave vessels matched in deadly fight   930
And fighting to the death, but I am pleased
More than a wise man ought to be; I wish,
I burn, I struggle, and in soul am there.
But me hath Nature tamed and bade me seek
For other agitations or be calm,
Hath dealt with me as with a turbulent stream –
Some nurseling of the mountains which she leads
Through quiet meadows after it has learned
Its strength and had its triumph and its joy,
Its desperate course of tumult and of glee.   940
That which in stealth by nature was performed
Hath reason sanctioned. Her deliberate voice
Hath said, 'Be mild and love all gentle things;
Thy glory and thy happiness be there.
Yet fear (though thou confide in me) no want
Of aspirations which have been – of foes
To wrestle with and victory to complete,
Bounds to be leapt and darkness to explore.
That which enflamed thy infant heart – the love,
The longing, the contempt, the undaunted quest –   950
These shall survive, though changed their office, these
Shall live; it is not in their power to die.'
Then farewell to the warrior's deeds, farewell
All hope, which once and long was mine, to fill
The heroic trumpet with the muse's breath!
Yet in this peaceful vale we will not spend
Unheard-of days, though loving peaceful thoughts;
A voice shall speak, and what will be the theme?
    On man, on nature, and on human life,
Thinking in solitude, from time to time   960
I feel sweet passions traversing my soul
Like music; unto these, where'er I may,

I would give utterance in numerous verse.
Of truth, of grandeur, beauty, love and hope –
Hope for this earth and hope beyond the grave –
Of virtue and of intellectual power,
Of blessed consolations in distress,
Of joy in widest commonalty spread,
Of the individual mind that keeps its own
Inviolate retirement, and consists   970
With being limitless the one great life –
I sing; fit audience let me find though few!
   Fit audience find though few – thus prayed the Bard,
Holiest of men. Urania, I shall need
Thy guidance, or a greater muse, if such
Descend to earth or dwell in highest heaven!
For I must tread on shadowy ground, must sink
Deep, and, aloft ascending, breathe in worlds
To which the heaven of heavens is but a veil.
All strength, all terror, single or in bands,   980
That ever was put forth in personal forms –
Jehovah, with his thunder, and the choir
Of shouting angels and the empyreal throne –
I pass them unalarmed. The darkest pit
Of the profoundest hell, chaos, night,
Nor aught of blinder vacancy scooped out
By help of dreams can breed such fear and awe
As fall upon us often when we look
Into our minds, into the mind of man,
My haunt and the main region of my song.   990
Beauty, whose living home is the green earth,
Surpassing the most fair ideal forms
The craft of delicate spirits hath composed
From earth's materials, waits upon my steps,
Pitches her tents before me when I move,
An hourly neighbour. Paradise and groves
Elysian, fortunate islands, fields like those of old
In the deep ocean – wherefore should they be
A history, or but a dream, when minds
Once wedded to this outward frame of things   1000
In love, find these the growth of common day?

I, long before the blessed hour arrives,
Would sing in solitude the spousal verse
Of this great consummation, would proclaim –
Speaking of nothing more than what we are –
How exquisitely the individual mind
(And the progressive powers perhaps no less
Of the whole species) to the external world
Is fitted; and how exquisitely too –
Theme this but little heard of among men –   1010
The external world is fitted to the mind;
And the creation (by no lower name
Can it be called) which they with blended might
Accomplish: this is my great argument.
Such pleasant haunts foregoing, if I oft
Must turn elsewhere, and travel near the tribes
And fellowships of men, and see ill sights
Of passions ravenous from each other's rage,
Must hear humanity in fields and groves
Pipe solitary anguish, or must hang   1020
Brooding above the fierce confederate storm
Of sorrow, barricadoed evermore
Within the walls of cities – may these sounds
Have their authentic comment, that even these
Hearing, I be not heartless or forlorn!
Come, thou prophetic spirit, soul of man,
Thou human soul of the wide earth that hast
Thy metropolitan temple in the hearts
Of mighty poets; unto me vouchsafe
Thy guidance, teach me to discern and part   1030
Inherent things from casual, what is fixed
From fleeting, that my verse may live and be
Even as a light hung up in heaven to cheer
Mankind in times to come! And if with this
I blend more lowly matter – with the thing
Contemplated describe the mind and man
Contemplating, and who and what he was,
The transitory being that beheld
This vision, when and where and how he lived,
With all his little realities of life –   1040

90

Be not this labour useless. If such theme
With highest things may mingle, then, Great God,
Thou who art breath and being, way and guide,
And power and understanding, may my life
Express the image of a better time,
More wise desires and simple manners; nurse
My heart in genuine freedom; all pure thoughts
Be with me and uphold me to the end!

1800   *The Recluse* (1888)

OLD MAN TRAVELLING

[Animal tranquillity and decay, a sketch]

   The little hedgerow birds,
That peck along the road, regard him not.
He travels on, and in his face, his step,
His gait, is one expression; every limb,
His look and bending figure, all bespeak   5
A man who does not move with pain, but moves
With thought – He is insensibly subdued
To settled quiet: he is one by whom
All effort seems forgotten, one to whom
Long patience has such mild composure given,   10
That patience now doth seem a thing, of which
He hath no need. He is by nature led
To peace so perfect, that the young behold
With envy, what the old man hardly feels.
– I asked him whither he was bound, and what   15
The object of his journey; he replied
'Sir! I am going many miles to take
A last leave of my son, a mariner,
Who from a sea-fight has been brought to Falmouth,
And there is dying in an hospital.'   20

1797   *Lyrical Ballads* (1798)

THE OLD CUMBERLAND BEGGAR

A Description

The class of beggars to which the old man here described belongs,
will probably soon be extinct. It consisted of poor, and, mostly, old
and infirm persons, who confined themselves to a stated round in
their neighbourhood, and had certain fixed days, on which, at differ-
ent houses, they regularly received charity; sometimes in money, but
mostly in provisions.

I saw an aged beggar in my walk,
And he was seated by the highway side
On a low structure of rude masonry
Built at the foot of a huge hill, that they
Who lead their horses down the steep rough road
May thence remount at ease. The aged man
Had placed his staff across the broad smooth stone
That overlays the pile, and from a bag
All white with flour the dole of village dames,
He drew his scraps and fragments, one by one,   10
And scanned them with a fixed and serious look
Of idle computation. In the sun,
Upon the second step of that small pile,
Surrounded by those wild unpeopled hills,
He sat, and ate his food in solitude;
And ever, scattered from his palsied hand,
That still attempting to prevent the waste,
Was baffled still, the crumbs in little showers
Fell on the ground, and the small mountain birds,
Not venturing yet to peck their destined meal,   20
Approached within the length of half his staff.

Him from my childhood have I known, and then
He was so old, he seems not older now;
He travels on, a solitary man,
So helpless in appearance, that for him
The sauntering horseman-traveller does not throw
With careless hands his alms upon the ground,
But stops, that he may safely lodge the coin

93

Within the old man's hat; nor quits him so,
But still when he has given his horse the rein   30
Towards the aged beggar turns a look,
Sidelong and half-reverted. She who tends
The toll gate, when in summer at her door
She turns her wheel, if on the road she sees
The aged beggar coming, quits her work,
And lifts the latch for him that he may pass.
The post-boy when his rattling wheels o'ertake
The aged beggar, in the woody lane,
Shouts to him from behind, and, if perchance
The old man does not change his course, the boy   40
Turns with less noisy wheels to the road-side,
And passes gently by, without a curse
Upon his lips, or anger at his heart.
He travels on, a solitary man,
His age has no companion. On the ground
His eyes are turned, and, as he moves along,
They move along the ground; and evermore,
Instead of common and habitual sight
Of fields with rural works, of hill and dale,
And the blue sky, one little span of earth   50
Is all his prospect. Thus, from day to day,
Bowbent, his eyes for ever on the ground,
He plies his weary journey, seeing still,
And never knowing that he sees, some straw,
Some scattered leaf, or marks which, in one track,
The nails of cart or chariot wheel have left
Impressed on the white road, in the same line,
At distance still the same. Poor traveller!
His staff trails with him, scarcely do his feet
Disturb the summer dust, he is so still   60
In look and motion that the cottage curs,
Ere he have passed the door, will turn away
Weary of barking at him. Boys and girls,
The vacant and the busy, maids and youths,
And urchins newly breeched all pass him by:
Him even the slow-paced waggon leaves behind.

94

But deem not this man useless. – Statesman! ye
Who are so restless in your wisdom, ye
Who have a broom still ready in your hands
To rid the world of nuisances; ye proud,   70
Heart-swoln, while in your pride ye contemplate
Your talents, power, and wisdom, deem him not
A burthen of the earth. 'Tis Nature's law
That none, the meanest of created things,
Of forms created the most vile and brute,
The dullest or most noxious, should exist
Divorced from good, a spirit and pulse of good,
A life and soul to every mode of being
Inseparably linked. While thus he creeps
From door to door, the villagers in him   80
Behold a record which together binds
Past deeds and offices of charity
Else unremembered, and so keeps alive
The kindly mood in hearts which lapse of years,
And that half-wisdom half-experience gives
Make slow to feel, and by sure steps resign
To selfishness and cold oblivious cares.
Among the farms and solitary huts,
Hamlets, and thinly-scattered villages,
Where'er the aged beggar takes his rounds,   90
The mild necessity of use compels
To acts of love; and habit does the work
Of reason, yet prepares that after-joy
Which reason cherishes. And thus the soul,
By that sweet taste of pleasure unpursued
Doth find itself insensibly disposed
To virtue and true goodness. Some there are,
By their good works exalted, lofty minds
And meditative, authors of delight
And happiness, which to the end of time   100
Will live, and spread, and kindle; minds like these,
In childhood, from this solitary being,
This helpless wanderer, have perchance received,
(A thing more precious far than all that books
Or the solicitudes of love can do!)

95

That first mild touch of sympathy and thought,
In which they found their kindred with a world
Where want and sorrow were. The easy man
Who sits at his own door, and like the pear
Which overhangs his head from the green wall,   110
Feeds in the sunshine; the robust and young,
The prosperous and unthinking, they who live
Sheltered, and flourish in a little grove
Of their own kindred, all behold in him
A silent monitor, which on their minds
Must needs impress a transitory thought
Of self-congratulation, to the heart
Of each recalling his peculiar boons,
His charters and exemptions; and perchance,
Through he to no one give the fortitude   120
And circumspection needful to preserve
His present blessings, and to husband up
The respite of the season, he, at least,
And 'tis no vulgar service, makes them felt.

Yet further. – Many, I believe, there are
Who live a life of virtuous decency,
Men who can hear the Decalogue and feel
No self-reproach, who of the moral law
Established in the land where they abide
Are strict observers, and not negligent,   130
Meanwhile, in any tenderness of heart
Or act of love to those with whom they dwell,
Their kindred, and the children of their blood.
Praise be to such, and to their slumbers peace!
– But of the poor man ask, the abject poor,
Go and demand of him, if there be here,
In this cold abstinence from evil deeds,
And these inevitable charities,
Wherewith to satisfy the human soul.
No – man is dear to man: the poorest poor   140
Long for some moments in a weary life
When they can know and feel that they have been
Themselves the fathers and the dealers out

Of some small blessings, have been kind to such
As needed kindness, for this single cause,
That we have all of us one human heart.
– Such pleasure is to one kind being known,
My neighbour, when with punctual care, each week
Duly as Friday comes, though pressed herself
By her own wants, she from her chest of meal   150
Takes one unsparing handful for the scrip
Of this old mendicant, and, from her door
Returning with exhilarated heart,
Sits by her fire and builds her hope in heaven.

Then let him pass, a blessing on his head!
And while, in that vast solitude to which
The tide of things has led him, he appears
To breathe and live but for himself alone,
Unblamed, uninjured, let him bear about
The good which the benignant law of heaven   160
Has hung around him, and, while life is his,
Still let him prompt the unlettered villagers
To tender offices and pensive thoughts.
Then let him pass, a blessing on his head!
And, long as he can wander, let him breathe
The freshness of the valleys, let his blood
Struggle with frosty air and winter snows,
And let the chartered wind that sweeps the heath
Beat his grey locks against his withered face.
Reverence the hope whose vital anxiousness   170
Gives the last human interest to his heart.
May never house, misnamed of industry,
Make him a captive; for that pent-up din,
Those life-consuming sounds that clog the air,
Be his the natural silence of old age.
Let him be free of mountain solitudes,
And have around him, whether heard or not,
The pleasant melody of woodland birds.
Few are his pleasures; if his eyes, which now
Have been so long familiar with the earth,   180
No more behold the horizontal sun

Rising or setting, let the light at least
Find a free entrance to their languid orbs.
And let him, *where* and *when* he will, sit down
Beneath the trees, or by the grassy bank
Of highway side, and with the little birds
Share his chance-gathered meal, and, finally,
As in the eye of Nature he has lived,
So in the eye of Nature let him die.

1798   *Lyrical Ballads*, 2nd edn (1801)

RESOLUTION AND INDEPENDENCE

There was a roaring in the wind all night;
The rain came heavily and fell in floods;
But now the sun is rising calm and bright;
The birds are singing in the distant woods;
Over his own sweet voice the stock-dove broods;
The jay makes answer as the magpie chatters;
And all the air is filled with pleasant noise of waters.

All things that love the sun are out of doors;
The sky rejoices in the morning's birth;
The grass is bright with rain-drops; on the moors   10
The hare is running races in her mirth;
And with her feet she from the plashy earth
Raises a mist; which, glittering in the sun,
Runs with her all the way, wherever she doth run.

I was a traveller then upon the moor;
I saw the hare that raced about with joy;
I heard the woods, and distant waters, roar;
Or heard them not, as happy as a boy:
The pleasant season did my heart employ:
My old remembrances went from me wholly;   20
And all the ways of men, so vain and melancholy.

But, as it sometimes chanceth, from the might
Of joy in minds that can no farther go,

98

As high as we have mounted in delight
In our dejection do we sink as low,
To me that morning did it happen so;
And fears, and fancies, thick upon me came;
Dim sadness, and blind thoughts I knew not nor could name.

I heard the skylark singing in the sky;
And I bethought me of the playful hare: 30
Even such a happy child of earth am I;
Even as these blissful creatures do I fare;
Far from the world I walk, and from all care;
But there may come another day to me,
Solitude, pain of heart, distress, and poverty.

My whole life I have lived in pleasant thought,
As if life's business were a summer mood;
As if all needful things would come unsought
To genial faith, still rich in genial good;
But how can he expect that others should   40
Build for him, sow for him, and at his call
Love him, who for himself will take no heed at all?

I thought of Chatterton, the marvellous boy,
The sleepless soul that perished in its pride;
Of him who walked in glory and in joy
Behind his plough, upon the mountain-side:
By our own spirits are we deified;
We poets in our youth begin in gladness;
But thereof comes in the end despondency and madness.

Now, whether it were by peculiar grace,   50
A leading from above, a something given,
Yet it befell, that, in this lonely place,
When up and down my fancy thus was driven,
And I with these untoward thoughts had striven,
I saw a man before me unawares:
The oldest man he seemed that ever wore grey hairs.

My course I stopped as soon as I espied
The old man in that naked wilderness:
Close by a pond, upon the further side,
He stood alone: a minute's space I guess   60
I watched him, he continuing motionless:
To the pool's further margin then I drew;
He being all the while before me full in view.

As a huge stone is sometimes seen to lie
Couched on the bald top of an eminence;
Wonder to all who do the same espy
By what means it could thither come, and whence;
So that it seems a thing endued with sense:
Like a sea-beast crawled forth, which on a shelf
Of rock or sand reposeth, there to sun itself.   70

Such seemed this man, not all alive nor dead,
Nor all asleep; in his extreme old age:
His body was bent double, feet and head
Coming together in their pilgrimage;
As if some dire constraint of pain, or rage
Of sickness felt by him in times long past,
A more than human weight upon his frame had cast.

Himself he propped, his body, limbs, and face,
Upon a long grey staff of shaven wood:
And, still as I drew near with gentle pace,   80
Beside the little pond or moorish flood
Motionless as a cloud the old man stood;
That heareth not the loud winds when they call;
And moveth altogether, if it move at all.

At length, himself unsettling, he the pond
Stirred with his staff, and fixedly did look
Upon the muddy water, which he conned,
As if he had been reading in a book:
And now such freedom as I could I took;
And, drawing to his side, to him did say,   90
'This morning gives us promise of a glorious day.'

100

A gentle answer did the old man make,
In courteous speech which forth he slowly drew:
And him with further words I thus bespake,
'What kind of work is that which you pursue?
This is a lonesome place for one like you.'
He answered me with pleasure and surprize;
And there was, while he spake, a fire about his eyes.

His words came feebly, from a feeble chest,
Yet each in solemn order followed each,   100
With something of a lofty utterance dressed;
Choice word, and measured phrase; above the reach
Of ordinary men; a stately speech!
Such as grave livers do in Scotland use,
Religious men, who give to God and man their dues.

He told me that he to this pond had come
To gather leeches, being old and poor:
Employment hazardous and wearisome!
And he had many hardships to endure:
From pond to pond he roamed, from moor to moor,   110
Housing, with God's good help, by choice or chance:
And in this way he gained an honest maintenance.

The old man still stood talking by my side;
But now his voice to me was like a stream
Scarce heard; nor word from word could I divide;
And the whole body of the man did seem
Like one whom I had met with in a dream;
Or like a man from some far region sent;
To give me human strength, and strong admonishment.

My former thoughts returned: the fear that kills;   120
The hope that is unwilling to be fed;
Cold, pain, and labour, and all fleshly ills;
And mighty poets in their misery dead.
And now, not knowing what the old man had said,
My question eagerly did I renew,
'How is it that you live, and what is it you do?'

He with a smile did then his words repeat;
And said, that, gathering leeches, far and wide
He travelled; stirring thus about his feet
The waters of the ponds where they abide.   130
'Once I could meet with them on every side;
But they have dwindled long by slow decay;
Yet still I persevere, and find them where I may.'

While he was talking thus, the lonely place,
The old man's shape, and speech, all troubled me:
In my mind's eye I seemed to see him pace
About the weary moors continually,
Wandering about alone and silently.
While I these thoughts within myself pursued,
He, having made a pause, the same discourse renewed.   140

And soon with this he other matter blended,
Cheerfully uttered, with demeanour kind,
But stately in the main; and, when he ended,
I could have laughed myself to scorn, to find
In that decrepit man so firm a mind.
'God,' said I, 'be my help and stay secure;
I'll think of the leech-gatherer on the lonely moor.'

1802   *Poems, in Two Volumes* (1807)

The Prelude 1798–9, First Part

                    Was it for this
That one, the fairest of all rivers, loved
To blend his murmurs with my nurse's song,
And from his alder shades, and rocky falls,
And from his fords and shallows, sent a voice
That flowed along my dreams? For this didst thou
O Derwent, travelling over the green plains
Near my 'sweet birthplace', didst thou beauteous stream
Make ceaseless music through the night and day,
Which with its steady cadence tempering   10
Our human waywardness, composed my thoughts
To more than infant softness, giving me,
Among the fretful dwellings of mankind,
A knowledge, a dim earnest of the calm
Which Nature breathes among the fields and groves?
    Beloved Derwent! fairest of all streams!
Was it for this that I, a four year's child,
A naked boy, among thy silent pools
Made one long bathing of a summer's day?
Basked in the sun, or plunged into thy streams,   20
Alternate, all a summer's day, or coursed
Over the sandy fields, and dashed the flowers
Of yellow grunsel, or when crag and hill,
The woods and distant Skiddaw's lofty height
Were bronzed with a deep radiance, stood alone,

A naked savage in the thunder shower?
  And afterwards, 'twas in a later day
Though early, when upon the mountain-slope
The frost and breath of frosty wind had snapped
The last autumnal crocus, 'twas my joy   30
To wander half the night among the cliffs
And the smooth hollows, where the woodcocks ran
Along the moonlight turf. In thought and wish,
That time, my shoulder all with springes hung,
I was a fell destroyer. Gentle Powers!
Who give us happiness and call it peace!
When scudding on from snare to snare I plied
My anxious visitation, hurrying on,
Still hurrying hurrying onward, how my heart
Panted; among the scattered yew-trees, and the crags   40
That looked upon me, how my bosom beat
With expectation. Sometimes strong desire,
Resistless, overpowered me, and the bird
Which was the captive of another's toils
Became my prey; and when the deed was done
I heard among the solitary hills
Low breathings coming after me, and sounds
Of undistinguishable motion, steps
Almost as silent as the turf they trod.
  Nor less, in springtime, when on southern banks   50
The shining sun had from his knot of leaves
Decoyed the primrose-flower, and when the vales
And woods were warm, was I a rover then
In the high places, on the lonesome peaks,
Among the mountains and the winds. Though mean
And though inglorious were my views, the end
Was not ignoble. Oh, when I have hung
Above the raven's nest, by knots of grass,
Or half-inch fissures in the slipp'ry rock,
But ill sustained, and almost, as it seemed,   60
Suspended by the blast which blew amain,
Shouldering the naked crag, oh at that time,
While on the perilous ridge I hung alone,
With what strange utterance did the loud dry wind

Blow through my ears! the sky seemed not a sky
Of earth, and with what motion moved the clouds!
   The mind of man is fashioned and built up
Even as a strain of music: I believe
That there are spirits, which, when they would form
A favoured being, from his very dawn   70
Of infancy do open out the clouds
As at the touch of lightning, seeking him
With gentle visitation; quiet Powers!
Retired and seldom recognized, yet kind,
And to the very meanest not unknown;
With me, though rarely in my early days
They communed: others too there are who use,
Yet haply aiming at the self-same end,
Severer interventions, ministry
More palpable, and of their school was I.   80
   They guided me: one evening, led by them,
I went alone into a shepherd's boat,
A skiff that to a willow-tree was tied
Within a rocky cave, its usual home;
The moon was up, the lake was shining clear
Among the hoary mountains: from the shore
I pushed, and struck the oars, and struck again
In cadence, and my little boat moved on
Just like a man who walks with stately step
Though bent on speed. It was an act of stealth   90
And troubled pleasure; not without the voice
Of mountain-echoes did my boat move on,
Leaving behind her still on either side
Small circles glittering idly in the moon
Until they melted all into one track
Of sparkling light. A rocky steep uprose
Above the cavern of the willow tree,
And now, as suited one who proudly rowed
With his best skill, I fixed a steady view
Upon the top of that same craggy ridge,   100
The bound of the horizon, for behind
Was nothing – but the stars and the grey sky.
– She was an elfin pinnace; twenty times

105

I dipped my oars into the silent lake,
And, as I rose upon the stroke, my boat
Went heaving through the water, like a swan –
When from behind that rocky steep, till then
The bound of the horizon, a huge cliff,
As if with voluntary power instinct,
Upreared its head: I struck, and struck again, 110
And, growing still in stature, the huge cliff
Rose up between me and the stars, and still
With measured motion, like a living thing,
Strode after me. With trembling hands I turned,
And through the silent water stole my way
Back to the cavern of the willow-tree.
There, in her mooring-place I left my bark,
And through the meadows homeward went with grave
And serious thoughts: and after I had seen
That spectacle, for many days my brain 120
Worked with a dim and undetermined sense
Of unknown modes of being: in my thoughts
There was a darkness, call it solitude
Or blank desertion; no familiar shapes
Of hourly objects, images of trees,
Of sea or sky, no colours of green fields:
But huge and mighty forms, that do not live
Like living men, moved slowly through my mind
By day, and were the trouble of my dreams.
　　Ah! not in vain ye Beings of the hills! 130
And ye that walk the woods and open heaths
By moon or star-light, thus from my first dawn
Of childhood did ye love to intertwine
The passions that build up our human soul,
Not with the mean and vulgar works of man,
But with high objects, with eternal things,
With life and nature, purifying thus
The elements of feeling and of thought,
And sanctifying by such discipline
Both pain and fear, until we recognize 140
A grandeur in the beatings of the heart.
　　Nor was this fellowship vouchsafed to me

With stinted kindness. In November days,
When vapours, rolling down the valleys, made
A lonely scene more lonesome, among woods
At noon, and 'mid the calm of summer nights
When by the margin of the trembling lake
Beneath the gloomy hills I homeward went
In solitude, such intercourse was mine.

   And in the frosty season when the sun   150
Was set, and, visible for many a mile,
The cottage windows through the twilight blazed,
I heeded not the summons: clear and loud
The village clock tolled six; I wheeled about
Proud and exulting like an untired horse
That cares not for its home. – All shod with steel
We hissed along the polished ice, in games
Confederate, imitative of the chase
And woodland pleasures, the resounding horn,
The pack loud bellowing, and the hunted hare.   160
So through the darkness and the cold we flew,
And not a voice was idle: with the din,
Meanwhile, the precipices rang aloud,
The leafless trees and every icy crag
Tinkled like iron, while the distant hills
Into the tumult sent an alien sound
Of melancholy not unnoticed while the stars,
Eastward, were sparkling clear, and in the west
The orange sky of evening died away.

   Not seldom from the uproar I retired   170
Into a silent bay, or sportively
Glanced sideway leaving the tumultuous throng
To cut across the shadow of a star
That gleamed upon the ice: and oftentimes
When we had given our bodies to the wind
And all the shadowy banks on either side
Came sweeping through the darkness, spinning still
The rapid line of motion, then at once
Have I, reclining back upon my heels,
Stopped short; yet still the solitary cliffs   180
Wheeled by me, even as if the earth had rolled

With visible motion her diurnal round;
Behind me did they stretch in solemn train
Feebler and feebler, and I stood and watched
Till all was tranquil as a summer sea.

   Ye Powers of earth! ye Genii of the springs!
And ye that have your voices in the clouds
And ye that are Familiars of the lakes
And of the standing pools, I may not think
A vulgar hope was yours when ye employed   190
Such ministry, when ye through many a year
Thus by the agency of boyish sports
On caves and trees, upon the woods and hills,
Impressed upon all forms the characters
Of danger or desire, and thus did make
The surface of the universal earth
With meanings of delight, of hope and fear,
Work like a sea.

           Not uselessly employed
I might pursue this theme through every change
Of exercise and sport to which the year   200
Did summon us in its delightful round.
We were a noisy crew: the sun in heaven
Beheld not vales more beautiful than ours
Nor saw a race in happiness and joy
More worthy of the fields where they were sown.
I would record with no reluctant voice
Our home amusements by the warm peat fire
At evening, when with pencil, and with slate
In square divisions parcelled out, and all
With crosses and with ciphers scribbled o'er,   210
We schemed and puzzled, head opposed to head
In strife too humble to be named in verse,
Or round the naked table, snow-white deal,
Cherry or maple, sat in close array
And to the combat – Lu or Whist – led on
A thick-ribbed army, not as in the world
Discarded and ungratefully thrown by
Even for the very service they had wrought,
But husbanded through many a long campaign.

108

Oh with what echoes on the board they fell –   220
Ironic diamonds, hearts of sable hue,
Queens gleaming through their splendour's last decay,
Knaves wrapped in one assimilating gloom,
And Kings indignant at the shame incurred
By royal visages. Meanwhile abroad
The heavy rain was falling, or the frost
Raged bitterly with keen and silent tooth,
And interrupting the impassioned game
Oft from the neighbouring lake the splitting ice
While it sank down towards the water sent   230
Among the meadows and the hills its long
And frequent yellings, imitative some
Of wolves that howl along the Bothnic main.
   Nor with less willing heart would I rehearse
The woods of autumn and their hidden bowers
With milk-white clusters hung; the rod and line,
True symbol of the foolishness of hope,
Which with its strong enchantment led me on
By rocks and pools where never summer-star
Impressed its shadow, to forlorn cascades   240
Among the windings of the mountain-brooks;
The kite, in sultry calms from some high hill
Sent up, ascending thence till it was lost
Among the fleecy clouds, in gusty days
Launched from the lower grounds, and suddenly
Dashed headlong – and rejected by the storm.
All these and more with rival claims demand
Grateful acknowledgement. It were a song
Venial, and such as if I rightly judge
I might protract unblamed; but I perceive   250
That much is overlooked, and we should ill
Attain our object if from delicate fears
Of breaking in upon the unity
Of this my argument I should omit
To speak of such effects as cannot here
Be regularly classed, yet tend no less
To the same point, the growth of mental power
And love of Nature's works.

Ere I had seen
Eight summers (and 'twas in the very week
When I was first transplanted to thy vale,   260
Beloved Hawkshead! when thy paths, thy shores
And brooks were like a dream of novelty
To my half-infant mind) I chanced to cross
One of those open fields which, shaped like ears,
Make green peninsulas on Esthwaite's lake.
Twilight was coming on, yet through the gloom
I saw distinctly on the opposite shore
Beneath a tree and close by the lake side
A heap of garments, as if left by one
Who there was bathing: half an hour I watched   270
And no one owned them: meanwhile the calm lake
Grew dark with all the shadows on its breast,
And now and then a leaping fish disturbed
The breathless stillness. The succeeding day
There came a company, and in their boat
Sounded with iron hooks and with long poles.
At length the dead man 'mid that beauteous scene
Of trees, and hills, and water, bolt upright
Rose with his ghastly face. I might advert
To numerous accidents in flood or field,   280
Quarry or moor, or 'mid the winter snows,
Distresses and disasters, tragic facts
Of rural history that impressed my mind
With images, to which in following years
Far other feelings were attached, with forms
That yet exist with independent life
And, like their archetypes, know no decay.

   There are in our existence spots of time
Which with distinct pre-eminence retain
A fructifying virtue, whence, depressed   290
By trivial occupations and the round
Of ordinary intercourse, our minds
(Especially the imaginative power)
Are nourished, and invisibly repaired.
Such moments chiefly seem to have their date
In our first childhood. I remember well

('Tis of an early season that I speak,
The twilight of rememberable life)
While I was yet an urchin, one who scarce
Could hold a bridle, with ambitious hopes   300
I mounted, and we rode towards the hills;
We were a pair of horsemen: honest James
Was with me, my encourager and guide.
We had not travelled long ere some mischance
Disjoined me from my comrade, and through fear
Dismounting, down the rough and stony moor
I led my horse and, stumbling on, at length
Came to a bottom where in former times
A man, the murderer of his wife, was hung
In irons; mouldered was the gibbet-mast,   310
The bones were gone, the iron and the wood,
Only a long green ridge of turf remained
Whose shape was like a grave. I left the spot,
And, reascending the bare slope, I saw
A naked pool that lay beneath the hills,
The beacon on the summit, and more near
A girl who bore a pitcher on her head
And seemed with difficult steps to force her way
Against the blowing wind. It was in truth
An ordinary sight, but I should need   320
Colours and words that are unknown to man
To paint the visionary dreariness
Which, while I looked all round for my lost guide,
Did, at that time, invest the naked pool,
The beacon on the lonely eminence,
The woman and her garments vexed and tossed
By the strong wind. Nor less I recollect
(Long after, though my childhood had not ceased)
Another scene which left a kindred power
Implanted in my mind.   330
                              One Christmas time,
The day before the holidays began,
Feverish, and tired and restless, I went forth
Into the fields, impatient for the sight
Of those three horses which should bear us home,

111

My brothers and myself. There was a crag,
An eminence which from the meeting point
Of two highways ascending overlooked
At least a long half-mile of those two roads,
By each of which the expected steeds might come,
The choice uncertain. Thither I repaired   340
Up to the highest summit; 'twas a day
Stormy, and rough, and wild, and on the grass
I sat, half-sheltered by a naked wall;
Upon my right hand was a single sheep,
A whistling hawthorn on my left, and there,
Those two companions at my side, I watched
With eyes intensely straining as the mist
Gave intermitting prospects of the wood
And plain beneath. Ere I to school returned
That dreary time, ere I had been ten days   350
A dweller in my father's house, he died,
And I and my two brothers, orphans then,
Followed his body to the grave. The event
With all the sorrow which it brought appeared
A chastisement, and when I called to mind
That day so lately passed when from the crag
I looked in such anxiety of hope,
With trite reflections of morality
Yet with the deepest passion, I bowed low
To God, who thus corrected my desires;   360
And afterwards the wind, and sleety rain,
And all the business of the elements,
The single sheep, and the one blasted tree,
And the bleak music of that old stone wall,
The noise of wood and water, and the mist
Which on the line of each of those two roads
Advanced in such indisputable shapes,
All these were spectacles and sounds to which
I often would repair, and thence would drink
As at a fountain, and I do not doubt   370
That in this later time when storm and rain
Beat on my roof at midnight, or by day
When I am in the woods, unknown to me

The workings of my spirit thence are brought.
        Nor sedulous to trace
How Nature by collateral interest
And by extrinsic passion peopled first
My mind with forms, or beautiful or grand,
And made me love them, may I well forget
How other pleasures have been mine, and joys   380
Of subtler origin, how I have felt
Not seldom, even in that tempestuous time,
Those hallowed and pure motions of the sense
Which seem in their simplicity to own
An intellectual charm, that calm delight
Which, if I err not, surely must belong
To those first-born affinities that fit
Our new existence to existing things
And in our dawn of being constitute
The bond of union betwixt life and joy.   390
    Yes, I remember when the changeful earth
And twice five seasons on my mind had stamped
The faces of the moving year, even then,
A child, I held unconscious intercourse
With the eternal beauty, drinking in
A pure organic pleasure from the lines
Of curling mist or from the level plain
Of waters coloured by the steady clouds.
    The sands of Westmorland, the creeks and bays
Of Cumbria's rocky limits, they can tell   400
How when the sea threw off his evening shade
And to the shepherd's hut beneath the crags
Did send sweet notice of the rising moon,
How I have stood to images like these
A stranger, linking with the spectacle
No body of associated forms
And bringing with me no peculiar sense
Of quietness or peace, yet I have stood
Even while my eye has moved o'er three long leagues
Of shining water, gathering, as it seemed,   410
Through the wide surface of that field of light
New pleasure, like a bee among the flowers.

Thus often in those fits of vulgar joy
Which through all seasons on a child's pursuits
Are prompt attendants, 'mid that giddy bliss
Which like a tempest works along the blood
And is forgotten, even then I felt
Gleams like the flashing of a shield; the earth
And common face of Nature spake to me
Remembrable things: sometimes, 'tis true,   420
By quaint associations, yet not vain
Nor profitless if haply they impressed
Collateral objects and appearances,
Albeit lifeless then, and doomed to sleep
Until maturer seasons called them forth
To impregnate and to elevate the mind.
—— And if the vulgar joy by its own weight
Wearied itself out of the memory,
The scenes which were a witness of that joy
Remained, in their substantial lineaments   430
Depicted on the brain, and to the eye
Were visible, a daily sight: and thus
By the impressive agency of fear,
By pleasure and repeated happiness,
So frequently repeated, and by force
Of obscure feelings representative
Of joys that were forgotten, these same scenes
So beauteous and majestic in themselves,
Though yet the day was distant, did at length
Become habitually dear, and all   440
Their hues and forms were by invisible links
Allied to the affections.
                              I began
My story early, feeling, as I fear,
The weakness of a human love for days
Disowned by memory, ere the birth of spring
Planting my snow-drops among winter snows.
Nor will it seem to thee, my friend, so prompt
In sympathy, that I have lengthened out
With fond and feeble tongue a tedious tale.
Meanwhile my hope has been that I might fetch   450

114

Reproaches from my former years, whose power
May spur me on, in manhood now mature,
To honourable toil. Yet, should it be
That this is but an impotent desire,
That I by such inquiry am not taught
To understand myself, nor thou to know
With better knowledge how the heart was framed
Of him thou lovest, need I dread from thee
Harsh judgments if I am so loth to quit
Those recollected hours that have the charm   460
Of visionary things, and lovely forms
And sweet sensations that throw back our life
And make our infancy a visible scene
On which the sun is shining? –
   Here we pause
Doubtful; or lingering with a truant heart
Slow and of stationary character
Rarely adventurous, studious more of peace
And soothing quiet which we here have found.

1798–9

'THERE WAS A BOY'

There was a boy, ye knew him well, ye rocks
And islands of Winander and ye green
Peninsulas of Esthwaite! many a time
When the stars began
To move along the edges of the hills
Rising or setting, would he stand alone
Beneath the trees or by the glimmering lakes
And through his fingers woven in one close knot
Blow mimic hootings to the silent owls
And bid them answer him. And they would shout   10
Across the wat'ry vale and shout again
Responsive to my call with tremulous sobs
And long halloos and screams and echoes loud
Redoubled and redoubled, a wild scene
Of mirth and jocund din. And when it chanced
That pauses of deep silence mocked my skill
Then, often, in that silence while I hung
Listening a sudden shock of mild surprize
Would carry far into my heart the voice
Of mountain torrents: or the visible scene   20
Would enter unawares into my mind
With all its solemn imagery, its rocks
Its woods and that uncertain heaven received
Into the bosom of the steady lake.

1798   rev. text, *Lyrical Ballads*, 2nd edn (1801)

'THERE WAS A SPOT'

There was a spot,
My favourite station when the winds were up,
Three knots of fir-trees small and circular
Which with smooth space of open plain between
Stood single, for the delicate eye of taste   5
Too formally arranged. Right opposite
The central clump I loved to stand and hear
The wind come on and touch the several groves
Each after each, and thence in the dark night
Elicit all proportions of sweet sounds   10
As from an instrument. 'The strains are passed,'
Thus often to myself I said, 'the sounds
Even while they are approaching are gone by
And now they are more distant, more and more,
O listen, listen how they wind away   15
Still heard they wind away, heard yet and yet
While the last touch they leave upon the sense
Is sweeter than whate'er was heard before
And seems to say that they can never die.'

1798

THE DISCHARGED SOLDIER

                    I love to walk
Along the public way when for the night,
Deserted in its silence, it assumes
A character of deeper quietness
Than pathless solitudes. At such a time
I slowly mounted up a steep ascent
Where the road's wat'ry surface to the ridge
Of that sharp rising glittered in the moon
And seemed before my eyes another stream
Stealing with silent lapse to join the brook   10
That murmured in the valley. On I passed
Tranquil, receiving in my own despite
Amusement, as I slowly passed along,

117

From such near objects as from time to time
Perforce disturbed the slumber of the sense
Quiescent, and disposed to sympathy,
With an exhausted mind worn out by toil
And all unworthy of the deeper joy
Which waits on distant prospect, cliff or sea,
The dark blue vault, and universe of stars.   20
Thus did I steal along that silent road,
My body from the stillness drinking in
A restoration like the calm of sleep
But sweeter far. Above, before, behind,
Around me, all was peace and solitude:
I looked not round, nor did the solitude
Speak to my eye, but it was heard and felt.
Oh happy state! What beauteous pictures now
Rose in harmonious imagery – they rose
As from some distant region of my soul   30
And came along like dreams, yet such as left
Obscurely mingled with their passing forms
A consciousness of animal delight,
A self-possession felt in every pause
And every gentle movement of my frame.

  While thus I wandered, step by step led on,
It chanced a sudden turning of the road
Presented to my view an uncouth shape
So near that, stepping back into the shade
Of a thick hawthorn, I could mark him well,   40
Myself unseen. He was in stature tall,
A foot above man's common measure tall,
And lank, and upright. There was in his form
A meagre stiffness. You might almost think
That his bones wounded him. His legs were long,
So long and shapeless that I looked at them
Forgetful of the body they sustained.
His arms were long and lean; his hands were bare;
His visage, wasted though it seemed, was large
In feature; his cheeks sunken; and his mouth   50
Showed ghastly in the moonlight. From behind

118

A milestone propped him, and his figure seemed
Half-sitting and half-standing. I could mark
That he was clad in military garb,
Though faded yet entire. His face was turned
Towards the road, yet not as if he sought
For any living thing. He appeared
Forlorn and desolate, a man cut off
From all his kind, and more than half detached
From his own nature.   60
                          He was alone,
Had no attendant, neither dog, nor staff,
Nor knapsack – in his very dress appeared
A desolation, a simplicity
That appertained to solitude. I think
If but a glove had dangled in his hand
It would have made him more akin to man.
Long time I scanned him with a mingled sense
Of fear and sorrow. From his lips meanwhile
There issued murmuring sounds as if of pain
Or of uneasy thought; yet still his form   70
Kept the same fearful steadiness. His shadow
Lay at his feet and moved not. In a glen
Hard by, a village stood, whose silent doors
Were visible among the scattered trees,
Scarce distant from the spot an arrow's flight.
I wished to see him move, but he remained
Fixed to his place, and still from time to time
Sent forth a murmuring voice of dead complaint,
A groan scarce audible. Yet all the while
The chained mastiff in his wooden house   80
Was vexed, and from among the village trees
Howled never ceasing. Not without reproach
Had I prolonged my watch, and now confirmed,
And my heart's specious cowardice subdued,
I left the shady nook where I had stood
And hailed the stranger. From his resting-place
He rose, and with his lean and wasted arm
In measured gesture lifted to his head

Returned my salutation. A short while
I held discourse on things indifferent 90
And casual matter. He meanwhile had ceased
From all complaint – his station had resumed,
Propped by the milestone as before, and when erelong
I asked his history, he in reply
Was neither slow nor eager, but unmoved,
And with a quiet uncomplaining voice,
A stately air of mild indifference,
He told a simple fact: that he had been
A soldier, to the tropic isles had gone,
Whence he had landed now some ten days past; 100
That on his landing he had been dismissed,
And with the little strength he yet had left
Was travelling to regain his native home.
At this I turned and through the trees looked down
Into the village – all were gone to rest,
Nor smoke nor any taper light appeared,
But every silent window to the moon
Shone with a yellow glitter. 'No one there,'
Said I, 'is waking; we must measure back
The way which we have come. Behind yon wood 110
A labourer dwells, an honest man and kind;
He will not murmur should we break his rest,
And he will give you food if food you need,
And lodging for the night.' At this he stooped,
And from the ground took up an oaken staff
By me yet unobserved, a traveller's staff,
Which I suppose from his slack hand had dropped,
And, such the languor of the weary man,
Had lain till now neglected in the grass,
But not forgotten. Back we turned and shaped 120
Our course toward the cottage. He appeared
To travel without pain, and I beheld
With ill-suppressed astonishment his tall
And ghostly figure moving at my side.
As we advanced I asked him for what cause
He tarried there, nor had demanded rest

At inn or cottage. He replied, 'In truth
My weakness made me loth to move, and here
I felt myself at ease and much relieved,
But that the village mastiff fretted me,   130
And every second moment rang a peal
Felt at my very heart. There was no noise,
Nor any foot abroad – I do not know
What ailed him, but it seemed as if the dog
Were howling to the murmur of the stream.'
While thus we travelled on I did not fail
To question him of what he had endured
From war and battle and the pestilence.
He all the while was in demeanour calm,
Concise in answer: solemn and sublime   140
He might have seemed, but that in all he said
There was a strange half-absence and a tone
Of weakness and indifference, as of one
Remembering the importance of his theme,
But feeling it no longer. We advanced
Slowly, and ere we to the wood were come
Discourse had ceased. Together on we passed
In silence through the shades gloomy and dark,
Then turning up along an open field
We gained the cottage. At the door I knocked,   150
And called aloud, 'My friend, here is a man
By sickness overcome; beneath your roof
This night let him find rest, and give him food –
The service if need be I will requite.'
Assured that now my comrade would repose
In comfort, I entreated that henceforth
He would not linger in the public ways
But at the door of cottage or of inn
Demand the succour which his state required,
And told him, feeble as he was, 'twere fit   160
He asked relief or alms. At this reproof
With the same ghastly mildness in his look
He said, 'My trust is in the God of heaven,
And in the eye of him that passes me.'

By this the labourer had unlocked the door,
And now my comrade touched his hat again
With his lean hand, and in a voice that seemed
To speak with a reviving interest
Till then unfelt, he thanked me. I returned
The blessing of the poor unhappy man,   170
And so we parted.

1798   rev. text, *The Prelude* (1850)

THE SIMPLON PASS

—— Brook and road
Were fellow-travellers in this gloomy pass,
And with them did we journey several hours
At a slow step. The immeasurable height
Of woods decaying, never to be decayed,   5
The stationary blasts of waterfalls,
And in the narrow rent, at every turn,
Winds thwarting winds bewildered and forlorn,
The torrents shooting from the clear blue sky,
The rocks that muttered close upon our ears,   10
Black drizzling crags that spake by the wayside
As if a voice were in them, the sick sight
And giddy prospect of the raving stream,
The unfettered clouds and region of the heavens
Tumult and peace, the darkness and the light –   15
Were all like workings of one mind, the features
Of the same face, blossoms upon one tree,
Characters of the great Apocalypse,
The types and symbols of Eternity,
Of first, and last, and midst, and without end.   20

1799   *The Poems of William Wordsworth* (1845)

THE ASCENT OF SNOWDON

from: The Prelude *('1805'), Book Thirteenth*

In one of these excursions, travelling then
Through Wales on foot, and with a youthful friend,
I left Bethkelet's huts at couching-time,
And westward took my way to see the sun
Rise from the top of Snowdon. Having reached
The cottage at the mountain's foot, we there
Rouzed up the shepherd, who by ancient right
Of office is the stranger's usual guide,
And after short refreshment sallied forth.

It was a summer's night, a close warm night,   10
Wan, dull and glaring, with a dripping mist
Low-hung and thick that covered all the sky,
Half threatening storm and rain; but on we went
Unchecked, being full of heart and having faith
In our tried pilot. Little could we see,
Hemmed round on every side with fog and damp,
And after ordinary travellers' chat
With our conductor, silently we sank
Each into commerce with his private thoughts.
Thus did we breast the ascent, and by myself   20
Was nothing either seen or heard the while
Which took me from my musings, save that once
The shepherd's cur did to his own great joy
Unearth a hedgehog in the mountain crags
Round which he made a barking turbulent.
This small adventure, for even such it seemed
In that wild place and at the dead of night,
Being over and forgotten, on we wound
In silence as before. With forehead bent
Earthward, as if in opposition set   30
Against an enemy, I panted up
With eager pace, and no less eager thoughts.
Thus might we wear perhaps an hour away,
Ascending at loose distance each from each,

And I, as chanced, the foremost of the band;
When at my feet the ground appeared to brighten,
And with a step or two seemed brighter still;
Nor had I time to ask the cause of this,
For instantly a light upon the turf
Fell like a flash: I looked about, and lo!   40
The moon stood naked in the heavens, at height
Immense above my head, and on the shore
I found myself of a huge sea of mist,
Which, meek and silent, rested at my feet.
A hundred hills their dusky backs upheaved
All over this still ocean, and beyond,
Far, far beyond, the vapours shot themselves,
In headlands, tongues, and promontory shapes,
Into the sea, the real sea, that seemed
To dwindle and give up its majesty,   50
Usurped upon as far as sight could reach.
Meanwhile, the moon looked down upon this show
In single glory, and we stood, the mist
Touching our very feet; and from the shore
At distance not the third part of a mile
Was a blue chasm; a fracture in the vapour,
A deep and gloomy breathing-place, through which
Mounted the roar of waters, torrents, streams
Innumerable, roaring with one voice.
The universal spectacle throughout   60
Was shaped for admiration and delight,
Grand in itself alone, but in that breach
Through which the homeless voice of waters rose,
That dark deep thoroughfare, had Nature lodged
The soul, the imagination of the whole.

1804   rev. text, *The Prelude* (1850)

BEGGARS

She had a tall man's height, or more;
No bonnet screened her from the heat;
A long drab-coloured cloak she wore,

A mantle reaching to her feet:
What other dress she had I could not know;
Only she wore a cap that was as white as snow.

In all my walks, through field or town,
Such figure had I never seen:
Her face was of Egyptian brown:
Fit person was she for a queen,   10
To head those ancient Amazonian files:
Or ruling bandit's wife, among the Grecian Isles.

Before me begging did she stand,
Pouring out sorrows like a sea;
Grief after grief: – on English land
Such woes I knew could never be;
And yet a boon I gave her; for the creature
Was beautiful to see; a weed of glorious feature!

I left her, and pursued my way;
And soon before me did espy   20
A pair of little boys at play,
Chasing a crimson butterfly;
The taller followed with his hat in hand,
Wreathed round with yellow flow'rs, the gayest of the land.

The other wore a rimless crown,
With leaves of laurel stuck about:
And they both followed up and down,
Each whooping with a merry shout;
Two brothers seemed they, eight and ten years old;
And like that woman's face as gold is like to gold.   30

They bolted on me thus, and lo!
Each ready with a plaintive whine;
Said I, 'Not half an hour ago
Your mother has had alms of mine.'
'That cannot be,' one answered, 'She is dead.'
'Nay but I gave her pence, and she will buy you bread.'

125

'She has been dead, Sir, many a day.'
'Sweet boys, you're telling me a lie;
It was your mother, as I say – '
And in the twinkling of an eye,   40
    'Come, come!' cried one; and, without more ado,
Off to some other play they both together flew.

1802   *Poems, in Two Volumes* (1807)

TO THE CUCKOO

O blithe new-comer! I have heard,
I hear thee and rejoice:
O Cuckoo! shall I call thee bird,
Or but a wandering voice?

While I am lying on the grass,   5
I hear thy restless shout:
From hill to hill it seems to pass,
About, and all about!

To me, no babbler with a tale
Of sunshine and of flowers,   10
Thou tellest, Cuckoo! in the vale
Of visionary hours.

Thrice welcome, darling of the spring!
Even yet thou art to me
No bird; but an invisible thing,   15
A voice, a mystery.

The same whom in my school-boy days
I listened to; that cry
Which made me look a thousand ways;
In bush, and tree, and sky.   20

To seek thee did I often rove
Through woods and on the green;
And thou wert still a hope, a love;
Still longed for, never seen!

126

And I can listen to thee yet;   25
Can lie upon the plain
And listen, till I do beget
That golden time again.

O blessed bird! the earth we pace
Again appears to be   30
An unsubstantial, faery place;
That is fit home for thee!

1802   *Poems, in Two Volumes* (1807)

STEPPING WESTWARD

While my fellow-traveller and I were walking by the side of Loch
Ketterine, one fine evening after sun-set, on our road to a hut where
in the course of our tour we had been hospitably entertained some
weeks before, we met, in one of the loneliest parts of that solitary
region, two well-dressed women, one of whom said to us, by way of
greeting, 'What, you are stepping westward?'

'What, you are stepping westward?' – 'Yea'
– 'Twould be a wildish destiny,
If we, who thus together roam
In a strange land and far from home,
Were in this place the guests of chance: 5
Yet who would stop, or fear to advance,
Though home or shelter he had none,
With such a sky to lead him on?

The dewy ground was dark and cold;
Behind, all gloomy to behold;   10
And stepping westward seemed to be
A kind of *heavenly* destiny;
I liked the greeting; 'twas a sound
Of something without place or bound;
And seemed to give me spiritual right   15
To travel through that region bright.

The voice was soft, and she who spake
Was walking by her native lake:
The salutation had to me
The very sound of courtesy: 20
Its power was felt; and while my eye
Was fixed upon the glowing sky,
The echo of the voice enwrought
A human sweetness with the thought
Of travelling through the world that lay   25
Before me in my endless way.

1805   *Poems, in Two Volumes* (1807)

THE SOLITARY REAPER

Behold her, single in the field,
Yon solitary Highland lass!
Reaping and singing by herself;
Stop here, or gently pass!
Alone she cuts, and binds the grain,   5
And sings a melancholy strain;
O listen! for the vale profound
Is overflowing with the sound.

No nightingale did ever chaunt
So sweetly to reposing bands   10
Of travellers in some shady haunt,
Among Arabian sands:
No sweeter voice was ever heard
In springtime from the cuckoo-bird,
Breaking the silence of the seas   15
Among the farthest Hebrides.

Will no one tell me what she sings?
Perhaps the plaintive numbers flow
For old, unhappy, far-off things,
And battles long ago: 20
Or is it some more humble lay,
Familiar matter of today?

Some natural sorrow, loss, or pain,
That has been, and may be again!

Whate'er the theme, the maiden sang   25
As if her song could have no ending;
I saw her singing at her work,
And o'er the sickle bending;
I listened till I had my fill:
And, as I mounted up the hill,   30
The music in my heart I bore,
Long after it was heard no more.

1805   *Poems, in Two Volumes* (1807)

ELEGIAC STANZAS

*Suggested by a picture of Peele Castle, in a storm,
painted by Sir George Beaumont*

I was thy neighbour once, thou rugged pile!
Four summer weeks I dwelt in sight of thee:
I saw thee every day; and all the while
Thy form was sleeping on a glassy sea.

So pure the sky, so quiet was the air!
So like, so very like, was day to day!
Whene'er I looked thy image still was there;
It trembled, but it never passed away.

How perfect was the calm! it seemed no sleep;
No mood, which season takes away, or brings: 10
I could have fancied that the mighty deep
Was even the gentlest of all gentle things.

Ah! *then*, if mine had been the painter's hand,
To express what then I saw; and add the gleam,
The light that never was, on sea or land,
The consecration, and the poet's dream;

I would have planted thee, thou hoary pile!
Amid a world how different from this!

129

Beside a sea that could not cease to smile;
On tranquil land, beneath a sky of bliss: 20

Thou shouldst have seemed a treasure-house, a mine
Of peaceful years; a chronicle of heaven: –
Of all the sunbeams that did ever shine
The very sweetest had to thee been given.

A picture had it been of lasting ease,
Elysian quiet, without toil or strife;
No motion but the moving tide, a breeze,
Or merely silent Nature's breathing life.

Such, in the fond delusion of my heart,
Such picture would I at that time have made: 30
And seen the soul of truth in every part;
A faith, a trust, that could not be betrayed.

So once it would have been, – 'tis so no more;
I have submitted to a new control:
A power is gone, which nothing can restore;
A deep distress hath humanized my soul.

Not for a moment could I now behold
A smiling sea and be what I have been:
The feeling of my loss will ne'er be old;
This, which I know, I speak with mind serene.   40

Then, Beaumont, friend! who would have been the friend,
If he had lived, of him whom I deplore,
This work of thine I blame not, but commend;
This sea in anger, and that dismal shore.

Oh 'tis a passionate work! – yet wise and well;
Well chosen is the spirit that is here;
That hulk which labours in the deadly swell,
This rueful sky, this pageantry of fear!

And this huge castle, standing here sublime,
I love to see the look with which it braves,   50

130

Cased in the unfeeling armour of old time,
The light'ning, the fierce wind, and trampling waves..

Farewell, farewell the heart that lives alone,
Housed in a dream, at distance from the kind!
Such happiness, wherever it be known,
Is to be pitied; for 'tis surely blind.

But welcome fortitude, and patient cheer,
And frequent sights of what is to be borne!
Such sights, or worse, as are before me here. –
Not without hope we suffer and we mourn.   60

1806   *Poems, in Two Volumes* (1807)

ST PAUL'S

Pressed with conflicting thoughts of love and fear
I parted from thee, friend! and took my way
Through the great city, pacing with an eye
Downcast, ear sleeping, and feet masterless
That were sufficient guide unto themselves,   5
And step by step went pensively. Now, mark!
Not how my trouble was entirely hushed,
(That might not be) but how by sudden gift,
Gift of imagination's holy power,
My soul in her uneasiness received   10
An anchor of stability. It chanced
That while I thus was pacing I raised up
My heavy eyes and instantly beheld,
Saw at a glance in that familiar spot,
A visionary scene – a length of street   15
Laid open in its morning quietness,
Deep, hollow, unobstructed, vacant, smooth,
And white with winter's purest white, as fair,
As fresh and spotless as he ever sheds
On field or mountain. Moving form was none   20
Save here and there a shadowy passenger,
Slow, shadowy, silent, dusky, and beyond

And high above this winding length of street,
This noiseless and unpeopled avenue,
Pure, silent, solemn, beautiful, was seen   25
The huge majestic temple of St Paul
In awful sequestration, through a veil,
Through its own sacred veil of falling snow.

1808

Sonnets

'NUNS FRET NOT AT THEIR CONVENT'S NARROW ROOM'

Nuns fret not at their convent's narrow room;
And hermits are contented with their cells;
And students with their pensive citadels:
Maids at the wheel, the weaver at his loom,
Sit blithe and happy; bees that soar for bloom,   5
High as the highest peak of Furniss Fells,
Will murmur by the hour in foxglove bells:
In truth, the prison, unto which we doom
Ourselves, no prison is: and hence to me,
In sundry moods, 'twas pastime to be bound   10
Within the sonnet's scanty plot of ground:
Pleased if some souls (for such there needs must be)
Who have felt the weight of too much liberty,
Should find short solace there, as I have found.

1802   *Poems, in Two Volumes* (1807)

COMPOSED UPON WESTMINSTER BRIDGE

Sept. 2, 1802

Earth has not any thing to show more fair:
Dull would he be of soul who could pass by
A sight so touching in its majesty:

133

This city now doth like a garment wear
The beauty of the morning; silent, bare,   5
Ships, towers, domes, theatres, and temples lie
Open unto the fields, and to the sky;
All bright and glittering in the smokeless air.
Never did sun more beautifully steep
In his first splendour valley, rock, or hill;   10
Ne'er saw I, never felt, a calm so deep!
The river glideth at his own sweet will:
Dear God! the very houses seem asleep;
And all that mighty heart is lying still!

1802   *Poems, in Two Volumes* (1807)

'IT IS A BEAUTEOUS EVENING, CALM AND FREE'

It is a beauteous evening, calm and free;
The holy time is quiet as a nun
Breathless with adoration; the broad sun
Is sinking down in its tranquillity;
The gentleness of heaven is on the sea: 5
Listen! the mighty being is awake
And doth with his eternal motion make
A sound like thunder – everlastingly.
Dear child! dear girl! that walkest with me here,
If thou appear'st untouched by solemn thought,   10
Thy nature is not therefore less divine:
Thou liest in Abraham's bosom all the year;
And worshipp'st at the temple's inner shrine,
God being with thee when we know it not.

1802   *Poems, in Two Volumes* (1807)

'SURPRIZED BY JOY – IMPATIENT AS THE WIND'

Surprized by joy – impatient as the wind
I wished to share the transport – Oh! with whom
But thee, long buried in the silent tomb,
That spot which no vicissitude can find?

Love, faithful love recalled thee to my mind –   5
But how could I forget thee! – Through what power
Even for the least division of an hour,
Have I been so beguiled as to be blind
To my most grievous loss? – That thought's return
Was the worst pang that sorrow ever bore,   10
Save one, one only, when I stood forlorn,
Knowing my heart's best treasure was no more;
That neither present time, nor years unborn
Could to my sight that heavenly face restore.

1813   *Miscellaneous Poems* (1815)

THE RIVER DUDDON

AFTERTHOUGHT

I thought of thee, my partner and my guide,
As being passed away. – Vain sympathies!
For, *backward*, Duddon! as I cast my .eyes,
I see what was, and is, and will abide;
Still glides the stream, and shall for ever glide;   5
The form remains, the function never dies;
While *we*, the brave, the mighty, and the wise,
We men, who in our morn of youth defied
The elements, must vanish; – be it so!
Enough, if something from our hands have power   10
To live, and act, and serve the future hour;
And if, as tow'rd the silent tomb we go,
Through love, through hope, and faith's transcendent dower,
We feel that we are greater than we know.

1818–20   *The River Duddon: A Series of Sonnets* (1820)

MUTABILITY

From low to high doth dissolution climb,
And sinks from high to low, along a scale
Of awful notes, whose concord shall not fail;
A musical but melancholy chime,

Which they can hear who meddle not with crime, 5
Nor avarice, nor over-anxious care.
Truth fails not; but her outward forms that bear
The longest date do melt like frosty rime,
That in the morning whitened hill and plain
And is no more; drop like the tower sublime 10
Of yesterday, which royally did wear
Its crown of weeds, but could not even sustain
Some casual shout that broke the silent air,
Or the unimaginable touch of time.

1821   *Ecclesiastical Sketches* (1822)

'CALM IS THE FRAGRANT AIR, AND LOTH TO LOSE'

Calm is the fragrant air, and loth to lose
Day's grateful warmth, though moist with falling dews.
Look for the stars, you'll say that there are none;
Look up a second time, and, one by one,
You mark them twinkling out with silvery light,   5
And wonder how they could elude the sight.
The birds, of late so noisy in their bowers,
Warbled a while with faint and fainter powers,
But now are silent as the dim-seen flowers:
Nor does the village church-clock's iron tone   10
The time's and season's influence disown;
Nine beats distinctly to each other bound
In drowsy sequence; how unlike the sound
That, in rough winter, oft inflicts a fear
On fireside listeners, doubting what they hear!   15
The shepherd, bent on rising with the sun,
Had closed his door before the day was done,
And now with thankful heart to bed doth creep,
And join his little children in their sleep.
The bat, lured forth where trees the lane o'ershade,   20
Flits and reflits along the close arcade;
Far-heard the dor-hawk chases the white moth
With burring note, which industry and sloth
Might both be pleased with, for it suits them both.
Wheels and the tread of hoofs are heard no more;   25
One boat there was, but it will touch the shore
With the next dipping of its slackened oar;

Faint sound, that, for the gayest of the gay,
Might give to serious thought a moment's sway,
As a last token of man's toilsome day!   30

1832   *Yarrow Revisited and Other Poems* (1835)

AIREY-FORCE VALLEY

———— Not a breath of air
Ruffles the bosom of this leafy glen.
From this brook's margin, wide around, the trees
Are steadfast as the rocks; the brook itself,
Old as the hills that feed it from afar,   5
Doth rather deepen than disturb the calm
Where all things else are still and motionless.
And yet, even now, a little breeze, perchance
Escaped from boisterous winds that rage without,
Has entered, by the sturdy oaks unfelt,   10
But to its gentle touch how sensitive
Is the light ash! that, pendent from the brow
Of yon dim cave, in seeming silence makes
A soft eye-music of slow-waving boughs,
Powerful almost as vocal harmony   15
To stay the wanderer's steps and soothe his thoughts.

1835   *Poems, Chiefly of Early and Late Years* (1842)

EXTEMPORE EFFUSION UPON THE DEATH OF JAMES HOGG

When first, descending from the moorlands,
I saw the stream of Yarrow glide
Along a bare and open valley,
The Ettrick Shepherd was my guide.

When last along its banks I wandered,   5
Through groves that had begun to shed
Their golden leaves upon the pathways,
My steps the border minstrel led.

The mighty minstrel breathes no longer,
'Mid mouldering ruins low he lies;   10
And death upon the braes of Yarrow,
Has closed the shepherd-poet's eyes.

Nor has the rolling year twice measured,
From sign to sign, its steadfast course,
Since every mortal power of Coleridge   15
Was frozen at its marvellous source.

The rapt one, of the godlike forehead,
The heaven-eyed creature sleeps in earth:
And Lamb, the frolic and the gentle,
Has vanished from his lonely hearth.   20

Like clouds that rake the mountain-summits,
Or waves that own no curbing hand,
How fast has brother followed brother,
From sunshine to the sunless land!

Yet I, whose lids from infant slumbers   25
Were earlier raised, remain to hear
A timid voice, that asks in whispers,
'Who next will drop and disappear?'

Our haughty life is crowned with darkness,
Like London with its own black wreath,   30
On which with thee, O Crabbe! forth-looking,
I gazed from Hampstead's breezy heath.

As if but yesterday departed,
Thou too art gone before; but why,
O'er ripe fruit, seasonably gathered,   35
Should frail survivors heave a sigh?

Mourn rather for that holy spirit,
Sweet as the spring, as ocean deep;
For her who, ere her summer faded,
Has sunk into a breathless sleep.   40

No more of old romantic sorrows,
For slaughtered youth or love-lorn maid!
With sharper grief is Yarrow smitten,
And Ettrick mourns with her their poet dead.

1835   *Poetical Works* (1836, 1837)

Appendix

LINES WRITTEN IN EARLY SPRING

I heard a thousand blended notes,
While in a grove I sat reclined,
In that sweet mood when pleasant thoughts
Bring sad thoughts to the mind.

To her fair works did nature link   5
The human soul that through me ran;
And much it grieved my heart to think
What man has made of man.

Through primrose-tufts, in that sweet bower,
The periwinkle trailed its wreaths;   10
And 'tis my faith that every flower
Enjoys the air it breathes.

The birds around me hopped and played:
Their thoughts I cannot measure,
But the least motion which they made,   15
It seemed a thrill of pleasure.

The budding twigs spread out their fan,
To catch the breezy air;
And I must think, do all I can,
That there was pleasure there.   20

If I these thoughts may not prevent,
If such be of my creed the plan,
Have I not reason to lament
What man has made of man?

1798   *Lyrical Ballads* (1798)

LUCY GRAY

Oft had I heard of Lucy Gray,
And when I crossed the wild,
I chanced to see at break of day
The solitary child.

No mate, no comrade Lucy knew;   5
She dwelt on a wide moor,
The sweetest thing that ever grew
Beside a human door!

You yet may spy the fawn at play,
The hare upon the green;   10
But the sweet face of Lucy Gray
Will never more be seen.

'Tonight will be a stormy night,
You to the town must go,
And take a lantern, child, to light   15
Your mother through the snow.'

'That, father! will I gladly do;
'Tis scarcely afternoon –
The minster-clock has just struck two,
And yonder is the moon.'   20

At this the father raised his hook
And snapped a faggot-band;
He plied his work, and Lucy took
The lantern in her hand.

Not blither is the mountain roe,   25
With many a wanton stroke
Her feet disperse the powd'ry snow
That rises up like smoke.

The storm came on before its time,
She wandered up and down,   30
And many a hill did Lucy climb
But never reached the town.

The wretched parents all that night
Went shouting far and wide;
But there was neither sound nor sight   35
To serve them for a guide.

At day-break on a hill they stood
That overlooked the moor;
And thence they saw the bridge of wood
A furlong from their door.   40

And now they homeward turned, and cried
'In heaven we all shall meet!'
When in the snow the mother spied
The print of Lucy's feet.

Then downward from the steep hill's edge   45
They tracked the footmarks small;
And through the broken hawthorn-hedge,
And by the long stone-wall.

And then an open field they crossed,
The marks were still the same;   50
They tracked them on, nor ever lost,
And to the bridge they came.

They followed from the snowy bank
The footmarks, one by one,
Into the middle of the plank,   55
And further there were none.

Yet some maintain that to this day
She is a living child,
That you may see sweet Lucy Gray
Upon the lonesome wild.   60

O'er rough and smooth she trips along,
And never looks behind;
And sings a solitary song
That whistles in the wind.

1799   *Lyrical Ballads*, 2nd edn. (1801)

'SHE WAS A PHANTOM OF DELIGHT'

She was a phantom of delight
When first she gleamed upon my sight;
A lovely apparition, sent
To be a moment's ornament;
Her eyes as stars of twilight fair;   5
Like twilight's, too, her dusky hair;
But all things else about her drawn
From may-time and the cheerful dawn;
A dancing shape, an image gay,
To haunt, to startle, and way-lay.   10

I saw her upon nearer view,
A spirit, yet a woman too!
Her household motions light and free,
And steps of virgin liberty;
A countenance in which did meet   15
Sweet records, promises as sweet;
A creature not too bright or good
For human nature's daily food;
For transient sorrows, simple wiles,
Praise, blame, love, kisses, tears, and smiles.   20

And now I see with eyes serene
The very pulse of the machine;
A being breathing thoughtful breath;

144

A traveller betwixt life and death;
The reason firm, the temperate will,   25
Endurance, foresight, strength and skill;
A perfect woman; nobly planned,
To warn, to comfort, and command;
And yet a spirit still, and bright
With something of an angel light.   30

1803–4   *Poems, in Two Volumes* (1807)

'MY HEART LEAPS UP WHEN I BEHOLD'

My heart leaps up when I behold
    A rainbow in the sky;
So was it when my life began;
So is it now I am a man;
So be it when I shall grow old,   5
    Or let me die!
The child is father of the man;
And I could wish my days to be
Bound each to each by natural piety.

1802   *Poems, in Two Volumes* (1807)

'I WANDERED LONELY AS A CLOUD'

I wandered lonely as a cloud
That floats on high o'er vales and hills,
When all at once I saw a crowd
A host of dancing daffodils;
Along the lake, beneath the trees,   5
Ten thousand dancing in the breeze.

The waves beside them danced, but they
Outdid the sparkling waves in glee: –
A poet could not but be gay
In such a laughing company: 10
I gazed – and gazed – but little thought
What wealth the show to me had brought.

For oft when on my couch I lie
In vacant or in pensive mood,
They flash upon that inward eye 15
Which is the bliss of solitude,
And then my heart with pleasure fills,
And dances with the daffodils.

1804-7   *Poems, in Two Volumes* (1807)

LONDON

1802

Milton! thou should'st be living at this hour:
England hath need of thee: she is a fen
Of stagnant waters: altar, sword and pen,
Fireside, the heroic wealth of hall and bower,
Have forfeited their ancient English dower 5
Of inward happiness. We are selfish men;
Oh! raise us up, return to us again;
And give us manners, virtue, freedom, power.
Thy soul was like a star and dwelt apart:
Thou hadst a voice whose sound was like the sea; 10
Pure as the naked heavens, majestic, free,
So didst thou travel on life's common way,
In cheerful godliness; and yet thy heart
The lowliest duties on itself did lay.

1802   *Poems, in Two Volumes* (1807)

ODE: INTIMATIONS OF IMMORTALITY
FROM RECOLLECTIONS OF EARLY CHILDHOOD

Paulò majora canamus

There was a time when meadow, grove, and stream,
The earth, and every common sight,
        To me did seem
    Apparelled in celestial light,
The glory and the freshness of a dream.
It is not now as it has been of yore; –

146

Turn wheresoe'er I may,
        By night or day,
The things which I have seen I now can see no more.

'The rainbow comes and goes,   10
        And lovely is the rose,
        The moon doth with delight
    Look round her when the heavens are bare;
        Waters on a starry night
        Are beautiful and fair;
    The sunshine is a glorious birth;
    But yet I know, where'er I go,
That there hath passed away a glory from the earth.

Now, while the birds thus sing a joyous song,
    And while the young lambs bound   20
        As to the tabor's sound,
To me alone there came a thought of grief:
A timely utterance gave that thought relief,
        And I again am strong.
The cataracts blow their trumpets from the steep,
No more shall grief of mine the season wrong;
I hear the echoes through the mountains throng,
The winds come to me from the fields of sleep,
        And all the earth is gay,
            Land and sea   30
    Give themselves up to jollity,
        And with the heart of May
    Doth every beast keep holiday,
        Thou child of joy
Shout round me, let me hear thy shouts, thou happy shepherd
    boy!

Ye blessed creatures, I have heard the call
    Ye to each other make; I see
The heavens laugh with you in your jubilee;
    My heart is at your festival,
        My head hath its coronal,   40
The fullness of your bliss, I feel – I feel it all.

Oh evil day! if I were sullen
While the earth herself is adorning,
   This sweet May-morning,
And the children are pulling,
   On every side,
In a thousand valleys far and wide,
Fresh flowers; while the sun shines warm,
And the babe leaps up on his mother's arm: –
   I hear, I hear, with joy I hear!   50
   – But there's a tree, of many one,
A single field which I have looked upon,
Both of them speak of something that is gone:
   The pansy at my feet
   Doth the same tale repeat:
Whither is fled the visionary gleam?
Where is it now, the glory and the dream?

Our birth is but a sleep and a forgetting:
The soul that rises with us, our life's star,
   Hath had elsewhere its setting,   60
   And cometh from afar:
   Not in entire forgetfulness,
   And not in utter nakedness,
But trailing clouds of glory do we come
   From God, who is our home:
Heaven lies about us in our infancy!
Shades of the prison-house begin to close
   Upon the growing boy,
But he beholds the light, and whence it flows,
   He sees it in his joy;   70
The youth, who daily farther from the east
  Must travel, still is nature's priest,
   And by the vision splendid
   Is on his way attended;
At length the man perceives it die away,
And fade into the light of common day.

Earth fills her lap with pleasures of her own;
Yearnings she hath in her own natural kind,

148

And, even with something of a mother's mind,
    And no unworthy aim,   80
  The homely nurse doth all she can
To make her foster-child, her inmate man,
  Forget the glories he hath known,
And that imperial palace whence he came.

Behold the child among his new-born blisses,
A four years' darling of a pigmy size!
See, where 'mid work of his own hand he lies,
Fretted by sallies of his mother's kisses,
With light upon him from his father's eyes!
See, at his feet, some little plan or chart,   90
Some fragment from his dream of human life,
Shaped by himself with newly-learned art;
      A wedding or a festival,
      A mourning or a funeral;
        And this hath now his heart,
      And unto this he frames his song:
        Then will he fit his tongue
To dialogues of business, love, or strife;
      But it will not be long
      Ere this be thrown aside,   100
      And with new joy and pride
The little actor cons another part,
Filling from time to time his 'humorous stage'
With all the persons, down to palsied age,
That life brings with her in her equipage;
      As if his whole vocation
      Were endless imitation.

Thou, whose exterior semblance doth belie
      Thy soul's immensity;
Thou best philosopher, who yet dost keep   110
Thy heritage, thou eye among the blind,
That, deaf and silent, read'st the eternal deep,
Haunted for ever by the eternal mind, –
      Mighty prophet! seer blest!
      On whom those truths do rest,

Which we are toiling all our lives to find;
Thou, over whom thy immortality
Broods like the day, a master o'er a slave,
A presence which is not to be put by;
     To whom the grave   120
Is but a lonely bed without the sense or sight
   Of day or the warm light,
A place of thought where we in waiting lie;
Thou little child, yet glorious in the might
Of untamed pleasures, on thy being's height,
Why with such earnest pains dost thou provoke
The years to bring the inevitable yoke,
Thus blindly with thy blessedness at strife?
Full soon thy soul shall have her earthly freight,
And custom lie upon thee with a weight,   130
Heavy as frost, and deep almost as life!

      Oh joy! that in our embers
      Is something that doth live,
      That nature yet remembers
      What was so fugitive!

The thought of our past years in me doth breed
Perpetual benedictions: not indeed
For that which is most worthy to be blest;
Delight and liberty, the simple creed
Of childhood, whether fluttering or at rest,   140
With new-born hope for ever in his breast: –
    Not for these I raise
   The song of thanks and praise;
  But for those obstinate questionings
  Of sense and outward things,
  Fallings from us, vanishings;
  Blank misgivings of a creature
Moving about in worlds not realized,
High instincts, before which our mortal Nature
Did tremble like a guilty thing surprized: 150
  But for those first affections,
  Those shadowy recollections,

150

Which, be they what they may,
Are yet the fountain light of all our day,
Are yet a master light of all our seeing;
    Uphold us, cherish us, and make
Our noisy years seem moments in the being
Of the eternal silence: truths that wake,
        To perish never;
Which neither listlessness, nor mad endeavour,   160
        Nor man nor boy,
Nor all that is at enmity with joy,
Can utterly abolish or destroy!
    Hence, in a season of calm weather,
        Though inland far we be,
Our souls have sight of that immortal sea
        Which brought us hither,
        Can in a moment travel thither,
And see the children sport upon the shore,
And hear the mighty waters rolling evermore.   170

Then, sing ye birds, sing, sing a joyous song!
        And let the young lambs bound
        As to the tabor's sound!
    We in thought will join your throng,
        Ye that pipe and ye that play,
        Ye that through your hearts today
        Feel the gladness of the May!
What though the radiance which was once so bright
Be now for ever taken from my sight,
    Though nothing can bring back the hour   180
Of splendour in the grass, of glory in the flower;
        We will grieve not, rather find
        Strength in what remains behind,
        In the primal sympathy
        Which having been must ever be,
        In the soothing thoughts that spring
        Out of human suffering,
        In the faith that looks through death,
In years that bring the philosophic mind.

And oh ye fountains, meadows, hills, and groves,   190
Think not of any severing of our loves!
Yet in my heart of hearts I feel your might;
I only have relinquished one delight
To live beneath your more habitual sway.
I love the brooks which down their channels fret,
Even more than when I tripped lightly as they;
The innocent brightness of a new-born day
                    Is lovely yet;
The clouds that gather round the setting sun
Do take a sober colouring from an eye   200
That hath kept watch o'er man's mortality;
Another race hath been, and other palms are won.
Thanks to the human heart by which we live,
Thanks to its tenderness, its joys, and fears,
To me the meanest flower that blows can give
Thoughts that do often lie too deep for tears.

1802–4   *Poems, in Two Volumes* (1807)

Prose

PREFACE TO *LYRICAL BALLADS*

The first volume of these poems has already been submitted to general perusal. It was published as an experiment which, I hoped, might be of some use to ascertain, how far, by fitting to metrical arrangement a selection of the real language of men in a state of vivid sensation, that sort of pleasure and that quantity of pleasure may be imparted which a poet may rationally endeavour to impart.

I had formed no very inaccurate estimate of the probable effect of those poems: I flattered myself that they who should be pleased with them would read them with more than common pleasure: and on the other hand I was well aware that by those who should dislike them they would be read with more than common dislike. The result has differed from my expectation in this only, that I have pleased a greater number than I ventured to hope I should please.

For the sake of variety and from a consciousness of my own weakness I was induced to request the assistance of a friend, who furnished me with the poems of 'The Ancient Mariner', 'The Foster-Mother's Tale', 'The Nightingale', 'The Dungeon', and the poem entitled 'Love'. I should not, however, have requested this assistance had I not believed that the poems of my friend would in a great measure have the same tendency as my own, and that, though there would be found a

10

20

153

difference, there would be found no discordance in the colours
of our style; as our opinions on the subject of poetry do almost
entirely coincide.

Several of my friends are anxious for the success of these
poems from a belief that if the views, with which they were
composed, were indeed realized, a class of poetry would be
produced, well adapted to interest mankind permanently, and   30
not unimportant in the multiplicity and in the quantity of·its
moral relations: and on this account they have advised me to
prefix a systematic defence of the theory, upon which the
poems were written. But I was unwilling to undertake the
task, because I knew that on this occasion the reader would
look coldly upon my arguments, since I might be suspected of
having been principally influenced by the selfish and foolish
hope of *reasoning* him into an approbation of these particular
poems: and I was still more unwilling to undertake the task,
because adequately to display my opinions and fully to enforce   40
my· arguments would require a space wholly disproportionate
to the nature of a preface. For to treat the subject with the
clearness and coherence, of which I believe it susceptible, it
would be necessary to give a full account of the present state of
the public taste in this country, and to determine how far this
taste is healthy or depraved: which again could not be deter-
mined without pointing out in what manner language and the
human mind act and react on each other, and without retract-
ing the revolutions not of literature alone but likewise of
society itself. I have therefore altogether declined to enter   50
regularly upon this defence; yet I am sensible that there would
be some impropriety in abruptly obtruding upon the public,
without a few words of introduction, poems so materially dif-
ferent from those, upon which general approbation is at present
bestowed.

It is supposed, that by the act of writing in verse an author
makes a formal engagement that he will gratify certain known
habits of association, that he not only thus apprizes the reader
that certain classes of ideas and expressions will be found in his
book, but that others will be carefully excluded. This exponent   60
or symbol held forth by metrical language must in different eras
of literature have excited very different expectations: for

154

example in the age of Catullus, Terence and Lucretius, and that of Statius or Claudian, and in our own country, in the age of Shakespeare and Beaumont and Fletcher, and that of Donne and Cowley, or Dryden, or Pope. I will not take upon me to determine the exact import of the promise which by the act of writing in verse an author in the present day makes to his reader; but I am certain it will appear to many persons that I have not fulfilled the terms of an engagement thus voluntarily   70
contracted. I hope therefore the reader will not censure me, if I attempt to state what I have proposed to myself to perform, and also (as far as the limits of a preface will permit) to explain some of the chief reasons which have determined me in the choice of my purpose: that at least he may be spared any unpleasant feeling of disappointment, and that I myself may be protected from the most dishonourable accusation which can be brought against an author, namely, that of an indolence which prevents him from endeavouring to ascertain what is his duty, or, when his duty is ascertained, prevents him from performing it.   80

The principal object then which I proposed to myself in these poems was to make the incidents of common life interesting by tracing in them, truly though not ostentatiously, the primary laws of our nature: chiefly as far as regards the manner in which we associate ideas in a state of excitement. Low and rustic life was generally chosen because in that situation the essential passions of the heart find a better soil in which they can attain their maturity, are less under restraint, and speak a plainer and more emphatic language; because in that situation our elementary feelings exist in a state of greater simplicity and consequently   90
may be more accurately contemplated and more forcibly communicated; because the manners of rural life germinate from those elementary feelings; and from the necessary character of rural occupations are more easily comprehended; and are more durable; and lastly, because in that situation the passions of men are incorporated with the beautiful and permanent forms of nature. The language too of these men is adopted (purified indeed from what appear to be its real defects, from all lasting and rational causes of dislike or disgust) because such men hourly communicate with the best objects from which the best   100
part of language is originally derived; and because, from their

155

rank in society and the sameness and narrow circle of their intercourse, being less under the action of social vanity they convey their feelings and notions in simple and unelaborated expressions. Accordingly such a language arising out of repeated experience and regular feelings is a more permanent and a far more philosophical language than that which is frequently substituted for it by poets, who think that they are conferring honour upon themselves and their art in proportion as they separate themselves from the sympathies of men, and 110 indulge in arbitrary and capricious habits of expression in order to furnish food for fickle tastes and fickle appetites of their own creation.

I cannot be insensible of the present outcry against the triviality and meanness both of thought and language, which some of my contemporaries have occasionally introduced into their metrical compositions; and I acknowledge that this defect where it exists is more dishonourable to the writer's own character than false refinement or arbitrary innovation, though I should contend at the same time that it is far less pernicious in 120 the sum of its consequences. From such verses the poems in these volumes will be found distinguished at least by one mark of difference, that each of them has a worthy *purpose*. Not that I mean to say that I always begin to write with a distinct purpose formally conceived; but I believe that my habits of meditation have so formed my feelings, as that my descriptions of such objects as strongly excite those feelings, will be found to carry along with them a *purpose*. If in this opinion I am mistaken I can have little right to the name of a poet. For all good poetry is the spontaneous overflow of powerful feelings; but though this be 130 true, poems to which any value can be attached were never produced on any variety of subjects but by a man who being possessed of more than usual organic sensibility had also thought long and deeply. For our continued influxes of feeling are modified and directed by our thoughts, which are indeed the representatives of all our past feelings; and, as by contemplating the relation of these general representatives to each other, we discover what is really important to men, so by the repetition and continuance of this act feelings connected with important subjects will be nourished, till at length, if we be originally 140

156

possessed of much organic sensibility, such habits of mind will be produced that by obeying blindly and mechanically the impulses of those habits we shall describe objects and utter sentiments of such a nature and in such connection with each other, that the understanding of the being to whom we address ourselves, if he be in a healthful state of association, must necessarily be in some degree enlightened, his taste exalted, and his affections ameliorated.

I have said that each of these poems has a purpose. I have also informed my reader what this purpose will be found principally to be: namely to illustrate the manner in which our feelings and ideas are associated in a state of excitement. But speaking in less general language, it is to follow the fluxes and refluxes of the mind when agitated by the great and simple affections of our nature. This object I have endeavoured in these short essays to attain by various means; by tracing the maternal passion through many of its more subtle windings, as in the poems of 'The Idiot Boy' and 'The Mad Mother'; by accompanying the last struggles of a human being at the approach of death, cleaving in solitude to life and society, as in the poem of 'The Forsaken Indian'; by showing, as in the stanzas entitled 'We Are Seven', the perplexity and obscurity which in childhood attend our notion of death, or rather our utter inability to admit that notion; or by displaying the strength of fraternal, or to speak more philosophically, of moral attachment when early associated with the great and beautiful objects of nature, as in 'The Brothers'; or, as in the incident of 'Simon Lee', by placing my reader in the way of receiving from ordinary moral sensations another and more salutary impression than we are accustomed to receive from them. It has also been part of my general purpose to attempt to sketch characters under the influence of less impassioned feelings, as in the 'Old Man Travelling', 'The Two Thieves', etc., characters of which the elements are simple, belonging rather to nature than to manners, such as exist now and will probably always exist, and which from their constitution may be distinctly and profitably contemplated. I will not abuse the indulgence of my reader dwelling longer upon this subject; but it is proper that I should mention one other circumstance which distinguishes these poems from the popular

poetry of the day; it is this, that the feeling therein developed   180
gives importance to the action and situation and not the action
and situation to the feeling. My meaning will be rendered per-
fectly intelligible by referring my reader to the poems entitled
'Poor Susan' and 'The Childless Father', particularly to the last
stanza of the latter poem.

I will not suffer a sense of false modesty to prevent me from
asserting that I point my reader's attention to this mark of dis-
tinction far less for the sake of these particular poems than from
the general importance of the subject. The subject is indeed
important! For the human mind is capable of excitement with-   190
out the application of gross and violent stimulants; and he must
have a very faint perception of its beauty and dignity who does
not know this, and who does not further know that one being
is elevated above another in proportion as he possesses this
capability. It has therefore appeared to me that to endeavour to
produce or enlarge this capability is one of the best services in
which, at any period, a writer can be engaged; but this service,
excellent at all times, is especially so at the present day. For
a multitude of causes unknown to former times are now acting
with a combined force to blunt the discriminating powers of   200
the mind, and unfitting it for all voluntary exertion to reduce it
to a state of almost savage torpor. The most effective of these
causes are the great national events which are daily taking place,
and the increasing accumulation of men in cities, where the uni-
formity of their occupations produces a craving for extraordi-
nary incident which the rapid communication of intelligence
hourly gratifies. To this tendency of life and manners the litera-
ture and theatrical exhibitions of the country have conformed
themselves. The invaluable works of our elder writers, I had
almost said the works of Shakespeare and Milton, are driven   210
into neglect by frantic novels, sickly and stupid German trage-
dies, and deluges of idle and extravagant stories in verse. –
When I think upon this degrading thirst after outrageous sti-
mulation I am almost ashamed to have spoken of the feeble effort
with which I have endeavoured to counteract it; and reflecting
upon the magnitude of the general evil, I should be oppressed
with no dishonourable melancholy, had I not a deep impression
of certain inherent and indestructible qualities of the human

mind, and likewise of certain powers in the great and perma-
nent objects that act upon it which are equally inherent and   220
indestructible; and did I not further add to this impression a
belief that the time is approaching when the evil will be system-
atically opposed by men of greater powers and with far more
distinguished success.

Having dwelt thus long on the subjects and aim of these
poems, I shall request the reader's permission to apprize him of
a few circumstances relating to their *style*, in order, among
other reasons, that I may not be censured for not having per-
formed what I never attempted. Except in a very few instances
the reader will find no personifications of abstract ideas in these   230
volumes, not that I mean to censure such personifications: they
may be well fitted for certain sorts of composition, but in these
poems I propose to myself to imitate, and, as far as is possible,
to adopt the very language of men, and I do not find that such
personifications make any regular or natural part of that lan-
guage. I wish to keep my reader in the company of flesh and
blood, persuaded that by so doing I shall interest him. Not but
that I believe that others who pursue a different track may
interest him likewise: I do not interfere with their claim, I only
wish to prefer a different claim of my own. There will also be   240
found in these volumes little of what is usually called poetic dic-
tion; I have taken as much pains to avoid it as others ordinarily
take to produce it; this I have done for the reason already
alleged, to bring my language near to the language of men, and
further, because the pleasure which I have proposed to myself
to impart is of a kind very different from that which is supposed
by many persons to be the proper object of poetry. I do not
know how without being culpably particular I can give my
reader a more exact notion of the style in which I wished these
poems to be written than by informing him that I have at all   250
times endeavoured to look steadily at my subject, consequently
I hope it will be found that there is in these poems little false-
hood of description, and that my ideas are expressed in language
fitted to their respective importance. Something I must have
gained by this practice, as it is friendly to one property of all
good poetry, namely good sense; but it has necessarily cut me
off from a large portion of phrases and figures of speech which

from father to son have long been regarded as the common
inheritance of poets. I have also thought it expedient to restrict
myself still further, having abstained from the use of many   260
expressions, in themselves proper and beautiful, but which
have been foolishly repeated by bad poets till such feelings of
disgust are connected with them as it is scarcely possible by any
art of association to overpower.

If in a poem there should be found a series of lines, or even a
single line, in which the language, though naturally arranged
and according to the strict laws of metre, does not differ from
that of prose, there is a numerous class of critics who, when
they stumble upon these prosaisms as they call them, imagine
that they have made a notable discovery, and exult over the poet   270
as over a man ignorant of his own profession. Now these men
would establish a canon of criticism which the reader will
conclude he must utterly reject if he wishes to be pleased with
these volumes. And it would be a most easy task to prove to
him that not only the language of a large portion of every good
poem, even of the most elevated character, must necessarily,
except with reference to the metre, in no respect differ from
that of good prose, but likewise that some of the most interest-
ing parts of the best poems will be found to be strictly the lan-
guage of prose when prose is well written. The truth of this   280
assertion might be demonstrated by innumerable passages from
almost all the poetical writings, even of Milton himself. I have
not space for much quotation; but, to illustrate the subject in a
general manner, I will here adduce a short composition of Gray,
who was at the head of those who by their reasonings have
attempted to widen the space of separation betwixt prose and
metrical composition, and was more than any other man curi-
ously elaborate in the structure of his own poetic diction.

In vain to me the smiling mornings shine,
And reddening Phoebus lifts his golden fire: 290
The birds in vain their amorous descant join,
Or cheerful fields resume their green attire:
These ears alas! for other notes repine;
A different object do these eyes require;
My lonely anguish melts no heart but mine;

And in my breast the imperfect joys expire;
Yet morning smiles the busy race to cheer,
And new-born pleasure brings to happier men;
The fields to all their wonted tribute bear;
To warm their little loves the birds complain.   300
I fruitless mourn to him that cannot hear
And weep the more because I weep in vain.

It will easily be perceived that the only part of this sonnet
which is of any value is the lines printed in italics: it is equally
obvious that except in the rhyme, and in the use of the single
word 'fruitless' for fruitlessly, which is so far a defect, the
language of these lines does in no respect differ from that of
prose.

Is there then, it will be asked, no essential difference between
the language of prose and metrical composition? I answer that   310
there neither is nor can be any essential difference. We are fond
of tracing the resemblance between poetry and painting, and,
accordingly, we call them sisters: but where shall we find bonds
of connection sufficiently strict to typify the affinity betwixt
metrical and prose composition? They both speak by and to the
same organs; the bodies in which both of them are clothed may
be said to be of the same substance, their affections are kindred
and almost identical, not necessarily differing even in degree;
poetry sheds no tears 'such as angels weep,' but natural and
human tears; she can boast of no celestial ichor that distin-   320
guishes her vital juices from those of prose; the same human
blood circulates through the veins of them both.

If it be affirmed that rhyme and metrical arrangement of
themselves constitute a distinction which overturns what I have
been saying on the strict affinity of metrical language with that
of prose, and paves the way for other distinctions which the
mind voluntarily admits, I answer that the distinction of rhyme
and metre is regular and uniform, and not, like that which is
produced by what is usually called poetic diction, arbitrary and
subject to infinite caprices upon which no calculation whatever   330
can be made. In the one case the reader is utterly at the mercy of
the poet respecting what imagery or diction he may choose to
connect with the passion, whereas in the other the metre obeys

certain laws, to which the poet and reader both willingly submit because they are certain, and because no interference is made by them with the passion but such as the concurring testimony of ages has shown to heighten and improve the pleasure which co-exists with it.

It will now be proper to answer an obvious question, namely, why, professing these opinions have I written in verse? To this 340 in the first place I reply, because, however I may have restricted myself, there is still left open to me what confessedly constitutes the most valuable object of all writing whether in prose or verse, the great and universal passions of men, the most general and interesting of their occupations, and the entire world of nature, from which I am at liberty to supply myself with endless combinations of forms and imagery. Now, granting for a moment that whatever is interesting in these objects may be as vividly described in prose, why am I to be condemned if to such description I have endeavoured to superadd the charm which by 350 the consent of all nations is acknowledged to exist in metrical language? To this it will be answered, that a very small part of the pleasure given by poetry depends upon the metre, and that it is injudicious to write in metre unless it be accompanied with the other artificial distinctions of style with which metre is usually accompanied, and that by such deviation more will be lost from the shock which will be thereby given to the reader's associations than will be counterbalanced by any pleasure which he can derive from the general power of numbers. In answer to those who thus contend for the necessity of accompanying 360 metre with certain appropriate colours of style in order to the accomplishment of its appropriate end, and who also, in my opinion, greatly under-rate the power of metre in itself, it might perhaps be almost sufficient to observe that poems are extant, written upon more humble subjects, and in a more naked and simple style than what I have aimed at, which poems have continued to give pleasure from generation to generation. Now, if nakedness and simplicity be a defect, the fact here mentioned affords a strong presumption that poems somewhat less naked and simple are capable of affording pleasure at the present 370 day; and all that I am now attempting is to justify myself for having written under the impression of this belief.

162

But I might point out various causes why, when the style is manly, and the subject of some importance, words metrically arranged will long continue to impart such a pleasure to mankind as he who is sensible of the extent of that pleasure will be desirous to impart. The end of poetry is to produce excitement in coexistence with an overbalance of pleasure. Now, by the supposition, excitement is an unusual and irregular state of the mind; ideas and feelings do not in that state succeed each other 380 in accustomed order. But if the words by which this excitement is produced are in themselves powerful, or the images and feelings have an undue proportion of pain connected with them, there is some danger that the excitement may be carried beyond its proper bounds. Now the co-presence of something regular, something to which the mind has been accustomed when in an unexcited or a less excited state, cannot but have great efficacy in tempering and restraining the passion by an intertexture of ordinary feeling. This may be illustrated by appealing to the reader's own experience of the reluctance with which he comes 390 to the re-perusal of the distressful parts of *Clarissa Harlowe*, or *The Gamester*. While Shakespeare's writings, in the most pathetic scenes, never act upon us as pathetic beyond the bounds of pleasure – an effect which is in a great degree to be ascribed to small but continual and regular impulses of pleasurable surprise from the metrical arrangement. – On the other hand (what it must be allowed will much more frequently happen) if the poet's words should be incommensurate with the passion, and inadequate to raise the reader to a height of desirable excitement, then, (unless the poet's choice of his 400 metre has been grossly injudicious) in the feelings of pleasure which the reader has been accustomed to connect with metre in general, and in the feeling, whether cheerful or melancholy, which he has been accustomed to connect with that particular movement of metre, there will be found something which will greatly contribute to impart passion to the words, and to effect the complex end which the poet proposes to himself.

If I had undertaken a systematic defence of the theory upon which these poems are written, it would have been my duty to develop the various causes upon which the pleasure received 410 from metrical language depends. Among the chief of these

163

causes is to be reckoned a principle which must be well known
to those who have made any of the arts the object of accurate
reflection; I mean the pleasure which the mind derives from the
perception of similitude in dissimilitude. This principle is the
great spring of the activity of our minds and their chief feeder.
From this principle the direction of the sexual appetite, and all
the passions connected with it, take their origin: it is the life of
our ordinary conversation; and upon the accuracy with which
similitude in dissimilitude, and dissimilitude in similitude are   420
perceived, depend our taste and our moral feelings. It would
not have been a useless employment to have applied this prin-
ciple to the consideration of metre, and to have shown that
metre is hence enabled to afford much pleasure, and to have
pointed out in what manner that pleasure is produced. But my
limits will not permit me to enter upon this subject, and I must
content myself with a general summary.

I have said that poetry is the spontaneous overflow of power-
ful feelings: it takes its origin from emotion recollected in tran-
quillity: the emotion is contemplated till by a species of reaction   430
the tranquillity gradually disappears, and an emotion, similar to
that which was before the subject of contemplation, is gra-
dually produced, and does itself actually exist in the mind. In
this mood successful composition generally begins, and in a
mood similar to this it is carried on; but the emotion, of what-
ever kind and in whatever degree, from various causes is quali-
fied by various pleasures, so that in describing any passions
whatsoever, which are voluntarily described, the mind will
upon the whole be in a state of enjoyment. Now if Nature be
thus cautious in preserving in a state of enjoyment a being thus   440
employed, the poet ought to profit by the lesson thus held forth
to him, and ought especially to take care, that whatever pas-
sions he communicates to his reader, those passions, if his
reader's mind be sound and vigorous, should always be accom-
panied with an overbalance of pleasure. Now the music of
harmonious metrical language, the sense of difficulty over-
come, and the blind association of pleasure which has been
previously received from works of rhyme or metre of the same
or similar construction, all these imperceptibly make up a
complex feeling of delight, which is of the most important use   450

164

in tempering the painful feeling which will always be found intermingled with powerful descriptions of the deeper passions. This effect is always produced in pathetic and impassioned poetry; while in lighter compositions the ease and gracefulness with which the poet manages his numbers are themselves confessedly a principal source of the gratification of the reader. I might perhaps include all which it is *necessary* to say upon the subject by affirming what few persons will deny, that of two descriptions either of passions, manners, or characters, each of them equally well executed, the one in prose and the other in 460 verse, the verse will be read a hundred times where the prose is read once. We see that Pope, by the power of verse alone, has contrived to render the plainest common sense interesting, and even frequently to invest it with the appearance of passion. In consequence of these convictions I related in metre the tale of 'Goody Blake and Harry Gill', which is one of the rudest of this collection. I wished to draw attention to the truth that the power of the human imagination is sufficient to produce such changes even in our physical nature as might almost appear miraculous. The truth is an important one; the fact (for it is a 470 *fact*) is a valuable illustration of it. And I have the satisfaction of knowing that it has been communicated to many hundreds of people who would never have heard of it, had it not been narrated as a ballad, and in a more impressive metre than is usual in ballads.

Having thus adverted to a few of the reasons why I have written in verse, and why I have chosen subjects from common life, and endeavoured to bring my language near to the real language of men, if I have been too minute in pleading my own cause, I have at the same time been treating a subject of general 480 interest; and it is for this reason that I request the reader's permission to add a few words with reference solely to these particular poems, and to some defects which will probably be found in them. I am sensible that my associations must have sometimes been particular instead of general, and that, consequently, giving to things a false importance, sometimes from diseased impulses I may have written upon unworthy subjects; but I am less apprehensive on this account than that my language may frequently have suffered from those arbitrary

165

connections of feelings and ideas with particular words, from 490
which no man can altogether protect himself. Hence I have no
doubt that in some instances feelings even of the ludicrous may
be given to my readers by expressions which appeared to me
tender and pathetic. Such faulty expressions were I convinced
they were faulty at present, and that they must necessarily con-
tinue to be so, I would willingly take all reasonable pains to
correct. But it is dangerous to make these alterations on the
simple authority of a few individuals, or even of certain classes
of men; for where the understanding of an author is not con-
vinced, or his feelings altered, this cannot be done without 500
great injury to himself: for his own feelings are his stay and
support, and if he sets them aside in one instance, he may be
induced to repeat this act till his mind loses all confidence in
itself and becomes utterly debilitated. To this it may be added,
that the reader ought never to forget that he is himself exposed
to the same errors as the poet, and perhaps in a much greater
degree: for there can be no presumption in saying that it is not
probable he will be so well acquainted with the various stages of
meaning through which words have passed, or with the fickle-
ness or stability of the relations of particular ideas to each other; 510
and above all, since he is so much less interested in the subject,
he may decide lightly and carelessly.

Long as I have detained my reader, I hope he will permit me
to caution him against a mode of false criticism which has been
applied to poetry in which the language closely resembles that
of life and nature. Such verses have been triumphed over in
parodies of which Dr Johnson's stanza is a fair specimen.

I put my hat upon my head,
And walked into the Strand,
And there I met another man 520
Whose hat was in his hand.

Immediately under these lines I will place one of the most justly
admired stanzas of the 'Babes in the Wood'.

These pretty babes with hand in hand
Went wandering up and down;

But never more they saw the man
Approaching from the town.

In both of these stanzas the words, and the order of the words, in no respect differ from the most unimpassioned conversation. There are words in both, for example, 'the Strand', and 'the town', connected with none but the most familiar ideas; yet the one stanza we admit as admirable, and the other as a fair example of the superlatively contemptible. Whence arises this difference? Not from the metre, not from the language, not from the order of the words; but the *matter* expressed in Dr Johnson's stanza is contemptible. The proper method of treating trivial and simple verses to which Dr Johnson's stanza would be a fair parallelism is not to say this is a bad kind of poetry, or this is not poetry, but this wants sense; it is neither interesting in itself, nor can *lead* to anything interesting; the images neither originate in that sane state of feeling which arises out of thought, nor can excite thought or feeling in the reader. This is the only sensible manner of dealing with such verses: Why trouble yourself about the species till you have previously decided upon the genus? Why take pains to prove that an ape is not a Newton when it is self-evident that he is not a man?

I have one request to make of my reader, which is that in judging these poems he would decide by his own feelings genuinely, and not by reflection upon what will probably be the judgment of others. How common is it to hear a person say, 'I myself do not object to this style of composition or this or that expression, but to such and such classes of people it will appear mean or ludicrous.' This mode of criticism so destructive of all sound unadulterated judgment is almost universal: I have therefore to request that the reader would abide independently by his own feelings, and that if he finds himself affected he would not suffer such conjectures to interfere with his pleasure.

If an author by any single composition has impressed us with respect for his talents, it is useful to consider this as affording a presumption, that on other occasions where we have been displeased, he nevertheless may not have written ill or absurdly; and, further, to give him so much credit for this one composition as may induce us to review what has displeased us with more care than we should otherwise have bestowed upon it. This is not only an act of justice, but, in our decisions upon poetry especially, may conduce in a high degree to the improvement of our own taste: for an *accurate* taste in poetry and in all the other arts, as Sir Joshua Reynolds has observed, is an *acquired* talent, which can only be produced by thought and a long continued intercourse with the best models of composition. This is mentioned not with so ridiculous a purpose as to prevent the most inexperienced reader from judging for himself (I have already said that I wished him to judge for himself) but merely to temper the rashness of decision, and to suggest that if poetry be a subject on which much time has not been bestowed, the judgment may be erroneous, and that in many cases it necessarily will be so.

I know that nothing would have so effectually contributed to further the end which I have in view as to have shown of what kind the pleasure is, and how the pleasure is produced which is confessedly produced by metrical composition essentially different from what I have here endeavoured to recommend; for the reader will say that he has been pleased by such composition and what can I do more for him? The power of any art is limited and he will suspect that if I propose to furnish him with new friends it is only upon condition of his abandoning his old friends. Besides, as I have said, the reader is himself conscious of the pleasure which he has received from such composition, composition to which he has peculiarly attached the endearing name of poetry; and all men feel an habitual gratitude, and something of an honourable bigotry, for the objects which have long continued to please them: we not only wish to be pleased, but to be pleased in that particular way in which we have been accustomed to be pleased. There is a host of arguments in these feelings: and I should be the less able to combat them successfully, as I am willing to allow that, in order entirely to enjoy the poetry which I am recommending, it would be necessary to give up much of what is ordinarily enjoyed. But would my limits have permitted me to point out how this pleasure is produced, I might have removed many obstacles, and assisted my reader in perceiving that the powers

570

580

590

600

of language are not so limited as he may suppose; and that it is possible that poetry may give other enjoyments, of a purer, more lasting, and more exquisite nature. But this part of my subject I have been obliged altogether to omit: as it has been less my present aim to prove that the interest excited by some other kinds of poetry is less vivid, and less worthy of the nobler powers of the mind, than to offer reasons for presuming that, if the object which I have proposed to myself were adequately 610 attained, a species of poetry would be produced which is genuine poetry; in its nature well adapted to interest mankind permanently, and likewise important in the multiplicity and quality of its moral relations.

From what has been said, and from a perusal of the poems, the reader will be able clearly to perceive the object which I have proposed to myself: he will determine how far I have attained this object; and, what is a much more important question, whether it be worth attaining; and upon the decision of these two questions will rest my claim to the approbation of the 620 public.

1800   *Lyrical Ballads*, 2nd edn (1801)

APPENDIX TO PREFACE TO *LYRICAL BALLADS*

See page 161 – 'by what is usually called poetic diction'.

Perhaps, as I have no right to expect that attentive perusal, without which, confined, as I have been, to the narrow limits of a preface, my meaning cannot be thoroughly understood, I am anxious to give an exact notion of the sense in which the phrase poetic diction has been used; and for this purpose, a few words shall here be added, concerning the origin and characteristics of the phraseology which I have condemned under that name.

The earliest poets of all nations generally wrote from passion excited by real events; they wrote naturally, and as men: feeling 10 powerfully as they did, their language was daring, and figurative. In succeeding times, poets, and men ambitious of the fame of poets, perceiving the influence of such language, and desirous of producing the same effect without being animated by the same passion, set themselves to a mechanical adoption of these figures of speech, and made use of them, sometimes with propriety, but much more frequently applied them to feelings and thoughts with which they had no natural connection whatsoever. A language was thus insensibly produced, differing materially from the real language of men in *any situation*. The reader or hearer of this distorted language found himself in a perturbed and unusual state of mind: when affected by the genuine language of the passion he had been in a perturbed and unusual state of mind also: in both cases he was willing that his common judgment and understanding should be laid asleep, and he had no instinctive and infallible perception of the true to make him reject the false; the one served as a passport for the other. The emotion was in both cases delightful, and no wonder if he confounded the one with the other, and believed them both to be produced by the same, or similar causes. Besides, the poet spake to him in the character of a man to be looked up to, a man of genius and authority. Thus, and from a variety of other causes, this distorted language was received with admiration; and poets, it is probable, who had before contented themselves for the most part with misapplying only expressions which at first had been dictated by real passion, carried the abuse still further, and introduced phrases composed apparently in the spirit of the original figurative language of passion, yet altogether of their own invention, and characterised by various degrees of wanton deviation from good sense and nature.

It is indeed true, that the language of the earliest poets was felt to differ materially from ordinary language, because it was the language of extraordinary occasions; but it was really spoken by men, language which the poet himself had uttered when he had been affected by the events which he described, or which he had heard uttered by those around him. To this language it is probable that metre of some sort or other was early superadded. This separated the genuine language of poetry still further from common life, so that whoever read or heard the poems of these earliest poets felt himself moved in a way in which he had not been accustomed to be moved in real

170

life, and by causes manifestly different from those which acted upon him in real life. This was the great temptation to all the corruptions which have followed: under the protection of this feeling succeeding poets constructed a phraseology which had one thing, it is true, in common with the genuine language of poetry, namely, that it was not heard in ordinary conversation; that it was unusual. But the first poets, as I have said, spake a language which, though unusual, was still the language of men. This circumstance, however, was disregarded by their successors; they found that they could please by easier means: they became proud of modes of expression which they themselves had invented, and which were uttered only themselves. In process of time metre became a symbol or promise of this unusual language, and whoever took upon him to write in metre, according as he possessed more or less of true poetic genius, introduced less or more of this adulterated phraseology into his compositions, and the true and the false were inseparably interwoven until, the taste of men becoming gradually perverted, this language was received as a natural language: and at length, by the influence of books upon men, did to a certain degree really become so. Abuses of this kind were imported from one nation to another, and with the progress of refinement this diction became daily more and more corrupt, thrusting out of sight the plain humanities of nature by a motley masquerade of tricks, quaintnesses, hieroglyphics, and enigmas.

It would not be uninteresting to point out the causes of the pleasure given by this extravagant and absurd diction. It depends upon a great variety of causes, but upon none, perhaps, more than its influence in impressing a notion of the peculiarity and exaltation of the poet's character, and in flattering the reader's self-love by bringing him nearer to a sympathy with that character; an effect which is accomplished by unsettling ordinary habits of thinking, and thus assisting the reader to approach to that perturbed and dizzy state of mind in which if he does not find himself, he imagines that he is *balked* of a peculiar enjoyment which poetry can and ought to bestow.

The sonnet quoted from Gray, in the Preface, except the lines printed in italics, consists of little else but this diction, though not of the worst kind; and indeed, if one may be permitted to say so, it is far too common in the best writers both ancient and modern. Perhaps in no way, by positive example, could more easily be given a notion of what I mean by the phrase *poetic diction* than by referring to a comparison between the metrical paraphrases which we have of passages in the Old and New Testament, and those passages as they exist in our common translation. See Pope's 'Messiah' throughout; Prior's 'Did sweeter sounds adorn my flowing tongue,' etc. etc.; 'Though I speak with the tongues of men and of angels,' 100 etc. etc. 1st Corinthians, chap. xiii. By way of immediate example, take the following of Dr Johnson:

Turn on the prudent ant thy heedless eyes,
Observe her labours, sluggard, and be wise;
No stern command, no monitory voice,
Prescribes her duties, or directs her choice;
Yet, timely provident, she hastes away
To snatch the blessings of a plenteous day;
When fruitful summer loads the teeming plain,
She crops the harvest, and she stores the grain. 110
How long shall sloth usurp thy useless hours,
Unnerve thy vigour, and enchain thy powers?
While artful shades thy downy couch enclose,
And soft solicitation courts repose,
Amidst the drowsy charms of dull delight,
Year chases year with unremitted flight,
Till Want now following, fraudulent and slow,
Shall spring to seize thee, like an ambushed foe.

From this hubbub of words pass to the original. 'Go to the ant, thou sluggard, consider her ways, and be wise: which hav- 120 ing no guide, overseer, or ruler, provideth her meat in summer, and gathereth her food in the harvest. How long wilt thou sleep, O sluggard? when wilt thou arise out of thy sleep? Yet a little sleep, a little slumber, a little folding of the hands to sleep. So shall thy poverty come as one that travelleth, and thy want as an armed man.' Proverbs, chap. vi.

One more quotation, and I have done. It is from Cowper's verses supposed to be written by Alexander Selkirk:

Religion! what treasure untold
Resides in that heavenly word! 130
More precious than silver and gold,
Or all that this earth can afford.
But the sound of the church-going bell
These valleys and rocks never heard,
Ne'er sighed at the sound of a knell,
Or smiled when a sabbath appeared.

Ye winds, that have made me your sport
Convey to this desolate shore
Some cordial endearing report
Of a land I must visit no more. 140
My friends, do they now and then send
A wish or a thought after me?
O tell me I yet have a friend,
Though a friend I am never to see.

This passage is quoted as an instance of three different styles of composition. The first four lines are poorly expressed; some critics would call the language prosaic; the fact is, it would be bad prose, so bad, that it is scarcely worse in metre. The epithet 'church-going' applied to a bell, and that by so chaste a writer as Cowper, is an instance of the strange abuses which poets 150 have introduced into their language, till they and their readers take them as matters of course, if they do not single them out expressly as objects of admiration. The two lines 'Ne'er sighed at the sound,' etc., are, in my opinion, an instance of the language of passion wrested from its proper use, and, from the mere circumstance of the composition being in metre, applied upon an occasion that does not justify such violent expressions; and I should condemn the passage, though perhaps few readers will agree with me, as vicious poetic diction. The last stanza is throughout admirably expressed: it would be equally good 160 whether in prose or verse, except that the reader has an exquisite pleasure in seeing such natural language so naturally connected with metre. The beauty of this stanza tempts me to conclude with a principle which ought never to be lost sight of, and which has been my chief guide in all I have said, – namely, that in works of *imagination and sentiment*, for of these only have I been treating, in proportion as ideas and feelings are valuable, whether the composition be in prose or in verse, they require and exact one and the same language. Metre is but adventitious to composition, and the phraseology for which that passport is necessary, even where it may be graceful at all, will be little valued by the judicious.

1802   *Lyrical Ballads*, 3rd edn (1802)

Critical commentary

After Chaucer and Shakespeare, Wordsworth might well be accounted our greatest poet. This may seem too favourable a judgement; yet even those who dissent from it would probably agree that Wordsworth is widely respected and still read.

This is a tribute to his genius, for no poet has been worse arranged or, until recent times, edited more clumsily. The editions of the past followed an arbitrary system laid down by the author in his middle age. The poems were classified under heads in a manner which ensured that they were read with regard to neither chronology nor merit. Side by side, in the section titled 'Poems founded on the affections', 'Michael' and 'The idiot boy' rub uneasy flanks; one a masterpiece, the other a well-meant failure. Either of them, good or bad, might be as appropriately found under the heading 'Poems referring to the period of childhood' or, quite possibly, 'Poems of the imagination'. When one considers that this confusion was typical of the arbitrary arrangement followed by (say) the Oxford University Press *Poetical Works*, a standard edition for eighty years, it is a wonder that anyone read Wordsworth at all.

It can safely be said that no one read him in his entirety. In Wordsworth's case more than most it seems that the public has been content to rely upon the selection of critics and editors. When Wordsworth is raised, all too often the *œuvre* under discussion is what some nineteenth-century worthy has made of it.

The two most influential selections have been those of Tennyson and of Arnold respectively. *The Golden Treasury* (1861) was compiled by Francis Turner Palgrave on Tennyson's advice, and nowhere is Tennyson more influential than in the choice of pieces culled from Wordsworth. For Tennyson, Wordsworth was a master of simplicity, and he has no way of seeing when the older poet confuses simplicity with *simplesse*. As a result, the enormous selection of Wordsworth in *The Golden Treasury* is flawed by jejune efforts such as 'Simon Lee, the old huntsman' (1798):

> Few months of life has he in store
> As he to you will tell,
> For still, the more he works, the more
> Do his weak ankles swell.

This is the Wordsworth derided in such comic collections of bad verse as *The Stuffed Owl* (D.B. Wyndham Lewis and Charles Lee, eds, 1930); the Wordsworth in whom intention remains at a considerable distance from achievement. One can see an attempt to render compassion, but any understanding of the old man's predicament is baulked by the ludicrous details and the uneasy self-consciousness that the ballad manifests:

> My gentle reader, I perceive
> How patiently you've waited,
> And now I fear that you expect
> Some tale will be related.

This is emphatically not a Wordsworth who is readable nowadays. In company with such poems as this – some pieces about the schoolmaster 'Matthew' come to mind – the Miltonic sonnets which represent the literary and rhetorical side of Wordsworth's output must be downgraded. Most of them are a mixture of objurgation and clumsiness, and the awkward rhyme in the fourth line here is quite characteristic:

> The world is too much with us; late and soon,
> Getting and spending, we lay waste our powers:
> Little we see in Nature that is ours;
> We have given our hearts away, a sordid boon!

176

Milton was certainly living at that hour,and it was Wordsworth who resuscitated him. Here is all the worst aspect of Miltonic verse: exhortation, generalizing, literary phraseology. Tennyson's choice of poems for *The Golden Treasury* suggests that Wordsworth occupied no territory between a simplified narrative of rustic doings and an oratorical proclamation of abstract universals.

Matthew Arnold was equivocal about this selection from Wordsworth: it 'surprised many readers, and gave offence to not a few' (*Selected Poems of Wordsworth*, 1879, p. vii). Arnold's own choice is far more intelligent, and influenced readers of Wordsworth until quite recently. We find, for example, the great Arnoldian of the earlier twentieth century, F. R. Leavis in *Revaluation* (1936), discounting Wordsworth's 'philosophy' and concentrating on the meditative-descriptive side of his work. There is some point in doing this: like Leavis, Arnold in his own time refused to be led astray by the moralistic aspects of *The Excursion* or the declamation of 'Ode: intimations of immortality'.

But, in spite of this, there is a concern with the tentative and minuscule in Arnold's approach, echoed as it has been by many critics since. 'His best work is in his shorter pieces . . . I have not ventured on detaching portions of poems . . . the *Excursion* and the *Prelude*, his poems of greatest bulk, are by no means Wordsworth's best work': this stressing of the exquisite, but essentially minor, went on almost until the present day. The 'Lucy' poems, 'The solitary reaper', these are excellent of their kind; but how far is their kind capable of sustaining major poetry? They are fragments of perception, beautifully caught, but without a context:

> No motion has she now, no force;
>   She neither hears nor sees,
> Rolled round in earth's diurnal course
>   With rocks and stones and trees.

('A slumber did my spirit seal', 1799)

It was possible for the late Hugh Sykes Davies to misread this quite egregiously (*Essays in Criticism* XV, 1965, p. 136), but one can see how the misunderstanding came about. Of what validity is Wordsworth's elegy unless we know, even if only within the terms of the poem, for whom it was composed? Where is the context in

177

which this 'she' exists? The reader need not go along with Sykes Davies, and identify the feminine pronoun with the mind, in order to have problems with this poem that take the attention too far away from the text, rapt and beautiful though it certainly is.

Wordsworth is a larger and more complex poet than either Arnold or the neo-Arnoldian apologists have made him. The tendency has been to mute his originality: to suggest that his roots were in the eighteenth century. There is, of course, a sense in which this is so. The poetic realism of Wordsworth had much to do with Langhorne's pioneering work in *The Country Justice* (1774–7); he can be related to the Goldsmith of *The Deserted Village* (1770) and to the Cowper of *The Task* (1785), notably the narrative of 'Crazy Kate', which also influenced Southey's 'Hannah' (1799). None of this, however, explains the horror with which *Lyrical Ballads* (1798) was received by the reviewers. It was in the course of a critique of Crabbe, because of his formalism still acceptable to an Augustan ear, that Francis Jeffrey turned aside, in 1808, to deal with Wordsworth and Coleridge:

> The gentlemen of the new school, on the other hand, scarcely ever condescend to take their subjects from any description of persons that are at all known to the common inhabitants of the world; but invent for themselves certain whimsical and unheard of beings, to whom they impute some fantastical combinations of feelings, and labour to excite our sympathy for them, either by placing them in incredible situations, or by some strained and exaggerated moralization of a vague and tragical description.
>
> (*Edinburgh Review* xii, p. 133)

Of course, *Lyrical Ballads*, as the Preface to the Second Edition suggests, was conceived as something of a pioneering enterprise, and there are poems as exaggerated as the showpieces of any other new school of poetry; 'Simon Lee' and the 'Matthew' poems among them. But the piece upon which Jeffrey particularly turns his outraged attention is one with far more tenacious claims on our sympathy: the incomparable, lovely

> There was a boy, ye knew him well, ye cliffs
> And islands of Winander! many a time,
> At evening, when the stars had just begun

To move along the edges of the hills,
Rising or setting, would he stand alone,
Beneath the trees, or by the glimmering lake,
And there, with fingers interwoven, both hands
Pressed closely palm to palm and to his mouth
Uplifted, he, as through an instrument,
Blew mimic hootings to the silent owls
That they might answer him. And they would shout
Across the wat'ry vale and shout again
Responsive to his call, with quivering peals,
And long halloos, and screams.

('There was a boy', 1798)

What impresses us about this passage is its rightness, its inevitability. It is therefore hard to remember that, in 1808, poetry such as this could upset a critic through being original. Jeffrey's expectations are outraged; and, in commenting upon the poem, he seems to be looking everywhere but in the appropriate direction. In particular, he is obsessed by a passage not so far quoted, concerning the death of the child:

> The sports of childhood, and the untimely death of promising youth, is also a common topic of poetry. Mr Wordsworth has made some blank verse about it; but, instead of the delightful and picturesque sketches with which so many authors of moderate talents have presented us on this inviting subject, all that he is pleased to communicate of the rustic child, is, that he used to amuse himself with shouting to the owls, and hearing them answer. To make amends for this brevity, the process of his mimicry is most accurately described. . . . This is all we hear of him; and for the sake of this one accomplishment, we are told, that the author has frequently stood mute, and gazed on his grave for half an hour together!

(*Edinburgh Review*, xii, pp. 135–6)

After the conventional portraits of eighteenth-century poetry, sketched plainly enough in Jeffrey's expectations, this piece evidently seemed *outré*, even arbitrary. But possibly there is an explanation for its failure to make him look in the right direction. Jeffrey is, for instance, worried by the way in which the description of the bird-calls leads on to the boy's death. But though the connection is made in the version that Jeffrey was reading and that is usually published, the first draft of the poem shows that the death is extraneous. In its original version, the poem is autobiographical; a straight recollection of Wordsworth's own childhood. The account of the child's death is therefore an addendum. Perhaps a case could be made out for it; the boy is, after all, received into the nature which he was imitating.

But, as Jeffrey's adverse reaction shows, the end of the poem has been a source of critical deflection, and certainly has no deep-rooted connection with the rest of it. Possibly, if confronted with the original draft, Jeffrey would have had less to say about the piece's tendency towards dramatic inflation; though there is no evidence that he could have responded to its mythopoeia, those elements that lie beyond the story line. For him, and this is clear from his comments on Crabbe as well, a succession of events can have no more than its literal significance. To do Jeffrey justice, he concedes that the mimicry is 'accurately described'; but he does not see there is more to it than that. Wordsworth is depicting a boy who wills himself into the woodland, into the life of the trees; it is no accident that he does not merely disturb the owls but actively and successfully imitates them, recreating something of their nature in himself. In the passage which Jeffrey ignores we find

> a gentle shock of mild surprize
> Has carried far into his heart the voice
> Of mountain torrents, or the visible scene
> Would enter unawares into his mind.

The boy becomes part of the lake and the woodlands with which he is communing.

Even as it stands, the poem shows the astonishing mythopoeic power of the early Wordsworth, as well as indicating the direction in which his greatness lies. No wonder that, in his own lifetime, the public gave in to the popular vogue of Byron, Scott, and Moore. But Coleridge held out against the tide; recognizing, as we should expect from so fine a critic, the master-spirit of the age.

Yet, even granted his originality, Wordsworth had dreadful luck with the reviewers. It is quite possible that the reviews of *The*

Excursion caused him to suppress much of his other discursive work in blank verse. Some commentators have tried to whitewash Jeffrey, who wrote the most damaging critique of *The Excursion*. But consider his words:

> The volume before us, if we were to describe it very shortly, we should characterize as a tissue of moral and devotional ravings, in which innumerable changes are rung upon a few very simple and familiar ideas: – but with such an accompaniment of long words, long sentences, and unwieldy phrases – and such a hubbub of strained raptures and fantastical sublimities, that it is often extremely difficult for the most skilful and attentive student to obtain a glimpse of the author's meaning – and altogether impossible for an ordinary reader to conjecture what he is about.
>
> (*Edinburgh Review*, xxiv, 1814, p. 4)

These strictures were occasioned by grave faults in the poem, but they cannot justify Jeffrey's brutality. He had used more measured terms in reviewing work that was far inferior to *The Excursion*. Clearly there was something in Wordsworth that outraged him; and his outrage brought about some heavy consequences. Wordsworth had been expecting great things of *The Excursion*, and the probability is that he was deeply hurt by the reception accorded to this first instalment of what he still considered to be his life's work, *The Recluse*. There can be little doubt that it was the failure of *The Excursion* that determined him to leave *The Prelude*, a far greater poem, unpublished till after his death. After all, it was similar enough in mode to invite attack, and much more personal. Some portions of it, such as 'There was a boy', had already been separately published and been mocked. One cannot blame Wordsworth for seeking to avoid a chorus of ridicule that might have had repercussions on his sanity.

However, though he never published *The Prelude*, Wordsworth subjected the poem to intense redrafting, culminating in the wholesale revisions of 1831–2, and 1838–9. He ironed out its early colloquialisms, strengthened its moralistic links, and turned his youthful perceptions into the otiose Miltonicism that dogged his later poetry. By a poignant irony, it is this later version that has been promulgated.

Readers had difficulty with it even in the later nineteenth century.

Arnold, as has been indicated, avoided choosing passages from it for his selection and some early editors of Wordsworth excluded it altogether, because of what they took to be its manifest inferiority to the poet's other work. Only gradually did *The Prelude* become current, and then as much through an interest in the poet's life as in his writings.

The promulgation of the so-called 1850 text is a matter for regret. Ernest de Selincourt, a textual pioneer in the matter of Wordsworth's revisions, claimed it as a much better composition than the A-text, a fair copy made by Dorothy Wordsworth in 1805–6 and used as the basis for twentieth-century editions of the 1805 text. But the reasons de Selincourt gives for his preference are odd. He seems to feel that Wordsworth strengthened his poem by taking out the idioms that 'leave the impression of a man . . . talking to his friend' (*The Prelude*, edition of 1926, p. xliv). Instead, de Selincourt favours the later version's Miltonic inversion and heavy explicitness. His preference was followed by F. R. Leavis: 'No one is likely to dispute that the later version is decidedly the more satisfactory' (*Revaluation*, 1936, p. 158). This may be taken as a general judgement, though it should be said that the passage most immediately under discussion is the one in Book Second beginning 'Blessed the infant babe'. Leavis's preference in this instance was challenged by Donald Davie (*Articulate Energy*, 1957, pp. 114–15). But the dissension is hardly worth taking up: the passage in question is discursive and didactic, and a comparison between its two existing versions is likely to be no more than a discrimination between modes of mediocrity. The case is rather that Wordsworth was essentially a narrative poet, the greatest since Chaucer, and that therefore we should consider him at his best. Such a consideration could be developed, through differentiating between the '1805' and '1850' versions of *The Prelude* by way of analysing, with comparisons, the efficacy of the earlier one.

This can be done initially in terms of language; it is language, after all, that makes the poet. Wordsworth is not usually credited with exactness or precision in this sphere; still less with sensuous vitality. Yet if we consider one of the key episodes of the '1805' *Prelude* and see how Wordsworth maltreated it in later years, we can give the lie to any such deprecation.

A crucial example is the account of Wordsworth's expedition to Snowdon while staying with Robert Jones in North Wales after their

Continental tour of 1790. It may be found in Book Thirteenth of the '1805' version and Book Fourteenth of the '1850' version; neither among the most frequented parts of *The Prelude*. Yet in the earlier version, at least, the account exhibits a preternatural keenness of eye and ear. It begins briskly enough:

> In one of these excursions, travelling then
> Through Wales on foot.

But, in the later version, 'Wales' is atrophied into 'the Northern tracts / Of Cambria', and to the simple word 'excursions' is added the pious hope '(may they ne'er / Fade from remembrance)'.

There is a frankly tactile description of the evening:

> It was a summer's night, a close warm night,
> Wan, dull and glaring, with a dripping mist.

But the older Wordsworth mashes up the rhythm into an unrelieved chain of adjectives: 'It was a close, warm, breezeless summer night'. No wonder Wordsworth has a reputation for failure in sensuous detail!

The real success of the earlier version, however, is the mystical illumination that flashes upon the poet in this scene; an illumination greatly superior to the much-fêted 'Simplon Pass' of Book Sixth. Here the concrete particulars of the summer night assume startling urgency as they impinge upon the young traveller's mind:

>   and lo!
> The moon stood naked in the heavens, at height
> Immense above my head.
>
> Far, far beyond, the vapours shot themselves,
> In headlands, tongues, and promontory shapes,
> Into the sea, the real sea.
>
> Meanwhile, the moon looked down upon this show
> In single glory, and we stood, the mist
> Touching our very feet.

But, as forecast by Wordsworth's 'Ode: intimations of immortality', the things that he had seen, he in later life could see no more. The moon of the '1850' *Prelude* did not stand naked in the heavens but 'hung naked in a firmament', and we lose the sense of immense height in favour of a description of this same firmament, 'azure without cloud'.

Again, the 'vapours' of the earlier version are in flux: they 'shot themselves, / In headlands, tongues, and promontory shapes'. But, in the later version, they appear as '*solid* vapours *stretched*, / In headlands, tongues,' etc. Now this is confused: the vapours cannot be solid, and, if they were, could not be stretched; and, if they *could* be stretched, they would hardly stretch into forms as various as those of headlands, tongues and promontories, not if they were 'solid' in the first place. Such images as these could only be appropriate to something flexuous and evanescent.

Worst of all, however, Wordsworth's stark simplicity – 'the moon looked down upon this show' – is Miltonized into this cumbrous periphrasis:

> the full-orbed moon,
> Who, from her sovereign elevation, gazed
> Upon the billowy ocean.

Personality is drained off; we are left with received gestures, such as 'full-orbed' and 'sovereign elevation', which give us no idea of how things looked to the young Wordsworth – indeed, there is no sense of that passionate spectator at all. These verbal points are not small ones, even in the local context of a single episode; and, multiplied as they are throughout the '1850' *Prelude*, they serve to blur and dissipate the sharp impressions of the original. This is not deliberate falsification so much as a desire in the aging Wordsworth to restore the literary decorum which his younger self had so sharply outraged. These verbal changes, however, often produced an entire dislocation of narrative.

One of the finest narratives Wordsworth ever accomplished is the encounter, in Book Fourth of the *Prelude*, with the discharged soldier. This was originally written as an independent poem, a companion-piece to 'The old Cumberland beggar', in January–February 1798, before any plans for *The Prelude* had taken shape. It is best, perhaps, read as an independent poem, and as such the spectral figure of its protagonist is thrust at us with stark directness:

He was in stature tall,
A foot above man's common measure tall,
And lank, and upright. There was in his form
A meagre stiffness. You might almost think
That his bones wounded him. His legs were long,
So long and shapeless that I looked at them
Forgetful of the body they sustained.
His arms were long and lean; his hands were bare;
His visage, wasted though it seemed, was large
In feature; his cheeks sunken; and his mouth
Showed ghastly in the moonlight. From behind
A milestone propped him, and his figure seemed
Half-sitting and half-standing. I could mark
That he was clad in military garb,
Though faded yet entire. His face was turned
Towards the road, yet not as if he sought
For any living thing. He appeared
Forlorn and desolate, a man cut off
From all his kind, and more than half detached
From his own nature.
          He was alone,
Had no attendant, neither dog, nor staff,
Nor knapsack – in his very dress appeared
A desolation, a simplicity
That appertained to solitude. I think
If but a glove had dangled in his hand
It would have made him more akin to man.
Long time I scanned him with a mingled sense
Of fear and sorrow. From his lips meanwhile
There issued murmuring sounds as if of pain
Or of uneasy thought; yet still his form
Kept the same fearful steadiness. His shadow
Lay at his feet and moved not.

These sharp detached details never lapse into catalogue: what fuses them together is the sense of the man's vulnerability and loneliness. It is Wordsworth's greatness that he can make so static a mode as description – description, moreover, of a stationary object – develop in the manner of narrative. This effect of development is partly owing to the poet's sense of the beholder: we are keenly aware of Wordsworth himself watching the old man.

Unfortunately this awareness has faded out in revision, and, with it, half the significance of the events recorded:

> There was in his form
> A meagre stiffness. You might almost think
> That his bones wounded him

becomes, in the '1850' *Prelude*, merely assertion:

> Stiff, lank, and upright; a more meagre man
> Was never seen before by night or day.

This latter is no more than prosaic. Not only has the sense of observation been blunted but the intimacy with the reader has been lost and all expressiveness removed from the rhythm.

With the effect of ghostliness in the original goes the fear that the young Wordsworth has of the man:

> Long time I scanned him with a mingled sense
> Of fear and sorrow

but this is omitted from the revision. In its stead, we have a moralistic reflection upon the contrast between the soldier and 'the trappings of a gaudy world'. This is an awkward dispersion of one faculty Wordsworth excelled in, the sense of place.

It could, of course, be argued that some contrast with the soldier is necessary, if only to set his lank figure in perspective. But this, in fact, was provided in the original poem of 1798:

> In a glen
> Hard by, a village stood, whose silent doors
> Were visible among the scattered trees,
> Scarce distant from the spot an arrow's flight.

This at once sets off the loneliness of the old soldier and also suggests that help is nearer than he supposes. It is missing from the revised text, and is replaced by mere circumstance – 'we reached a cottage' –

as though Wordsworth were no more acquainted with the country than the old soldier himself.

The narrative is more than its literal detail. For instance, the soldier at first sight appears wholly vulnerable, without a staff; but, after Wordsworth makes an approach, he picks his staff up out of the grass where it had lain neglected. The soldier himself has been at fault in giving way to self-pity; help was at hand. Further, the poet, seen as an instrument of that help, was himself mistaken in imagining the soldier to be utterly vulnerable; the staff may not have been immediately apparent, but it was there. The inference is that no man is entirely alone: the very word 'staff', coupled with the soldier's biblical diction, has an unmistakable echo of the psalmist.

One cannot quite call this symbolism. Rather one might adopt a phrase suggested in conversation by Judith Hutchinson, late of Queen's University, Belfast, and call the staff a 'significance' or 'significant object'; bearing a meaning, that is to say, beyond the immediate situation, without necessarily following a one-to-one pattern of symbolism.

This 'significance' is blurred by Wordsworth's changes in revision: by the suppression, for instance, of the fact that shelter was close at hand. This suppression leaves us with a sense of arbitrariness, as though the poet was able to offer help merely by accident; while in the original he appears an agent of providence.

Narrative of this order, the order of the earlier versions of *The Prelude*, was lost to writers of the time; partly through the stupidity of reviewers, partly through Wordsworth's own diffidence. The poems leading up to the '1805' version – 'There was a boy', 'The discharged soldier', 'The ascent of Snowdon' and the first part of the text of 1798–9 – stand as pointers to all that narrative verse should have been able to accomplish in the nineteenth century. Their suppression was one of the great set-backs of literature; as great, in its way, as the premature deaths of Keats and Shelley, and those of the poets of the First World War. A vital link in a great tradition was thereby missing; a crucial example was denied the poets of the rising generation. For the *Prelude* poems represent a major advance in the handling of narrative: a decisive move forward from Goldsmith and Cowper; more far-reaching than Crabbe. These poems could have been the basis for a revival of narrative verse.

Such a revival never took place. Since *The Prelude* was not published, writers had to turn elsewhere for their inspiration. Clearly Crabbe himself could offer little: though a great poet, he was at the end of a long tradition; as his eclipse, after his death, palpably shows. His perceptions were hard and particular, but his backward-looking technique prevented him from making the fullest use of them. Further, the other poets of the time were far more circumscribed in subject-matter: Keats, no escapist himself, gave rise to a curiously Parnassian school of poetry, which excluded the grittiness of fiction. No, if writers had to learn, they could learn only from the greatest poet of the age; and, since they could not go to *The Prelude*, they went to *The Excursion*.

Among Wordsworth's greatest disciples are John Stuart Mill and George Eliot. It is no coincidence that these are writers of prose; a political philosopher and a novelist, respectively. This suggests there is more in the sheer content of Wordsworth's verse than has generally been acknowledged: Mill, in his *Autobiography* (1860s) describes it as the very culture of the feelings; and his social concern, like that of Arnold, has a Wordsworthian root.

But the greatest disciple was George Eliot. The silent suffering of Maggie in *The Mill on the Floss* (1860), the deliberate stylization of rustic simplicity in *Silas Marner* (1861), the massively heroic figures of Adam Bede and Caleb Garth – these owe much, in moral perception, to Wordsworth; to say nothing of the sheer technique of presenttion. If we agree with Leavis (*The Great Tradition*, 1947) that they represent a foreshortening of George Eliot's art – moral fable rather than realistic narrative – this is only to say that the novel had to grow away from Wordsworth if it was ever to take account of the necessities of prose.

But such a growing away, while it increased the possibilities of 'naturalism', also brought an unavoidable tendency towards disruption. One can say that Victorian novels carry up to half their bulk in waste matter; mostly by way of explanatory links between episodes or material relating to character which is imaginatively extraneous. George Eliot herself built up the realistic, circumstantial side of fiction, and achieved a masterpiece in this vein in *Middlemarch* (1871–2); the poetic vision has gone, but the massive observation commands respect; all that need be done in the form of realistic fiction is done here. But any attempt to go beyond realism results in fragmentation. It is the attempt to include ideal characters in a naturalistic framework that brings about the disruption of *Felix Holt* (1866) and *Daniel Deronda* (1874–6); novels whose interest lies away from their titular heroes. Such a form as that of *The Prelude* of 1798–9 or the forms of its related poems could accommodate heightened perceptions and short-cuts across narrative; but such advantages were not available to the novelists who were, in some sense, Wordsworth's successors.

It is, then, not too much to suggest that, had *The Prelude* been published in its earlier versions, those of 1798–9 or 1804–5, these successors would not have used prose as the medium for their fictions. On the contrary, the weight of narrative would have rested upon verse; as, indeed, had been the case in previous civilizations. The prose tale has usually been identified with light reading; its rise and decay during the last two hundred years as the central medium for fiction has been a divagation. All its greatest achievements – *Wuthering Heights*, *Moby-Dick*, *Our Mutual Friend*, *The Rainbow* – aspire towards the condition of dramatic poetry. But dramatic poetry, for obvious reasons, is not readily accomplished in the form of prose. The failures usually occur at what should be climaxes; intensifications of reality when the prose tale reaches out after a concentration which is essentially unproselike. Ahab's pseudo-Shakespearian soliloquies, for example, coarsen the flexibility of the blank verse which they imitate. Think of the celebrated Egdon Heath passage in *The Return of the Native* (1878). Prose encourages a plethora of description here: its otiosity has no parallel in the austere treatment of landscape in Hardy's verse. Even *The Rainbow* (1915), masterpiece though it is, has many pages which are highly patterned in rhythm and heavily charged in imagery, which strive after the power of poetry and which, in so doing, present insoluble problems to the reader. Ultimately the difficulty is one of density: the eye travels too quickly over the prose to be able to take in the concentration of meaning: the work demands to be read aloud, and, being in prose, affords little guide or oppor-tunity for the reader to do this.

The Prelude, on the other hand, was, in its earlier versions, com-posed for the voice: Wordsworth recited it on his marches over the hills, dictated it to his sister, and, ever afterward, lost no opportunity of speaking it to select groups of friends. There is an insistent quality of rhythm in *The Prelude*, at least in its earlier stages, that confirms the feeling that heightened narrative or dramatic poetry cannot be taken in through the eye alone. Consider the great scenes of the early *Prelude*, such as the ones just discussed: these have an intensifying of vision that is impossible to prose. This may be because prose is a medium where explanations are necessary and where the decisive patterning of rhythm is next to impossible without making heavy demands upon the reader. Therefore attempts to go outside the limits of explanatory naturalism are bound to bring about lapses in execution, if not in imagination.

The great narrators of the nineteenth century wrote prose because there was no way open to them in verse: the crucial documents were suppressed , and it is a credit to them that they used the available tradition as well as they did. But the tradition was, in fact, one near to prose: there are lapses in *Lyrical Ballads* not dissimilar to those which occur in George Eliot, Hardy, and Lawrence. Jeffrey pointed out similar lapses in *The Excursion*; insensitively, because he could not put the faults of the poem in perspective. Faults it certainly has, however, and they are largely the faults of prose. For instance, it is noticeable that in *The Excursion* Jeffrey particularly objects to the detail spent upon exploring the character of the old pedlar in Book First and to the moral drawn at the end of that book.

But it must be remarked that what Jeffrey was reviewing in itself was a revision; one of several attempts Wordworth made to rewrite what seems to have been his first really great poem, 'The ruined cottage'. The earliest complete draft we have of this dates from January–February 1798 (Ms. B), but an even earlier draft was read to Coleridge at Racedown in 1797; and it seems to have been considerably shorter. One would give a great deal for this original draft, which inspired Coleridge with the conviction that his new friend was the greatest poet of the age; but it is probable that, to some extent, this can be reconstructed.

For all his pejorative remarks upon the rest of *The Excursion*, Jeffrey was favourably disposed towards the account of Margaret and her desertion by her husband: 'We must say that there is very considerable pathos in the telling of this simple story.' There can be no doubt that this is the central core of the poem. It follows that the portions to which Jeffrey objected, the pedlar and the moralizing, are accretions upon the original plot.

Even the earliest draft we have, that of 1798, has flaws: the story of the pedlar's life disrupts the narrative. It is, for instance, noticeable that Wordsworth had considerable trouble with a passage beginning 'he from his native hills / Had wandered far': lines 58ff. give rise to an addendum of 250 lines intended in some way to be inserted into the poem. This alone would suggest a wandering of imaginative attention. But the pedlar's story also adds a great deal which is immaterial to the plot; and it operates at a much lower pressure than the rest of the poem. It is therefore reasonable to suppose that lines 47 to 103 together with the addendum, which explain the pedlar's background and which represent the aspect of the poem most disliked by Jeffrey, are extraneous. Weight is given to this supposition by a textual variant in a transcript which Coleridge got Dorothy to make of the conclusion to the earliest draft; he sent it in a letter dated 10 June 1797 to his Unitarian friend, the Reverend John Prior Estlin. This transcript has the pedlar addressing Wordsworth as 'Stranger', which suggests that the pedlar was, in the first version of the poem, a person unknown to Wordsworth, who would not, therefore, have been acquainted with his story. This is supported by an apparent inconsistency in line 40 of the 1798 draft, which states that Wordsworth had seen the old man for the first time only the day before. It would seem, then, that the pedlar is an accretion upon an original which was exclusively concerned with the story of Margaret. Since the process of revision was largely a matter of expanding the moralistic side of the poem, it would seem that it was only from the second draft onward, the one represented by the 1798 manuscript, that Wordsworth felt the temptation to build the pedlar up into a major figure with a story of his own. This is borne out by the fact that each successive revision, between 1798 and 1813, expands the story of the pedlar and adds a further layer of moralizing. A draft of 1799, reprinted by Jonathan Wordsworth in his *Music of Humanity* (1969), separates the two stories but retains a good deal of moralizing in each of them and in many ways is verbally inferior. Later the stories were reunited. But certainly the version of 1798 (Ms. B) is nearest to the original. Even as we have it, this 'Ruined cottage' is free of much extraneous matter that later accumulated: there is, for instance, nothing to compare with the egregious passage in *The Excursion* which begins 'Oh! many are the poets that are sown / By nature'. It is possible that the pedlar (or Wanderer, as he is in *The Excursion*) could be defended as providing a sort of moral equipoise to Margaret: he has wandered far from his home, like her husband, but to some purpose. But ultimately it is to the story of Margaret that we turn; and, if we omit the pedlar's story from the 1798 draft, what we will be left with is something approximating to the 'Ruined cottage' of 1797. The approximation can be made even closer by drawing upon the evidence afforded by fragmentary drafts in notebooks of spring 1797, of January–February 1798 (the 'Christabel' Notebook) and of January–March 1798 (the 'Alfoxden' Notebook), together with Dorothy's transcript of the conclusion attached to the letter Coleridge wrote to Thelwall in June 1797.

'The ruined cottage' is a very great poem indeed. All the more pity, then, that its publication history has been more chequered even than that of *The Prelude*. The two versions that used to be most frequently referred to, both inferior, were Book First of *The Excursion*, with all its moralizings, and a sort of cento of Ms. B and Book First prepared by Arnold for his selection from Wordsworth. Even Ms. B, which seems more satisfactory than either, was for many years available only in the notes to Volume Five of the edition of Wordsworth by de Selincourt and Darbishire; who say, grudgingly, that it seems worth while to reproduce it *in extenso*!

Successive revisions made 'The ruined cottage' seem more prosaic than it is. It may not have the flash of vivid illumination that characterizes *The Prelude* in its earlier manifestations; but it does share with the poems associated with that work the accurate observation of detail that is *more* than detail – description which enacts a moral vision. In a real sense, Margaret *is* her cottage: as her life is disrupted, her cottage, too, decays. There is nothing occult about this: the gradual deterioration can be accounted for naturalistically. Yet it is more than realistic description; so much more that, when we first encounter the cottage, there is something demoralized about it, almost to the point of anthropomorphism:

> It was a plot
> Of garden-ground, now wild, its matted weeds
> Marked with the steps of them who as they pass
> The gooseberry trees that shot in long lank slips
> Or currants showing on a leafless stem
> In scanty strings had tempted to o'erleap
> The broken wall.

This is the characteristic reaction of an observer. The advantage of having the poet himself viewing the landscape is that we do not rest with commentary: the cottage impinges alarmingly on his uninformed gaze. Margaret's story is all the richer by being narrated through another dramatized consciousness: that of the old pedlar, who knows, as the poet does not, the steps that led to the ruin so vividly set before the spectator's eye; and the remainder of the poem, after this initial confrontation, is his retelling of these past circumstances.

The story is a simple one: a family falling upon hard times and sickness, the woman being deserted by her husband, her baby dying. But the poem gains in focus through the device of narrating all this in terms of the cottage. Thus we see, before the bad times come upon them, a thriving family whose husband kept the cottage and its grounds in order:

> 'They who passed
> At evening, from behind the garden fence
> Might hear his busy spade which he would ply
> After his daily work till the daylight
> Was gone, and every leaf and every flower
> Were lost in the dark hedges.'

But the harvest fails, and the countryside is reduced to destitution in time of war. A fever shatters Margaret's husband and, during his sickness, their savings are consumed. The husband's labours now assume a disordered, frenetic quality:

> 'He blended where he might the various tasks
> Of summer, autumn, winter and of spring.'

From now on, the story acquires a seasonal pattern: we see only intermittent glimpses of the cottage, on the old pedlar's infrequent visits to the district. This, however, enables us to judge the decay of the cottage, and of the family; we see the various stages of dissolution. The pedlar next comes by in early spring:

> 'At the door arrived
> I knocked, and when I entered with the hope
> Of usual greeting Margaret looked at me
> A little while, then turned her head away
> Speechless, and sitting down upon a chair
> Wept bitterly.'

The action is as graphic as that of a stage play. Her husband has deserted her; but she is courageous, and attempts to carry on his work as well as her own:

> 'We parted. 'Twas the early spring,
> I left her busy with her garden tools.'

But a family deprived of its head cannot keep order for long; and, on his next visit, in the 'wane of summer', though all appears much the same, the pedlar notices signs of decay:

> 'Her cottage in its outward look appeared
> As cheerful as before; in any show
> Of neatness little changed, but that I thought
> The honeysuckle crowded round the door
> And from the wall hung down in heavier tufts . . .
> The unprofitable bindweed spread his bells
> From side to side, and with unwieldy wreaths
> Had dragged the rose from its sustaining wall
> And bowed it down to earth.'

The detail is not only sharp and accurate but, in Judith Hutchinson's sense of the term, 'significant'. Margaret herself is bowed with grief, now that she is unprotected. Just as her cottage and garden are out of order, so she spends her time wandering without purpose while her child cries, neglected in the cottage. The pedlar does what he can, but the case is hopeless:

> 'I left her then
> With the best hope and comfort I could give,
> She thanked me for my will, for my hope
> It seemed she did not thank me.'

The grim irony of the phrasing acts out the starkness of the facts: there is no future for this woman. Indeed, when the pedlar next returns, on the earliest day of spring, the decay is far advanced:

> 'her house
> Bespoke a sleepy hand of negligence . . .
> . . . of her herbs and flowers

194

        The better part were gnawed away
      Or trampled on the earth; a chain of straw
      Which had been twisted round the tender stem
      Of a young apple-tree lay at its root,
      The bark was nibbled round by truant sheep.
      Margaret stood near, her infant in her arms
      And seeing that my eye was on the tree
      She said "I fear it will be dead and gone
      Ere Robert come again."

We hardly need the explicit identification of tree and child: both are deprived of the bond that might have sustained them, both are eroded by suffering. Except for her baby, and her little boy now apprenticed away from her, Margaret has no wish to live; and 'many seasons pass' before the pedlar returns to these parts. By that time Margaret, who has been retreating as a character right through the poem, is dead; and we learn of her fate only though hearsay, without even the personal observation of the pedlar. Apparently, towards the end, she no longer even had the heart to wander:

        'Master! I have heard
      That in that broken arbour she would sit
      The idle length of half a sabbath day
      There – where you see the toadstool's lazy head . . .
            . . . See'st thou that path?
      The greensward now has broken its grey line;
      There, to and fro she paced through many a day
      Of the warm summer.'

Margaret's life has been encroached upon, just as the fungus has reared its head in the garden and the path has been obliterated by the greensward:

        'Meanwhile her poor hut
      Sunk to decay, for he was gone whose hand
      At the first nippings of October frost,
      Closed up each chink and with fresh bands of straw
      Chequered the green-grown thatch.'

We have reached, in the history of the cottage, the point at which the poet first came across it: sapped by frost and rain, open to the wind:

> 'and Stranger! here
> In sickness she remained, and here she died
> Last human tenant of these ruined walls.'

The graphic simplicity is characteristic and supreme: no embellishing metaphors are required here. The observed facts speak for themselves and beyond themselves, out to the human situation of which they are a dramatic summary.

'The ruined cottage' is, in one sense, richer than its companion poem, 'Michael', since it has the colouring of the intermediaries, Wordsworth and the pedlar: the narrative is seen through the dramatized consciousness of two spectators with varying degrees of dramatic involvement.

Nothing of this kind transmutes the austerity of 'Michael' (1800). This poem stands at the ultimate reach of Wordsworth's art, the reduction of all variousness of human experience to a stark simplicity. No further development along these lines could be imagined, and none came.

In plot, the poem is not dissimilar to 'The ruined cottage': a story of loss and desertion, no doubt drawing for its raw material upon what Wordsworth could envisage of the abandoned Annette Vallon, and feeding upon the root of his helpless remorse. At the same time, the situation in 'Michael' is set at a distance, and one might have guessed that an equipoise savouring of quietism was impending.

This is not to criticize the poem, though, which is surely the most flawless piece of work Wordsworth ever accomplished. It was certainly the most easily composed; alone among the great masterpieces it is not bedevilled with variant texts, endless revisions and needless addenda.

Like 'The ruined cottage', the poem begins, ends and is centred upon a 'significant object':

> Beside the brook
> There is a straggling heap of unhewn stones!
> And to that place a story appertains.

196

The story is, massively, Michael's; and, in a sense, it is an example against what is thought to be Wordsworth's general belief in the fortifying influence of nature. This is a man superbly in tune with his environment:

> Hence had he learned the meaning of all winds,
> Of blasts of every tone . . .
> . . . he had been alone
> Amid the heart of many thousand mists
> That came to him and left him on the heights.

Unusual self-reliance, great bodily strength: these are the keynotes of Michael's presentation, struck again and again throughout. The poem, in other words, even more than 'The ruined cottage', is concerned to show what happens when phenomenal courage and physique are sapped by adversity.

More even than with Margaret and her family is the positive cycle of Michael's life built up: his labouring with his young son, his helping his wife after the day's work in the field is over. The 'positive' is reinforced by the light from the cottage which beams out over the valley and gives the cottage its affectionate name, The Evening Star. This is an emblem of regularity, constancy, industry:

> The light was famous in its neighbourhood,
> And was a public symbol of the life
> The thrifty pair had lived.

The integration which Michael had achieved did not come about by chance; it has been hard-won. We are told that the fields he owns were burdened with debt when they came to him, and that the root of his industry lay in his efforts to clear them.

But in old age disaster overtakes him. A surety which the shepherd had given for his nephew has been broken, and the forfeit amounts to half his substance:

> This unlooked for claim
> At the first hearing, for a moment took
> More hope out of his life than he supposed
> That any old man ever could have lost.

It seems that some of the fields must be sold. But this he cannot endure; and perhaps his sorrow is mistaken:

> 'yet if these fields of ours
> Should pass into a stranger's hand, I think
> That I could not lie quiet in my grave.'

So, in a sense, he sacrifices, instead of the fields, his son, who is sent away to the city to make his fortune:

> 'Our Luke shall leave us, Isabel; the land
> Shall not go from us.'

This is tenacity gone wrong; yet Michael is not merely miserly. He is trying to leave the land to Luke as unencumbered 'as is the wind / That passes over it'. In a kind of guarantee of co-operation, the boy lays the first stone of a sheep-fold which the old man had been intending to build with him.

Unluckily, the boy goes to the bad; the episode is treated perfunctorily, as befits a report from 'the dissolute city'. Once torn up from his environment, Luke has no real identity, and eventually loses himself 'beyond the seas'.

As with Margaret, so with Michael: the body appears to endure while the mind is broken. His routine, in outward appearance, looks much the same:

> Among the rocks
> He went, and still looked up upon the sun,
> And listened to the wind.

But the 'significant object' is the sheep-fold, that emblem of co-operation. He goes, indeed, to the fold; but it is never built:

> and 'tis believed by all
> That many and many a day he thither went,
> And never lifted up a single stone.

This justly admired master-stroke suggests the breaking of a spring: there is no purpose in the old man's life now his son is gone. His life, like that of Margaret, has been encroached upon; and, as in 'The ruined cottage', all that is left to the beholder is the wreck of Michael's hope:

> the remains
> Of the unfinished sheep-fold may be seen
> Beside the boisterous brook of Green-head Gill.

The brook and the wind sweep through the poem: it is only humanity, anchored to its small inheritance and material possessions, that is beaten down; and human works along with it.

This lofty subject is matched by its style, which is very much that of the Authorized Version; indeed, as H. A. Mason demonstrated (*Delta*, no. 30, 1963, p. 8), a few alterations would serve to give one the exact rhythm and accent of the Bible. Mr Mason feels that behind the poem stands the book of Ruth; otherwise the sustaining inspiration seems to be the sacrifice of Isaac.

Just for once, however, Wordsworth was not impelled to alleviate the grimness of the poem with a patched-on moral. There are few differences between the text as it appears in the *Collected Poems* and that first published in *Lyrical Ballads*. It seems that this was a poem Wordsworth was prepared to stand by.

However, it is not surprising that its influence has been mainly upon prose, since the austerity of the style derives from a prose inspiration. The same may be true of the influence of 'The ruined cottage'; though, since this was circulated only in adulterated versions, it is hard to be sure.

Influence apart, however, there can be no doubt that the poems discussed brought something new into literature. They show, for instance, a handling of narrative superior to anything since Shakespeare and the medieval poets; and an aspect of narrative unknown even to these great narrators: the concentration upon a single experience until all its implications are drawn out of it. In many respects, these poems unite the virtues of prose and poetry: clarity and definition on the one hand, emotional heightening and dramatic rhythm on the other. The supremacy of these poems, however, should not be taken as a denial of the presence in Wordsworth's *œuvre* of several other major works: 'Resolution and independence' (1802) and 'Tintern Abbey' (1798), for example. But the first is flawed by its discursive beginning and a jaunty moral at the end, not unlike that tacked on to 'The ruined cottage' in later versions; and 'Tintern Abbey' is rendered highly ambiguous by its absence of discernible plot. F. W. Bateson in his book on Wordsworth (1954) suggests that the poem amounts to a love poem written to his sister Dorothy by Wordsworth; who, rather disquieteningly, identifies himself with the mountain winds blowing against her. But both 'Resolution and independence' and 'Tintern Abbey' are considerable works, even if they do not represent Wordsworth at his greatest.

There are, as well, a fair number of good secondary pieces; few of which have been given the attention they deserve. Some of them are overflows from other poems, such as the passage about the three knots of fir-trees (1798), in manner and rhythm akin to the earlier *Prelude*, which for many years could only be found in Appendix B of the de Selincourt and Darbishire edition, Volume Five. There is also an enchanting account of a boy playing in the snow (1798) which may have been intended for 'Michael'; this could be found in the notes to de Selincourt and Darbishire, Volume Two. More familiar will be the atmospheric nature-pieces, which are at their best when associated with Dorothy Wordsworth: 'Nutting' (1798), for example, and the 'Poems on the naming of places' (1799–1800), especially no. IV, with its unforgettable picture of the sick peasant. This last is one of many straight descriptions of rustic and vagrant life, such as 'Old man travelling' and 'The old Cumberland beggar' from *Lyrical Ballads*, and 'Beggars' from the far inferior *Poems, in Two Volumes* of 1807. These rural sketches have a good deal in common with Crabbe and Clare, but would hardly convert one to Wordsworth without the backing of the greater poems.

A critic must put his cards on the table and say what the poet he is writing about has achieved and what his greatest poems are. In all the work that has been produced on Wordsworth, surprisingly few people have come out unequivocally and done this.

The anthologies of the past assure us that it is the minor poems, especially those from the collection of 1807, that keep Wordsworth alive. It is therefore good tactics to conclude by reifying the contention with which this commentary began. Wordsworth is a narrative poet, more mythopoeic than Crabbe, more concentrated than Byron, with more human interest than Keats or Shelley, and fewer eccentricities than Coleridge. He has not the urbanity and insight of Chaucer nor the dramatic power of Shakespeare; but his handling of narrative is manifestly superior to that of Milton, and he is less fragmented than Dryden or Pope. His finest work reflects an intense focus upon a single situation so as to bring out all its overtones. Work of this order may be found in the first part of the 1798–9 *Prelude*, with its episodes of 'The stolen boat', 'The ice skater', and 'The mouldered gibbet'; in other poems related to *The Prelude*, such as 'The discharged soldier' and 'The ascent of Snowdon'; in the reconstruction of the 1797 'Ruined cottage'; and in 'Michael'.

Wordsworth deserves to be termed the first modern poet; partly because he was the first to be seriously out of step with the current literary establishment, but mainly because he placed enormous reliance upon his perceptions as an individual. The arresting, static quality of his figures is paralleled only by the extraordinary way in which they seem to develop under his unwavering gaze. Wordsworth's power to create fictions such as these equals that of any of the great novelists, and he is less flawed, in his actual narrative, than they are. He has access to a heightened speech which is impossible to prose. Because of this Wordsworth seems to be, as no novelist is, indefinitely re-readable.

Selected bibliography

WORDSWORTH AND HIS CIRCLE

Coleridge, S. T. *Biographia Literaria*, ed. James Engell and W. J. Bate, 2 vols., Princeton, N.J., 1983.
—— *Poems*, ed. E. H. Coleridge, Oxford, 1912.
De Quincey, Thomas, *Recollections of the Lakes and the Lake Poets*, ed. David Wright, Harmondsworth, Middlesex, 1970.
Southey, Robert, *Poems*, ed. M. H. Fitzgerald, Oxford, 1909.
Wordsworth, Dorothy, *Journals*, ed. Ernest de Selincourt, 2 vols., London, 1951.
—— *Journals*, ed. Mary Moorman, Oxford, 1971.
Wordsworth, William, *Poems*, ed. Matthew Arnold, London, 1879.
—— *Poetical Works*, ed. Thomas Hutchinson, Oxford, 1904.
—— *Poetical Works*, ed. Ernest de Selincourt and Helen Darbishire, 5 vols. Oxford, 1940–9.
—— *The Cornell Wordsworth*, ed. Stephen Parrish *et al.*, 13 vols.; in progress, Ithaca, New York, 1975–.
—— *The Oxford Authors: Wordsworth*, ed. Stephen Gill, Oxford, 1984.
—— *Lyrical Ballads*, ed. R. L. Brett and A. R. Jones, London, 1963.
—— *The Prelude 1799, 1805, 1850*, ed. Jonathan Wordsworth, M. H. Abrams, and Stephen Gill, New York and London, 1979.
—— *Prose Works*, ed. W. J. B. Owen and J. W. Smyser, 3 vols., Oxford, 1974.

BIOGRAPHICAL WORKS

Curry, Kenneth, *Southey*, London and Boston, 1975.

Friedman, Michael H., *The Making of a Tory Humanist*, New York, 1979.

Gittings, Robert, and Manton, Jo, *Dorothy Wordsworth*, Oxford, 1985.

Hanson, Lawrence, *The Life of S. T. Coleridge: The Early Years*, London, 1938.

Moorman, Mary L., *William Wordsworth: The Early Years 1770–1803*, Oxford, 1957.

—— *William Wordsworth: The Later Years 1803–1850*, Oxford, 1965.

Reed, Mark L., *Wordsworth: The Chronology of the Early Years 1770–1799*, Cambridge, Mass., 1967.

—— *Wordsworth: The Chronology of the Middle Years 1800–1815*, Cambridge, Mass., 1975.

Thompson, T. W., *Wordsworth's Hawkshead*, ed. Robert Woof, Oxford, 1970.

CRITICISM

Bateson, F. W., *Wordsworth: A Re-Interpretation*, London, 1954, 1956.

Ellis, David, *Wordsworth, Freud and the Spots of Time*, Cambridge, 1988.

Fruman, Norman, *Coleridge, The Damaged Archangel*, New York and London, 1971.

Hartman, Geoffrey H., *Wordsworth's Poetry 1787–1814*, New Haven, Conn., and London, 1964.

Harvey, W. J., 'Vision and medium in *The Prelude*', in *Wordsworth: The Prelude*, ed. W. J. Harvey and Richard Gravil, London, 1972.

Hazlitt, William, *Lectures on the English Poets* and *The Spirit of the Age*, London, 1910; rep. 1959, with an introduction by C. M. Maclean.

Hobsbaum, Philip, 'The essential Wordsworth', *Poetry Review* LVII, Winter 1966–7.

—— *Tradition and Experiment in English Poetry*, London and Totowa, New Jersey, 1979.

Jacobus, Mary, *Tradition and Experiment in Wordsworth's 'Lyrical Ballads' (1798)*, Oxford, 1976.

Johnston, Kenneth R., *Wordsworth and 'The Recluse'*, New Haven, Conn., and London, 1984.

Leavis, F. R., 'Wordsworth', in *Revaluation*, London, 1936.

—— 'Wordsworth: the creative conditions', in *The Critic as Anti-Philosopher*, ed. G. Singh, London, 1982.

Macdonell, Diane C., 'The place of the device of expectation . . . in Book 1 of *The Excursion*', *Studies in Romanticism* 18, Fall, 1979.

McFarland, Thomas, *Romanticism and the Forms of Ruin*, Princeton, N.J., 1981.

Sheats, Paul D. *The Making of Wordsworth's Poetry, 1785–1798*, Cambridge, Mass., 1973.

Smith, James, 'Wordsworth: a preliminary survey', in *Shakespearian and Other Essays*, Cambridge, 1974.

Spivak, Gayatri Chakravorty, 'Sex and history in *The Prelude* (1805)', *In Other Worlds: Essays in Cultural Politics*, New York and London, 1987.

Winkler, R. O. C., 'Wordsworth's poetry', in *The Pelican Guide to English Literature*, vol. 5, ed. Boris Ford, Harmondsworth, Middlesex, 1957.

Wordsworth, Jonathan, *The Music of Humanity*, London, 1969.

—— *The Borders of Vision*, Oxford, 1982.

—— ed., *Bicentenary Wordsworth Studies in Memory of John Alban Finch*, Ithaca, New York, 1970.

Notes

D. W., *Alfoxden*	Dorothy Wordsworth, *Alfoxden Journal*
D. W., *Grasmere*	Dorothy Wordsworth, *Grasmere Journals*
Lyrical Ballads, 1798	William Wordsworth, Notes to *Lyrical Ballads* (1798)
Lyrical Ballads, 1801	William Wordsworth, Notes to *Lyrical Ballads* (2nd edn, 1801)
'Preface', 1815	William Wordsworth, Preface to *Poems* (1815)
Guide through . . . the Lakes	William Wordsworth, *Guide through the District of the Lakes* (5th edn, 1835)
I. F.	William Wordsworth, Notes dictated to Isabella Fenwick (1842–3), reprinted in *Poetical Works* (Oxford, 1940–9), ed. Ernest de Selincourt and Helen Darbishire

THE RUINED COTTAGE

The text of 'The ruined cottage' in this edition is basically that of the March 1798 version with the life of the pedlar (ll. 47–104 of Ms. B) left out. What remains is in effect the 'lost' version of 1797, except that possibly the introduction, in the present edition ll. 1–45, may

205

also be later than 1797. It is, however, based on the earlier poem, *An Evening Walk* (1793), especially ll. 53–88 which begin: 'When in the south, the wan moon brooding still, / Breathed a pale steam around the glaring hill, / And shades of deep embattled clouds were seen / Spotting the northern cliff with lights between'. The present editor has therefore followed the precedent of Stephen Gill in his edition of 'Adventures on Salisbury Plain', and included for narrative completeness the introduction, as Mr Gill did 'The female vagrant' in his text of Ms. 2. Purists, however, are welcome to begin reading at l. 29, 'I found a ruined cottage'; or l. 34, 'As I looked around'; or possibly l. 46, 'Now on the bench he lay'. When there has been a choice of readings in Ms. B the present editor has chosen the earlier one in each case as being likely to represent what Wordsworth wrote in 1797. Other, more fragmentary, manuscripts have been drawn upon when they provided evidence conducive to the reconstruction of the 1797 draft.

Verbal deviations from Ms. B are as follows:

5   *dappled* supplies a blank in Ms. B and is taken from Dorothy Wordsworth's transcript of 1799, Ms. D, the one in which the pedlar's life is left out altogether, to form an independent poem.

60   *lank slips* supplies a blank in Ms. B and is taken from Ms. D, as above.

66–9   *with weeds and grass ... a wooden bowl* supplies a blank in l. 125 of Ms. B and also adds three lines; all taken from the 'Christabel' notebook (so called because it contains the first version of Coleridge's poem of that name) which dates from late January 1798 or shortly after, and which therefore precedes Ms. B. The last phrase of l. 66 here, and ll. 68–9, are, in any case, verbally close to ll. 142–5 of Ms. B.

73   *'Oh! Master time has been.'* This is a reading from the 'Christabel' notebook, and is important as indicating that in a pre-Ms. B draft the narrator did not know the pedlar, who calls him – not, as in Ms. B 'my friend' – but, formally, 'Master'. In the poem at this earlier stage the narrator could not have told the story of the pedlar's life which disrupts later versions of the narrative. The portentous 'I see around me here / Things which you cannot see', ll. 129–30 of Ms.

B, is an addendum. The whole of this passage, in the present edition ll. 66–79, is from the 'Christabel' notebook, and represents a version of the poem closer to the 1797 draft than Ms. B.

79–141   *'Many a passenger . . . Ill fared it now with Robert.'* This passage is based on Ms. A, the earliest extant draft of 'The ruined cottage', dating from spring 1797 but unfortunately incomplete. There have been editorial interventions in the present text at l. 88 ('her' inserted between 'seen' and 'sit'); l. 90 ('offers' for 'offer'); l. 91 ('tricked' for 'trick'); l. 99 (where 'wall' supplies a blank and is taken from a variant later on in Ms. A). A repetition of l. 93, 'You see the swallow's nest has dropped away', which would have come between l. 100 and l. 101 of the present edition, has been omitted; also twelve attendant lines which Wordsworth has cancelled. In Ms. A they run, after 'A wretched covert 'tis for man or beast':

> And when the poor man's horse that shelters there
> Turns from the beating wind and open sky
> The iron links with which his feet are clogged
> Mix their dull clanking with the heavy sound
> Of falling rain a melancholy [noise.]
> And when the poor man's horse that hither comes
> For shelter turns
> And open sky the passenger may hear
> The iron links with which his feet are clogged
> Mix their dull clanking with the heavy sound
> Of falling rain, a melancholy thing
> To any man who has a heart to feel.

This is really a juxtaposition of two attempts at the same passage. It has considerable power but leads away from the narrative of 'The ruined cottage' and was incorporated into an early poem, 'Incipient madness': 'The poor man's horse that feeds along the lanes / Had hither come among these fractured walls / To weather out the night'.

106   editorial intervention: 'ere' for 'er' and 'mower's' for (in Ms. A) 'mower'.

141	Ms. A ends and the text returns to Ms. B from here to the end of Part One.
183	Ms. B reads '[ ] of Nature with our restless thoughts'. The blank is supplied with 'The tone', from Ms. B², a transcript of part of 'The ruined cottage' sent by Dorothy Wordsworth to Mary Hutchinson on 5 March 1798.
198	This line is taken from a passage otherwise very similar in the 'Alfoxden' notebook, also anterior to Ms. B, including drafts that Wordsworth wrote between January and March 1798. Ms. B has 'There was a heartfelt chillness in my veins'. The 'I' of 'I felt' in l. 198 of the present text is, however, an editorial emendation; the 'Alfoxden' original reads 'A felt'.
201	'Alfoxden' notebook; Ms. B has 'The comfort of the warmer sun'.
204	'Alfoxden' notebook; the same line is cancelled in Ms. B, as is the preceding 'and impelled'; for this latter, Ms. B substitutes 'I returned'.
210	*Even of the dead* The remainder of l. 210 and ll. 211 to 213 are from the 'Alfoxden' notebook: Ms. B reads 'contented thus to draw / A momentary pleasure never marked / By reason, barren of all future good. / We know that there is often to be found' ['In mournful thoughts', etc.].
222	*At your request* is the 'Alfoxden' reading. Ms. B has 'At your bidding'.
397	*winds* is the 'Christabel' notebook reading; Ms. B has 'wind'.
408	*'Master! I have heard'* this is as Dorothy Wordsworth's transcript in Coleridge's letter of 10 June 1797 to John Prior Estlin, and as originally written in Ms. B but later cancelled in favour of 'I have heard my Friend'. Dorothy's 1797 transcript, together with Ms. A, is the nearest we are likely to get to the orginal poem. All indications are that the pedlar was in that poem unknown to the narrator; see note to l. 73, above.
430	*sat* This is Dorothy Wordsworth's transcript of 1797; Ms. B has 'stood'.
439	*sat* Dorothy Wordsworth's transcript of 1797; Ms. B has 'lived', replacing a cancelled 'sat', presumably, like 'Master'

(l. 408 of the present text), a slip made in copying too sedulously the original 1797 poem.

446   *the* [wretched spot] is the original reading of Dorothy Wordsworth's 1797 transcript, emended to 'this' there and in Ms. B.

449   *Stranger* reading as Dorothy Wordsworth's 1797 transcript and also in Ms. B, presumably following the original of 1797, the latter emended to 'my friend'. The present reading, 'Stranger', is crucial to the reconstruction of the 1797 original.

Acknowledgements are due to the pioneering work of Ernest de Selincourt and Helen Darbishire and, more recently, to Jonathan Wordsworth and James Butler. However, the editor would like to draw attention to his essay in *The Poetry Review* LVll (Winter 1966–7) and his book, *Tradition and Experiment in English Poetry* (Macmillan, and Rowman and Littlefield, 1979).

Epigraph		Anglicized from 'Epistle to John Lapraik, An Old Scotch Bard' by Robert Burns (1759–96). The original reads 'Gie me ae spark o' Nature's fire,/ That's a' the learning I desire / . . . My Muse, tho' hamely in attire, / May touch the heart'.
17	*lot*	fate.
91	*tricked*	decorated.
236	*wist*	knew.
250	*A purse*	This was a sum of three guineas paid to each man enlisting in the army. Bread in 1797 was approximately one-twentieth of the price it is in the late 1980s, so the sum could be estimated as £60.60 in present-day money. Alternatively, since Robert could have earned as much as £2.00 a week, the sum could be seen as the equivalent of not quite a fortnight's wages.

317	*With dull red stains discoloured*	'4th [February 1798] . . . The moss rubbed by the sheep that leave locks of wool, and the red marks with which they are spotted, upon the wood' (D. W., *Alfoxden*).
418–21	*she paced through many a day / . . . spinning the long-drawn thread / With backward steps*	'The long fibres . . . were tied around the spinner's waist . . . the spinners walked backwards from the rotating hooks . . . playing out fibres with each hand as they went and so making two yarns at a time which, on the return journey, were twisted together' (Patricia Baines, *Spinning Wheels, Spinners, and Spinning*, 1977).
422	*the soldier's red*	British soldiers wore red until khaki, a woollen cloth dyed brown, pioneered by the British army in India in the 1840s, was adopted during the Boer War of 1899–1902.

MICHAEL

'The character and circumstances of Luke were taken from a family to whom had belonged, many years before, the house we lived in at Town-End, along with some fields and woodlands on the eastern shore of Grasmere. The name of the Evening Star was not in fact given to this house but to another on the same side of the valley more to the north' (I. F.).

| 2 | *Green-head Gill* | 'Saturday [11 October, 1800] . . . After Dinner we walked up Greenhead Gill in search of a sheepfold...The sheepfold is falling away it is built nearly in the form of a heart unequally divided . . . Tuesday 9th [December 1800] Wm finished his poem today' (D. W., *Grasmere*); 'It may be proper to inform some readers, that a sheepfold in these mountains is an unroofed building of stone walls, with different divisions. It |

		is generally placed by the side of a brook, for the convenience of washing the sheep; but it is also useful as a shelter for them, and as a place to drive them into' (*Lyrical Ballads*, 1801).
11	*kite*	a bird of prey with a long forked tail and long broad wings, belonging to the hawk family.
102	*a mess of pottage*	probably porridge; 'Esau selleth his birthright for a mess of pottage' (heading to Genesis 25, Geneva Bible).
179	*The Clipping Tree*	'Clipping is the word used in the North of England for shearing' (*Lyrical Ballads*, 1801).
220–1	*bound / In surety*	Michael, using his land as security, had undertaken to pay a debt incurred by his nephew, should his nephew himself fail to pay it. The nephew fails, so Michael's land is subject to the charge. About 50 per cent of the land is claimed from him.
254–5	*'Our Luke shall leave us, Isabel; the land / . . . shall be free . . .'*	The idea is that Luke will go to London and make his fortune, so paying the debt Michael has taken on.
268	*Richard Bateman*	'This chapel was begun to be rebuilt Anno Domini 1743 at the sole expense of Mr Robert Bateman, merchant at Leghorn, born in this hamlet' (inscription on the stone tablet over the west door of the chapel at Ings, on the road from Kendal to Ambleside, quoted in Wordsworth, *Poetical Works*, 1940–9, ed. Ernest de Selincourt and Helen Darbishire, vol. II).
334	*a sheep-fold*	see note to l. 2, pp. 208–9.
424	*a covenant*	a binding promise; 'I will make my covenant between me and thee, and will multiply thee exceedingly' (Genesis 17:2).

This is a rejected portion of 'Michael', originally intended to occur after l. 213. It was found in an interleaved copy of Coleridge's *Poems* (1796), but dates from late 1800, the period of the composition of 'Michael'.

LINES WRITTEN A FEW MILES ABOVE TINTERN ABBEY

Tintern Abbey, not explicitly mentioned in the poem itself, was a Cistercian monastery, established in 1131 but rebuilt and enlarged in the period between 1220 and 1320. It was de-roofed by Henry VIII in the course of his suppression of the monasteries, in 1536. Being situated in a remote place, it escaped the dilapidations of quarriers and survives, now as in Wordsworth's time, a romantic spectacle with its great arches and columns on a bend of the River Wye.

1	*Five years have passed*	Wordsworth had previously seen Tintern Abbey on his wild journey (see p. 4) from Salisbury Plain to the home of Robert Jones in North Wales, summer 1793.
4	*a sweet inland murmur*	'The river is not affected by the tide a few miles above Tintern' (*Lyrical Ballads*, 1798).
15–19	*Once again I see / . . . wreaths of smoke / Sent up, in silence, from among the trees*	'Many of the furnaces, on the banks of the river, consume charcoal, which is manufactured on the spot; and the smoke, which is frequently seen issuing from the sides of the hills, and spreading its thin veil over a part of them, beautifully breaks their lines, and unites them with the sky' (William Gilpin, *Tour of the Wye*, 1771).
44	*corporeal frame*	body; 'bodily frame' (Wordsworth, 'Michael', l. 463).
57	*sylvan*	wooded.
116	*my dearest friend*	Dorothy Wordsworth had not been

with her brother in his previous expedition to the Wye, and was now experiencing its delights for the first time.

NUTTING

'Written in Germany; intended as part of a poem on my own life but struck out as not being wanted there . . . These verses arose out of the remembrance of feelings I had often had as a boy, and particularly in the extensive woods that still stretch from the side of Esthwaite Lake towards Graythwaite, the seat of the ancient family of Sandys' (I. F.). Part of the poem was sent in a letter from William and Dorothy Wordsworth, then staying at Goslar, to Coleridge, dated either 14 or 21 December 1798. Some fifty-two lines of introduction, found in the 'Christabel' notebook (see p. 206) were discarded. They began: 'Ah! what a crash was that! with gentle hand / Touch these fair hazels'.

9   *my frugal dame*   Ann Dyson (1713–96), with whom Wordsworth boarded throughout the eight and a quarter years he was at Hawkshead Grammar School. It would seem that her 'frugality' consisted in her requiring her young lodgers to put on their oldest clothes for their rustic expeditions.

The 'Lucy' poems

'STRANGE FITS OF PASSION I HAVE KNOWN'

An Ms draft was sent from Goslar to Coleridge in a letter of 14 or 21 December 1798.

'A SLUMBER DID MY SPIRIT SEAL'

'Some months ago Wordsworth transmitted me a most sublime epitaph / whether it had any reality, I cannot say. – Most probably, in some gloomier moment he had fancied the moment in which his Sister might die' (Coleridge, letter to Thomas Poole, 6 April 1799).

SONG ('SHE DWELT AMONG TH'UNTRODDEN WAYS')

The poem appears as a draft in a letter of 14 or 21 December 1798, to Coleridge. There are two stanzas included there which were later discarded. In draft, the poem begins: 'My hope was one, from cities far, / Nursed on a lonesome heath; / Her lips were red as roses are, / Her hair a woodbine wreath'.

2	*the springs of Dove*	There are rivers called Dove in Derbyshire, Yorkshire, and Westmorland. None had any particular significance for Wordsworth so far as is known. The name was probably chosen as a convenient rhyme-word.

'I TRAVELLED AMONG UNKNOWN MEN'

This poem was not included with the other 'Lucy' poems in *Lyrical Ballads* and was sent as a recent work in a letter to Mary Hutchinson (later, Mary Wordsworth) on 29 April 1801, with a recommendation that it be read after 'She dwelt among th'untrodden ways'.

'THREE YEARS SHE GREW IN SUN AND SHOWER'

'Composed in the Harz Mountains' (I. F.).

Poems on the naming of places

'IT WAS AN APRIL MORNING: FRESH AND CLEAR'

'This poem was suggested on the banks of the brook that runs through Easedale, which is, in some parts of its course, as wild and beautiful as brook can be. I have composed thousands of verses by the side of it' (I. F.).

| 39 | *My Emma* | Emma was the name Wordsworth occasionally used in his poems to stand for that of Dorothy. |

TO JOANNA

Joanna Hutchinson (1780–1843) was Mary Wordsworth's youngest sister, but she was brought up in Penrith; hardly, in the 1780s, remarkable for the 'smoke of cities'.

| 13 | *two long years* | Joanna could not have visited the Wordsworths at Grasmere two years previously, since they had been settled there only since the December preceding. She had not even visited Grasmere by the time this poem was written: 'Saturday 22nd [August 1800] . . . William was composing all the morning . . . He read us the Poem of Joanna beside the Rothay by the roadside' (D. W., *Grasmere*). The fiction is manufactured for the sake of the slight story-line: 'I begin to relate the story in a certain degree to divert or partly play upon the Vicar' (Wordsworth, Ms. 2, a notebook of 1799 mostly concerned with *Peter Bell*); 'The effect of her laugh is an extravagance; though the effect of the reverberation of voices in some parts of the mountains is very striking' (I. F.). |
| 28 | *runic priest* | 'In Cumberland and Westmorland are several inscriptions upon the native rock which from the wasting of time and the rudeness of the workmanship have been mistaken for Runic. They are without doubt Roman' (*Lyrical Ballads*, 1801). This is, then, a double displacement. Wordsworth chisels out a name on the native rock which will |

be mistaken not for a Roman inscription but for one that is runic; that is to say, pertaining to the earliest Teutonic alphabet, used by the Saxons and also, perhaps, suggestive of magical rites.

31   *Rotha*   'The Rotha, mentioned in this poem, is the river which flowing through the Lakes of Grasmere and Rydal falls into Windermere' (*Lyrical Ballads*, 1801; and see note to l. 13, p. 215).

56   *That ancient woman*   'On Helm-Crag, that impressive single mountain at the head of the Vale of Grasmere, is a rock which from most points of view bears a striking resemblance to an old woman cowering' (*Lyrical Ballads*, 1801).

57–65   *Hammer-Scar, / And the tall steep of Silver-How sent forth / A noise of laughter / . . . And Kirkstone tossed it from his misty head*   Hammar-Scar, Silver-How, Loughrigg, Fairfield, Helvellyn, Skiddaw, Glaramara, and Kirkstone are mountains that 'either immediately surround the Vale of Grasmere, or belong to the same cluster' (*Lyrical Ballads*, 1801; see note to l. 13, p. 215).

'THERE IS AN EMINENCE, – OF THESE OUR HILLS'

'It is not accurate that the eminence here alluded to could be seen from our orchard-seat. It rises above the road by the side of Grasmere lake, towards Keswick, and its name is Stone-Arthur' (I. F.).

14   *she who dwells with me*   Dorothy Wordsworth.

'A NARROW GIRDLE OF ROUGH STONES AND CRAGS'

'The character of the eastern shore of Grasmere Lake is quite changed, since these verses were written, by the public road being carried along its side. The friends spoken of were Coleridge and my sister, and the fact occurred strictly as recorded' (I. F.).

216

16	*wreck*	wrack; river débris cast on shore.
36	*of the Queen Osmunda*	royal moonwort, Osmunda regalis; 'In the root of Osmund or Water fern every eye may discern the form of a Half Moon' (Sir Thomas Browne, *The Garden of Cyrus*, 1658).
38	*naiad*	water spirit; 'The Nymphs, who preside over springs and rivulets . . . Their origin is deduced from the first allegorical deities, or powers of nature . . . They are . . . considered as giving motion to the air and exciting summer-breezes' (Mark Akenside, Argument for 'Hymn to the Naiads', 1746).

TO M.H.

'To Mary Hutchinson, two years before our marriage. The pool alluded to is in Rydal Upper Park' (I. F.).

Home at Grasmere

This poem is sometimes known as 'The recluse' because it was intended to be Book One of Wordsworth's projected philosophical poem of that name (see p. 8). But really it is a celebration of William and Dorothy Wordsworth's return to the Lake District in 1800; begun that year, revised in 1806, and revised over again in 1814. Wordsworth did not publish the poem in his lifetime; after his death, owing to copyright difficulties, it figured in comparatively few editions of his work. This text is based on the first complete version, Ms. B, dating from 1800. It is chosen for the present selection in preference to *The Excursion*, many of whose aspects it anticipates and most of whose poetry it excels.

| 1 | *yonder hill* | Loughrigg Terrace, south of Grasmere Lake. |
| 8 | *and sighing said* | supplied from Ms. D, *c.* 1812, to complete the line which was left unfinished in 1800. |

58	*more bountiful*	Ms. B reads, illogically, 'less bountiful'.
98	*my Emma*	Dorothy Wordsworth.
106	*happy*	supplied from Ms. D, to fill a blank in Ms. B.
171	*we met to part no more*	Separated in childhood after the death of their mother and break-up of the family home, William and Dorothy Wordsworth were reunited in 1794 and, from the date of setting up their first permanent home in Dorset, were never apart for any length of time.
185–91		Seven lines are missing from Ms. B and cannot be supplied from later drafts.
206	*spot*	editorially supplied; to fill a blank in Ms. B.
218–56		In December 1799 William and Dorothy Wordsworth started the journey from Sockburn, where they had been staying with the Hutchinson family. They began on horseback, but from Richmond they walked, through Wensleydale and past Sedbergh, some forty miles in three wintry days, until they reached Kendal. From there they were able to proceed by post-chaise to Grasmere.
242	*the hunted beast*	This refers to a local legend told of a hart seeking to escape his hunters by leaping down a mountainside to a well. This well thereafter never prospered; the surrounding landscape presented an aspect of decay. Wordsworth was told the story as he and Dorothy passed the spot during their journey to Grasmere, and later versified it as 'Hart-Leap Well': ' "Three leaps have borne him from this lofty brow, / Down to the very fountain where he lies" '.

292–314	*Behold them, how they shape . . . As if they scorned both resting-place and rest*	A version of these lines was published in the fourth edition of Wordsworth's *Guide through . . . the Lakes*, and appeared in *Poetical Works*, 1827, as 'Water Fowl'.
469–606	*Yon cottage, would that it could tell a part . . . And the whole house is filled with gaiety*	This passage was the original of *The Excursion*, 6, ll. 1080–187.
680	*worthiest*	supplied from a cancellation, to fill a blank in Ms. B.
739	*Helvellyn's eagles*	Helvellyn is one of the highest mountains of the Lake District, standing to the north-east of Grasmere. See also note to 'To Joanna', ll. 57–65, p. 216.
742	*Owlet Crag*	a local name, now unidentifiable.
749	*A term*	supplied from Ms. R, to fill a blank in Ms. B.
829	*Arcadian*	Arcadia was a name for a mountainous region in the Peloponnese south of Corinth, taken by Virgil to be an ideal pastoral enclave. Sir Philip Sidney named his famous romance *Arcadia* (1580) after it.
864	*a stranger whom we love*	John Wordsworth, brother to William and Dorothy, who stayed with them from January to September 1800.
869	*sisters of our hearts*	Mary, Sara and Joanna Hutchinson.
870	*a brother of our hearts*	Samuel Taylor Coleridge.
917	*urged*	supplied from Ms. D, to fill a blank in Ms. B.
959–1048	*On man, on nature, and on human life . . . Be with me and uphold me to the end!*	This passage appeared with *The Excursion* in 1814 as a prospectus for *The Recluse*.

972–3	*fit audience . . . find*	'still govern thou my song, / Urania, and fit audience find though few' (Milton, *Paradise Lost*, 1667, VII, ll. 30–1).
974	*Urania*	the muse, or guiding spirit, of astronomy, invoked also by Milton; see note above.
986	*blinder*	supplied from Ms. D, to fill a blank in Ms. B.
1042	*mingle*	supplied from prospectus, Ms. 2, to fill a gap in Ms. B.

OLD MAN TRAVELLING

'If I recollect right these verses were an overflowing from ''The Old Cumberland Beggar'' ' (I. F.). There is a draft, 'Description of a beggar', dating from early 1797. Lines 16–20 of 'Old man travelling' were omitted after the fourth edition of *Lyrical Ballads*, published in 1804, and the title was changed to 'Animal tranquillity and decay'.

THE OLD CUMBERLAND BEGGAR

This poem, like the one preceding, was developed from a draft called 'Description of a beggar' composed early in 1797. 'Observed, and with great benefit to my own heart, when I was a child: written at Racedown and Alfoxden in my 28th year. The political economists were about that time beginning their war upon mendicity in all its forms, and by implication, if not directly, upon almsgiving also' (I. F.).

| 37 | *post-boy* | postillion; the person who, when four or more horses were harnessed together to draw a heavy carriage, would ride on the near (i.e. left) leading horse in order to guide the team. Alternatively, this could mean the postman, a functionary who in those days would bring the mail to the local post-office on horseback. |

115	*silent monitor*	a conscience; the term has an interesting provenance. 'That which I found to be the most efficient check upon inferior conduct, was the contrivance of a silent monitor for each one employed in the establishment. This consisted of a four-sided piece of wood, about two inches long and one broad, each side coloured – one side black, another blue, the third yellow, and the fourth white, tapered at the top, and finished with wire eyes, to hang upon a hook with either side to the front. One of these was suspended in a conspicuous place near to each of the persons employed, and the colour at the front told of the conduct of the individual during the preceding day, to four degrees of comparison. Bad, denoted by black and No. 4, – indifferent by blue, and No. 3, – good by yellow, and no. 2, – and excellent by white and No. 1' (*The Life of Robert Owen, Written by Himself*, 1857–8). Wordsworth's use of the term 'silent monitor' is hardly accidental. Robert Owen was a pioneer in methods of education, and mentions in his autobiography that 'Coleridge came occasionally from his college, during vacations to join us'; 'us' being Owen's Manchester circle of 'inquiring friends'.
127	*the Decalogue*	The Ten Commandments (Exodus 20:1–17).
138	*these inevitable charities*	As Dickens was to, Wordsworth opposed the nineteenth-century tendency to force the poor into workhouses; rather than allow them to

		make a show of independence, while in fact begging their bread.
172	*house, misnamed of industry*	workhouse; an organized shelter for the poor who were assigned such tasks as they were capable of fulfilling in return for their keep.

RESOLUTION AND INDEPENDENCE

'This old man I met a few hundred yards from my cottage at Town-End, Grasmere; and the account of him is taken from his own mouth. I was in the state of feeling described in the beginning of the poem, while crossing over Barton Fell from Mr Clarkson's, at the foot of Ullswater, towards Askam. The image of the hare I then observed on the ridge of the fell' (I. F.).

43	*I thought of Chatterton*	Thomas Chatterton (1752–70) wrote poems purporting to be those of a fifteenth-century monk from Bristol, the wholly fictitious Thomas Rowley. Chatterton impressed very few people with these efforts, and killed himself. Yet the poems have their own weird merits, and Wordsworth has adopted the metre of Chatterton's 'An excelente balade of charitie' for 'Resolution and independence'.
45–6	*him who walked ... / Behind his plough*	Robert Burns. See note to Epigraph, 'The ruined cottage', p. 209.
64–71	*As a huge stone / ... Such seemed this man*	'The stone is endowed with something of the power of life to approximate it to the sea-beast; and the sea-beast stripped of some of its vital qualities to assimilate it to the stone; which intermediate image is thus treated for the purpose of bringing the original image, that of the stone, to a nearer resemblance to the figure and condition of

the aged man; who is divested of so much of the indications of life and motion as to bring him to the point where the two objects unite and coalesce in that just comparison' ('Preface', 1815).

72–3 *in his extreme old age: / His body was bent double*
'Friday 3rd October [1800] . . . When Wm and I returned from accompanying [Robert] Jones we met an old man almost double . . . His trade was to gather leeches, but now leeches are scarce and he had not enough strength for it. He lived by begging . . . He had been hurt in driving a cart, his leg broke, his body driven over, his skull fractured' (D. W., *Grasmere*). Notice that Dorothy Wordsworth imputes to physical accident the spinal curvature which Wordsworth in the poem describes as a result of old age. Perhaps it should be added that leeches were a species of aquatic worm used over the centuries for sucking blood in the belief that noxious substances poisoning the patient could thereby be extracted.

104 *Such as grave livers do in Scotland use*
'He was of Scotch parents . . . and was making his way to Carlisle where he should buy a few godly books to sell' (D. W., *Grasmere*).

The Prelude 1798–9, First Part

The version here derives from a fair copy (Ms. V) made by Dorothy Wordsworth in 1799 from an original written at Goslar.

1 *Was it for this . . . ?*
What is implied is that the whole poem forms an antecedent to the reiterated 'this'. It was that the poem in question might be written that the influence

which Wordsworth describes worked upon him in youth.

7	*Derwent*	The river Derwent flowed behind the house in Cockermouth where Wordsworth was born.
8	*'sweet birthplace'*	'already had I dreamt / Of my sweet birthplace' (Coleridge, 'Frost at midnight', 1798).
23	*grunsel*	ragwort or ragweed, *Senecio Jacobaea*; 'the great Groundswel hath rough whitish leaves' (Henry Lyte, translator, *Dodoens' Niewe Herball or Historie of Plantes*, 1578).
24	*Skiddaw*	a peak east of Cockermouth; Wordsworth speaks of its 'solitary majesty' (*Guide through . . . the Lakes*).
32	*woodcocks*	The woodcock is a migratory bird of the snipe family; 'of a good temperaunce and metely lyght in dygestion' (Thomas Elyot, *The Castel of Helth*, 1539).
34	*springes*	snares; 'springes to catch woodcocks' (Shakespeare, *Hamlet*, 1601, I.iii. 115).
44	*toils*	Toil is at once a noun denoting labour, and a trap; 'she looks like sleep, / As she would catch another Antony / In the strong toil of grace' (Shakespeare, *Antony and Cleopatra*, 1606, V.ii. 343–5).
55–7	*Though mean / And though inglorious were my views, the end / Was not ignoble*	'The end justifies the means' (Herman Busenbaum, *Medulla Theologiae Moralis*, 1650). Wordsworth was about to deprive the ravens of their eggs, but gained insight into nature in the process.
58	*the raven's nest*	The raven is a large member of the crow family; there may have been a bounty or payment for the eggs taken, since at that time the raven was con-

		sidered to be vermin especially dangerous to livestock.
103	*elfin pinnace*	a small boat, suited to children or fairies.
109	*voluntary power instinct*	as though filled with the power to move at will.
127–8	*But huge and mighty forms, that do not live / Like living men*	'Forms which never deigned / In eyes or ears to dwell within the sense / Of earthly organs' (Mark Akenside, *The Pleasures of the Imagination*, 1757, II, ll. 103–5).
186–9	*Ye Powers of earth! ye Genii of the springs! / ... Familiars of the lakes / And of the standing pools*	Wordsworth is addressing the spirits which he believes are immanent in the living forms of nature; 'Ye elves of hills, brooks, standing lakes, and groves; / And ye that on the sands with printless foot / Do chase the ebbing Neptune and do fly him' (Shakespeare, *The Tempest*, 1611, V.i. 33–5).
215–22	*to the combat – Lu or Whist – led on / A thick-ribbed army / ... Ironic diamonds, hearts of sable hue, / Queens gleaming through their splendour's last decay*	Loo, abbreviated from 'lanterloo', a word of obscure origin, was a round card-game, played by a varying number of participants. A 'loo' was a fine or forfeit incurred in the course of the game by players losing a trick. Whist, on the other hand, is played by four participants and is a primitive form of contract bridge. In the game Wordsworth describes, the diamonds and hearts had been so thumbed that their original red has blackened to the colour of the spades and clubs; hence 'ironic' diamonds and the 'last decay' of the queens' splendours.
233	*Bothnic*	northern Baltic.
235–6	*The woods of autumn and their hidden bowers /*	see note to 'Nutting', p. 213. This may have been the point at which 'Nutting' was to have been inserted

	With milk-white clusters hung	into *The Prelude*.
261	*Hawkshead*	'The Reader will excuse a partiality produced by the recollections of more than 10 years of boyhood and youth passed in this valley, a period during which neither the eye was inattentive nor the imagination torpid' (Wordsworth, 'An unpublished tour', 1811–12, *The Prose Works of William Wordsworth*, ed. W. J. B. Owen and J. W. Smyser, 1974, vol. II). Wordsworth was a year or two older than he suggests in the poem.
265	*Esthwaite's lake*	near Hawkshead; 'Its waters are pure and crystalline; the breezes have room to play upon its surface, and the strong winds to agitate its depths' (Wordsworth, 'An unpublished tour', see note above). This lake was the subject of a poem Wordsworth wrote at the age of seventeen: 'Green isles, steep woods, emerge to view' ('The vale of Esthwaite', 1787).
277–9	*the dead man / ... Rose with his ghastly face*	A schoolmaster called Joseph Jackson who was employed in the villages of Near Sawrey and Far Sawrey to the south-east of Esthwaite Water (Hawkshead was to the north-west) was drowned on 18 June 1779, while bathing.
288	*There are in our existence spots of time*	This is important as a concept in its own right and as a clue to Wordsworth's procédé, in *The Prelude* as elsewhere. Events, especially those of early childhood, can persist, not only shaping the infant psyche but also repairing the sensibility later

on. 'Spots of time' could be loosely paraphrased as 'significant memories'. It is easy to see how this ties in with the central statement of Wordsworth's Preface to *Lyrical Ballads* – 'emotion recollected in tranquillity'. The latter phrase might well serve as a generic sub-title for such poems as *The Prelude*, 'Tintern Abbey' and 'Home at Grasmere'. They are collocations of spots of time.

302   *honest James*   servant to Wordsworth's grandparents. At the period of the narrative, the young Wordsworth would have been about five years of age, staying with his grandparents at Penrith. Two different murders are in question, both anterior to the presumed date of the incident. One involved a local butcher in 1767; the other, a wife poisoned in 1672.

310   *gibbet-mast*   A gibbet was an upright post with a projecting arm from which the bodies of criminals were hung in chains or irons after they had been executed. 'Gibbet-*mast*', presumably to emphasize the wooden upright semblance of the structure, whose memory persists even though the gibbet itself has gone.

316   *The beacon on the summit*   The beacon was built in 1719, four years after the Jacobite rising intended to place the son of James II, who was later known as the Old Pretender, on the throne his father had occupied. When lit, the beacon would serve as a signal to warn against any further invasion from Scotland. In fact, there was an abortive invasion, in 1745.

332–5	*I went forth / Into the fields, impatient for the sight / Of those three horses which should bear us home, / My brothers and myself*	There was no way of travelling between Hawkshead and Penrith other than by horseback. Wordsworth describes himself looking out for the horses his grandfather would have sent to fetch himself and his brothers home from school at the end of the autumn term. The three brothers would at this time have been Richard, William, and John.
350–1	*ere I had been ten days / A dweller in my father's house, he died*	John Wordsworth died on 30 December 1783. Wordsworth's mother had died in March 1778.
447	*my friend*	S. T. Coleridge.
464–8	*Here we pause / . . . soothing quiet which we here have found*	Added from Dove Cottage Ms. 16 which also includes the earlier lines, 'To honourable toil / . . . On which the sun is shining? – ', found in Ms. V, the base-text for the version of *The Prelude* 1798–9, First Part, given here.

'THERE WAS A BOY'

This account of the poet's own boyhood occurs first in Ms. JJ, written during Wordsworth's sojourn at Goslar, October 1798 to January 1799. A copy was received by Coleridge who acknowledged it in a letter back to Wordsworth, dated 10 December 1798: 'the lines are very beautiful and leave an affecting impression'. The lines in question were published as an independent poem in *Lyrical Ballads* (1801) in a form adapted from first-person autobiography to what appears to be an elegy on some other boy, lying in Hawkshead Churchyard. John Tyson, who died in August 1782 aged 12, has been suggested (T. W. Thompson, *Wordsworth's Hawkshead*, ed. Robert Woof, 1970). In this elegaic form the piece was incorporated into *The Prelude* ('1805'), V, ll. 389–413, and, later, with a few Miltonizing alterations, into the '1850' version.

| 1–3 | *ye rocks / And islands of Winander and ye green / Peninsulas of Esthwaite* | Winandermere is an alternative name for Windermere: 'the water is . . . of crystalline purity; so that . . . a delusion might be felt, by a person resting quietly in a boat on the bosom of Winandermere . . . that his boat was suspended in an element as pure as air, or rather that the air and water were one' (*Guide through . . . the Lakes*). For Esthwaite, see note to *The Prelude* 1798–9, l. 265, p. 226. |

'THERE WAS A SPOT'

This is one of several pieces of blank verse in the 'Alfoxden' notebook dating from January 1798 to March of the same year. It relates to but is not integrally a section of *The Prelude* 1798–9, First Part.

| 5 | *for the delicate eye of taste* | There is an addendum in the manuscript which perhaps should go in: 'And for the poet's or the painter's eye'. Wordsworth has rejected the artificial notion of landscape associated in the eighteenth century with patrons such as Lord Burlington and designers such as William Kent. |

THE DISCHARGED SOLDIER

The incident upon which this piece is based took place during Wordsworth's first Long Vacation from Cambridge in the summer of 1788 when he revisited Hawkshead and his 'dame', Ann Tyson, with whom he had boarded as a schoolboy. It was composed as a separate piece, though it may have been intended for Wordsworth's projected philosophical epic, *The Recluse* (see note to 'Home at Grasmere', p. 217) which was under discussion at the time of writing, with Coleridge at Alfoxden. The narrative–autobiographical shape of 'The discharged soldier' relates it to the 1798–9 *Prelude*; later, the poem was incorporated into the '1805' version.

| 61 and see 115–16 | *Had no attendant neither dog, nor staff* | 'Yea, though I walk through the valley of the shadow of death, I will fear no evil: for thou art with me; thy rod and thy staff they comfort me' (Psalm 23). |
| 98–101 | *he had been / A soldier / ... on his landing he had been dismissed* | At this period, that of the French Revolutionary Wars, a soldier could be dropped at a British port when he was no longer capable of further service, to make his own way back home. This particular soldier had evidently served in the West Indies ('the tropic isles'). His wasted condition is a symptom of yellow fever. |

THE SIMPLON PASS

This was published as an independent poem and took its place among the 'Poems of the imagination' in the 1845 edition of Wordsworth's *Poetical Works*. It was incorporated into *The Prelude* ('1805'), VI, ll. 553–72 and, later, into *The Prelude* ('1850'), neither of which was published in Wordsworth's lifetime. The passage is based on the Swiss part of the European tour Wordsworth undertook with Robert Jones in the summer of 1790. There is a prototype of this passage in the record of the tour that Wordsworth wrote and published in 1793 as *Descriptive Sketches*.

THE ASCENT OF SNOWDON

This was written towards the end of 1804 for a five-book version of *The Prelude* which no longer exists, having been cannibalized into the '1805' version. It would have formed the opening of the last (i.e. fifth) book of the five-book *Prelude*, as it now forms the opening of the last (i.e. thirteenth) book of the '1805' *Prelude* and, in a revised form, the opening of the last (i.e. fourteenth) book of the '1850' *Prelude*. The episode is based on a tour of North Wales with Robert Jones at whose home Wordsworth had been staying during the summer of 1791 after his residence in London in the early months of that year.

2	*a youthful friend*	Robert Jones. See note above, and pp. 3, 4.
3	*Bethkelet*	Bethgelert or Beddgelert, a village in the foothills, and to the south, of Mount Snowdon. It would seem that Wordsworth and Jones tacked westward in their ascent.
11	*glaring*	'the wan moon brooding still, / Breathed a pale steam around the glaring hill' (Wordsworth, *An Evening Walk*, 1793, ll. 53–4); 'Along the south the uplands feebly glared' (Wordsworth, 'The ruined cottage', 1797–8, l. 2). It is the kind of evening when such light as there is seems to be dispersed and blurred by the 'dripping mist'.
53–6	*we stood, the mist / Touching our very feet; and from the shore / . . . Was a blue chasm*	The prototype of these lines may be found in Wordsworth's *Descriptive Sketches*, 1793, ll. 494–8, which in its turn owes something to *The Minstrel* (1771) by James Beattie; see especially I, ll. 185–6: 'Th' enormous waste of vapour, tossed / In billows, lengthening to th' horizon round'.

BEGGARS

'Saturday [13 March 1802]. William wrote the poem of the beggar woman taken from a woman whom I had seen in May – now nearly two years ago' (D. W., *Grasmere*). This poem, more than most, seems to be an adaptation from the writings of Dorothy Wordsworth; see her journal entry for 27 May 1800: 'a very tall woman, tall much beyond the measure of tall women, called at the door. She had a very long brown cloak, and a very white cap', etc.

11	*Amazonian*	pertaining to the Amazons who, according to ancient Greek mythology, were a nation of women warriors.

They lived in the Caucasus which is
now the southernmost part of the
Soviet Union in Europe.

TO THE CUCKOO

'Tuesday [23 March 1802]. A mild morning. William worked at the
Cuckoo poem . . . At the closing in of day went to sit in the orchard.
He came to me, and walked backwards and forwards . . . Wm
repeated the poem to me' (D. W., *Grasmere*); 'The cuckoo is almost
perpetually heard throughout the season of spring, but seldom
becomes an object of sight' ('Preface', 1815).

3–4	*shall I call thee bird, / Or but a wanderiing voice?*	'This concise interrogation characterizes the seeming ubiquity of the voice of the cuckoo, and dispossesses the creature almost of a corporeal existence' ('Preface', 1815).

STEPPING WESTWARD

Dorothy Wordsworth adds: 'I cannot describe how affecting this
simple expression was in that remote place, with the western sky in
front, *yet* glowing with the departed sun. Wm. wrote the . . . poem
long after, in remembrance of his feelings and mine.'

THE SOLITARY REAPER

'September 13th, Tuesday [1803]. It was harvest-time, and the fields
were quietly (might I be allowed to say pensively?) enlivened by small
companies of reapers. It is not uncommon in the more lonely parts of
the Highlands to see a single person so employed. The . . . poem was
suggested to Wm. by a beautiful sentence in Thomas Wilkinson's
Tour in Scotland.' Dorothy Wordsworth's *Recollections of a Tour Made
in Scotland A.D. 1803*, from which the previous two notes are drawn,
were written well after the events they describe; begun in September
1803 and finished, after many interruptions, in May 1805. The
sentence in question here may be found in Thomas Wilkinson's *Tours
to the British Mountains* (1824) which Wordsworth had read in

232

manuscript: 'Passed by a female who was reaping alone: she sung in Erse as she bended over her sickle; the sweetest human voice I ever heard: her strains were tenderly melancholy and felt delicious, long after they were heard no more.'

21	*lay*	A lyrical narrative, having the qualities both of song and story; 'Where the pen and the press are wanting, the flow of numbers impresses upon the memory of posterity the deeds and sentiments of their forefathers. Verse is naturally connected with music; and among a rude people the union is seldom broken' (Sir Walter Scott, *Minstrelsy of the Scottish Border*, 1802–3).

ELEGAIC STANZAS

This is one of several elegies Wordsworth wrote commemorating his brother John, drowned off Portland Bill in February 1805. It is addressed to a friend of Coleridge's who had become a friend of Wordsworth as well. Sir George Beaumont (1753–1827) was a rich patron of the arts and amateur painter. The painting referred to in this poem, *A Storm: Peele Castle*, was reproduced as the frontispiece for the second volume of Wordsworth's *Poems* (1815). Wordsworth wrote concerning his brother to Beaumont, saying: 'His taste in all the arts, music and poetry in particular . . . was exquisite. And his eye for the beauties of Nature was as fine and delicate as ever poet or painter was gifted with' (25 February 1805).

1	*thou rugged pile*	Peele (or Peile) is opposite the coast of Furness.
41	*Beaumont*	See note above.

ST PAUL'S

Written in April 1808 but not published until nearly a century after Wordsworth's death. Wordsworth wrote to Sir George Beaumont: 'I left Coleridge at 7 o'clock on Sunday morning; and walked

towards the city in a very thoughtful and melancholy state of mind
. . . when looking up, I saw before me the avenue of Fleet Street,
silent, empty, and pure white, with a sprinkling of new-fallen snow,
not a cart or a carriage to obstruct the view, no noise, only a few
soundless and dusky foot-passengers, here and there' (8 April 1808).

| 27 | *sequestration* | being set aside, isolated, taken away from a previous owner or incumbent, excommunicated. |

Sonnets

'NUNS FRET NOT AT THEIR CONVENT'S NARROW ROOM'

Wordsworth was one of the first poets regularly to practise the
sonnet form, which had been relatively neglected, since the time of
Milton: 'it has an energetic and varied flow of sound crowding into
narrow room more of the combined effect of rhyme and blank verse
than can be done by any kind of verse I know of' (Wordsworth,
letter to Charles Lamb or to Coleridge, 1 November 1802).

| 6 | *Furniss Fells* | Furness is an area at the south-west tip of the Lake District, 'lying out of the way of communication with other parts of the Island, and upon the edge of a hostile kingdom [Scotland]' (*Guide through . . . the Lakes*). |
| 11 | *the sonnet's scanty plot of ground* | The remark suggests that there is a freedom in constraint; demonstrated by the fact that the tightness of the sonnet form does not impede the flow of Wordsworth's verse. This is a self-reflexive poem. |

COMPOSED UPON WESTMINSTER BRIDGE

'On Thursday morning, 29th [July 1802], we arrived in London . . .
We mounted the Dover Coach at Charing Cross. It was a beautiful
morning. The City, St Paul's with the river and a multitude of little

boats made a most beautiful sight as we crossed Westminster Bridge. The houses were not overhung by their cloud of smoke and they were spread out endlessly, yet the sun shone so brightly with such a pure light that there was even something like the purity of one of nature's own grand spectacles' (D. W., *Grasmere*). Wordsworth and Dorothy were *en route* to Calais, to see Annette Vallon and Wordsworth's illegitimate daughter, Caroline.

'IT IS A BEAUTEOUS EVENING, CALM AND FREE'

Written in August 1802, when Wordsworth and Dorothy met Annette Vallon and her daughter in Calais. It is the daughter who is addressed. Wordsworth shows understanding of her incapacity to be moved by natural phenomena, of which she seems to be one.

12	*Abraham's bosom*	A term denoting heaven: 'And it came to pass, that the beggar died, and was carried by the angels into Abraham's bosom; the rich man also died and was buried' (Luke 16:22).
13	*the temple's inner shrine*	The inner shrine of the temple that Solomon built (2 Chronicles 4) was a most holy place, a temple within the temple, in which stood the Ark containing the tablets of the Law dictated by God to Moses. The implication here is that only the pure in heart would have access to the innermost shrine.

'SURPRIZED BY JOY – IMPATIENT AS THE WIND'

'This was in fact suggested by my daughter Catharine, long after her death' (I. F.). The poem was most probably written in 1813; Catharine had died in June 1812.

THE RIVER DUDDON: AFTERTHOUGHT

This sonnet is the conclusion of a sequence concerned with the River Duddon which flows through the south-western area of the Lake

District, past Seathwaite and Broughton. 'I first became acquainted with the Duddon, as I have good reason to remember, in early boyhood . . . I attached myself to a person living in the neighbourhood of Hawkshead, who was going to try his fortune as an angler near the source of the Duddon. We fished a great part of the day with very sorry success, the rain pouring torrents, and long before we got home I was worn out with fatigue; and, if the good man had not carried me on his back, I must have lain down under the best shelter I could find' (I. F.).

Published as one of the 'Ecclesiastical sketches', later known as 'Ecclesiastical sonnets'. This is a poem about entropy, the tendency of a closed system to break down.·

'CALM IS THE FRAGRANT AIR, AND LOTH TO LOSE'

Published as one of the 'Evening voluntaries'. Like several of Wordsworth's better poems in his later years, this is really a recollection of earlier work, *An Evening Walk* (1793), ll. 301–14: 'Sweet are the sounds that mingle from afar, / Heard by calm lakes, as peeps the folding star', etc.

22	*dor-hawk*	'The goatsucker or nightjar which feeds on moths, gnats, and dors or chaffers' (Thomas Pennant, *British Zoology*, 1768–70); the term 'dor', as in 'dor-beetle', applied to insects that made a distinct sound, such as a buzz or whirr, at night.

AIREY-FORCE VALLEY

'There are two roads by which this Lake [Ullswater] may be visited from Keswick. That which is adapted for travellers on horseback, or on foot, crosses the lower part of St John's Vale, and brings you through the valley and scattered village of Matterdale into Gowbarrow Park, unfolding at once a magnificent view of the two higher reaches of the lake. Airey Force thunders down the Ghyll or Gill, on the left, at a small distance from the road' (*Guide through . . . the Lakes*). 'Force' is a dialect word for waterfall.

EXTEMPORE EFFUSION UPON THE DEATH OF JAMES HOGG

'These verses were written extempore, immediately after reading a notice of the Ettrick Shepherd's death in the Newcastle paper' (I. F.).

2	*the stream of Yarrow*	Wordsworth and Dorothy had not visited the river Yarrow, a stream of famed beauty, on their first Scottish tour (1803), but in 1814 the river was shown to Wordsworth by James Hogg. Dorothy did not accompany her brother to Scotland on this later trip.
4	*The Ettrick Shepherd*	James Hogg (1770–1835), a.k.a. the Ettrick Shepherd after Ettrick Forest where he was born, 'was undoubtedly a man of original genius, but of coarse manners and low and offensive opinions' (I. F.). His death appears to have sparked in Wordsworth the realization that seven poets, all but one younger than himself, had died between 1832 and the time of writing, November 1835.
8	*the border minstrel*	Sir Walter Scott (1771–1832): his first major publication had been an edition of Scots ballads, *Minstrelsy of the Scottish Border* (1802–3).
15	*every mortal power*	In spite of the quarrel of 1810–12 (see p. 12), Wordsworth here pays tribute to Coleridge as a lifelong friend and mentor. They had gone to Belgium, Germany, and Holland together in 1828. Coleridge died in 1834.

19	*Lamb*	Charles Lamb (1775–1834), a school-friend of Coleridge's at Christ's Hospital, had died six months after Coleridge, in December 1834. He acquired a largely posthumous reputation as an essayist after his death. In his lifetime he was valued by his friends for his gentle humour. 'Frolic' is a Wordsworthian pun on his name.
31	*Crabbe*	George Crabbe was a narrative poet in the social-realistic vein initiated by John Langhorne (1735–79) and continued by Cowper; see the latter's tale of 'Crazy Kate' in *The Task* (1785). Wordsworth met Crabbe only upon occasion: 'After being silent for more than twenty years, he again applied himself to poetry, upon the spur of applause he received from the periodical publications of the day, as he himself tells us in one of his prefaces. Is it not to be lamented that a man who was so conversant with permanent truth, and whose writings are so valuable an acquisition to our country's literature, should have *required* an impulse from such a quarter?' (I. F.). This is a strange remark to come from Wordsworth, who had been sitting on *The Prelude* for more than thirty years at the time of writing. Maybe he required an 'impulse' from the periodicals.
39	*her who, ere her summer faded*	Felicia Hemans (1793–1835). 'Mrs Hemans was unfortunate as a poetess in being obliged by circumstances to write for money, and that so frequently and so much, that she was compelled to look out for subjects wherever she could find them, and to

238

write as expeditiously as possible' (I. F.). She is remembered, if at all, for her poem 'Casablanca': 'The boy stood on the burning deck / Whence all but he had fled . . .'.

41-2	*old romantic sorrows, / For slaughtered youth or love- lorn maid*	A reference to Hogg's tales in verse, such as 'The Pilgrims of the Sun': 'She only felt a shivering throb, / A pang defined that may not be; / And up she rose, a naked form, / More lightsome, pure and fair than he'.

Appendix

LINES WRITTEN IN EARLY SPRING

'Composed while I was sitting by the side of a brook that runs down from the Comb, in which stands the village of Alford, through the grounds of Alfoxden' (I. F.).

LUCY GRAY

Not one of the canonical 'Lucy' poems but related to them and written at Goslar during Wordsworth's German sojourn. 'It was founded on a circumstance told me by my sister, of a little girl who, not far from Halifax in Yorkshire, was bewildered in a snowstorm' (I. F.).

'SHE WAS A PHANTOM OF DELIGHT'

Written after the Scottish tour of 1803. 'The germ of this poem was four lines composed as a part of the verses on the Highland Girl' (I. F). Wordsworth had his wife, Mary, in mind: 'She came, no more a phantom to adorn / A moment, but an inmate of the heart' (*The Prelude*, '1850', XIV, ll. 268-9).

22	*The very pulse of the machine*	'At the return of the morning, by the powerful influence of light, the pulse of nature becomes more active, and the

universal vibration of life insensibly and irresistibly moves the wondrous machine' (William Bartram, *Travels through North and South Carolina*, 2nd edn, 1784); in Wordsworth's sense, the word 'machine' is a term applied to the human frame as a combination of several parts.

'MY HEART LEAPS UP WHEN I BEHOLD'

'Friday [26 March 1802] . . . While I was getting into bed he wrote the Rainbow' (D. W., *Grasmere*).

| 7 | *The child is father of the man* | 'We are ungrateful to others only when they have ceased to look back on their former selves with joy and tenderness. They exist in fragments' (Coleridge, *The Friend*, Essay V, 1809, 1818); Coleridge is using the word 'ungrateful' in its secondary sense of 'disagreeable'. |

'I WANDERED LONELY AS A CLOUD'

'Thursday 15th [April 1802] . . . When we were in the woods beyond Gowbarrow Park . . . I never saw daffodils so beautiful, they grew among the mossy stones about and about them, some rested their heads upon these stones as on a pillow for weariness and the rest tossed and reeled and danced and seemed as if they verily laughed with the wind that blew upon them over the Lake, they looked so gay ever glancing ever changing' (D. W., *Grasmere*).

| 15–16 | *They flash upon that inward eye / Which is the bliss of solitude* | 'The two best lines in it are by Mary [Wordsworth]' (I. F.). |

'Written immediately after my return from France to London, when I could not but be struck, as here described, with the vanity and parade of our own country, especially in great towns and cities, as contrasted with the quiet, and I may say the desolation, that the revolution had produced in France' (I. F.).

1	*Milton*	John Milton (1609–74), the great poet of the Puritan Revolution, for whose character and work Wordsworth had an especial regard: 'that sanctity of civil and religious duty, with which the tyranny of Charles the First was struggled against . . . that circle of glorious patriots' (Wordsworth, letter to *The Friend*, 14 December 1809).

ODE: INTIMATIONS OF IMMORTALITY FROM RECOLLECTIONS OF EARLY CHILDHOOD

'This was composed during my residence at Town-End, Grasmere; two years at least passed between the writing of the four first stanzas and the remaining part . . . To that dream-like vividness and splendour which invest objects of sight in childhood, every one, I believe, if he would look back, could bear testimony . . . Accordingly, a pre-existent state has entered into the popular creeds of many nations; and, among all persons acquainted with classic literature is known as an ingredient in Platonic philosophy' (I. F.).

Epigraph:	*'Pauló majora canamus'*	'Let us sing a loftier strain' (Virgil, *Eclogues* IV i).
58–65	*Our birth is but a sleep and a forgetting / . . . God, who is our home*	'Happy those early days when I / Shined in my angel-infancy. / Before I understood this place / Appointed for my second race, / Or taught my mind to fancy ought / But a white, celestial thought, / When yet I had not walked above / A mile, or two, from my first love, / And looking back (at that short

		space,) / Could see a glimpse of his bright face' (Henry Vaughan, 1622–95, 'The Retreat').
85	*Behold the child*	'A little child, a limber elf, / Singing, dancing to itself / . . . Makes such a vision to the sight / As fills a father's eyes with light' (Coleridge, 'Christabel', 1797).
103	*'humorous stage'*	'I do not here upon this hum'rous stage / Bring my transformed verse, apparelléd / With others' passions / . . . But here present thee, only modelled / In this poor frame, the form of mine own heart' (Samuel Daniel, 'To the right worthy and judicious . . . Fulke Greville', *Musophilus*, 1599).
117–19	*Thou, over whom thy immortality / Broods like the day . . . / A presence which is not to be put by*	'If we look back upon the days of childhood, we shall find that the time is not in remembrance when, with respect to our own individual being, the mind was without this assurance' ['that some part of our nature is imperishable'] (Wordsworth, 'Essay upon Epitaphs', 1810).
120–3	*To whom the grave / Is but a lonely bed / . . . A place of thought where we in waiting lie*	'Thursday 29th [April 1802] . . . We then went to John's Grove, sat a while at first. Afterwards William lay, and I lay in the trench under the fence – he with his eyes shut and listening to the waterfalls and the birds . . . He thought that it would be as sweet to lie so in the grave, to hear the peaceful sounds of the earth and just to know that our dear friends were near' (D. W., *Grasmere*).
144–8	*obstinate questionings / . . . Blank misgivings of a*	'I remember Mr Wordsworth saying that, at a particular stage of his mental progress, he used to be frequently so

	creature / Moving about in worlds not realized	rapt into an unreal transcendental world of ideas that the external world seemed no longer to exist in relation to him and he had to reconvince himself of its existence by clasping a tree, or something that happened to be near him' (R. P. Graves, quoted by Christopher Wordsworth, nephew of the poet, in his *Memoirs of William Wordsworth*, 1851, vol. II, p. 480).
149–50	*our mortal Nature / Did tremble like a guilty thing*	'It started like a guilty thing / Upon a fearful summons' (Shakespeare, *Hamlet*, 1601, I.i. 148–9).

Prose

PREFACE TO *LYRICAL BALLADS*

17–18	*a friend who furnished me with the poems of 'The Ancient Mariner'*	Samuel Taylor Coleridge.
27	*Several of my friends are anxious for the success of these poems*	presumably Coleridge.
63	*in the age of Catullus, Terence, and Lucretius*	These Roman poets are contrasted with those of a later age deemed inferior, Statius and Claudian. Similarly, Wordsworth contrasts the age of Shakespeare with that of Cowley, Dryden, and Pope.
107	*a far more philosophical language*	a language capable of denoting all the concepts formulated by mankind; Wordsworth is here following the philosopher David Hartley (1705–57).
112–3	*fickle appetites of their own creation*	At this point Wordsworth appended a footnote: 'It is worthwhile here to observe that the affecting parts of Chaucer are almost always expressed in language pure and universally intel-

ligible even to this day': Wordsworth here follows a judgement of Spenser, that Chaucer is a 'well of English undefiled'. This is in contradistinction to Dryden, who found him a 'rough diamond' and his verse 'not harmonious'.

211	*frantic novels*	The 'gothic' novels of such writers as Horace Walpole (1717–97) and Anne Radcliffe whose *Mysteries of Udolpho* (1794) is a prototype of horror stories up to the video shockers of our own time. The 'stupid German tragedies' are probably those of August von Kotzebue (1761–1819) whom Jane Austen was to pillory in *Mansfield Park* (1814).
284	*a short composition of Gray*	Thomas Gray (1716–71) had composed odes in irregular metres and exalted diction. He wrote in a letter to Richard West, the subject of the poem Wordsworth quotes, 'the language of the age is never the language of poetry'. Gray is now mostly remembered for his 'Elegy in a country churchyard', also thought to be in memory of Richard West.
318	*differing even in degree*	There follows at this point a footnote: 'I here use the word "poetry" (though against my own judgement) as opposed to the word "prose", and synonymous with metrical composition. But much confusion has been introduced into criticism by this contradistinction of poetry and prose, instead of the more philosophical one of poetry and matter of fact, or science. The only strict antithesis to prose is metre; nor is this, in truth, a *strict* antithesis; because lines and passages of

metre so naturally occur in writing prose, that it would be scarcely possible to avoid them, even were it desirable.'

319	*such as angels weep*	*Paradise Lost* (1667), I.l.620.
391	*'Clarissa Harlowe'*	Nowadays usually called *Clarissa*; a novel by Samuel Richardson (1689–1761), remarkable for its pathos.
392	*'The Gamester'*	A tragedy by Edward Moore (1712–57), concerned with the vice of gambling.
420	*similitude in dissimilitude*	'differences among things where resemblance prevails, and resemblances where difference prevails' (Henry Home, Lord Kames, *Elements of Criticism*, 1762).
428–30	*poetry is the spontaneous overflow of powerful feelings: it takes its origin from emotion recollected in tranquillity*	This, Wordsworth's central tenet in criticism, has parallels in 'Ueber Bürgers Gedichte' by Friedrich Schiller (1754–1805) and Coleridge's *Notebooks*: 'recalling of passion in tranquillity'. It is important to remember that Wordsworth's practice far excels his theory.
462	*Pope*	Alexander Pope (1688–1744), leading poet of the 'classical' school in Britain; seen by Coleridge as well as Wordsworth as being wedded to form.
517	*'Dr Johnson's stanza'*	Wordsworth may have found this in *The London Magazine*, April 1785. Samuel Johnson (1709–84), poet and critic much influenced by Pope, strongly opposed the Romantic tendencies of his day, including the interest in old ballads.
523	*'The Babes in the Wood'*	*sc.* 'The Children in the Wood'; an anonymous ballad printed by Thomas Percy in his *Reliques of English Poetry* (1765), itself an influential document of the Romantic Revolution.

| 545 | *Why take pains to prove an ape is not a Newton...?* | 'Superior beings, when of late they saw / A mortal man unfold all Nature's law, / Admired such wisdom in an earthly shape, / And showed a Newton as we show an ape'. Sir Isaac Newton (1642–1727) was a renowned mathematician credited with formulating the Laws of Gravitation: 'The marble index of a mind for ever / Voyaging through strange seas of thought alone' *The Prelude* '1850', III, ll. 62–3). |
| 569 | *Sir Joshua Reynolds* | Reynolds (1723–92) was a portrait painter of great eminence in his time; a friend of Johnson, and author of *Discourses on Art*. |

APPENDIX TO PREFACE TO *LYRICAL BALLADS*

98	*Pope's 'Messiah'*	This is an imitation of Virgil's 'Pollio', named after the nobleman to whom it is dedicated. It is an eclogue, or pastoral poem, welcoming the birth of a male child as signalling a new age.
99	*Prior*	Matthew Prior (1664–1721); Wordsworth alludes to his 'Charity. A Paraphrase on the Thirteenth Chapter of the First Epistle to the Corinthians'.
102–3	*Dr Johnson ... the prudent ant*	The poem is called 'The Ant' and first appeared in Anna Williams, *Miscellanies in Verse and Prose* (1766). It is important to remember that Johnson was also the author of 'The Vanity of Human Wishes'.
127	*Cowper's verses*	William Cowper (1731–1800), author of *The Task*, a discursive poem incorporating some memorable 'spots of time', that considerably influenced *The Prelude*.
148–9	*The epithet 'church-going' applied to a bell*	'The church-inviting bells' delightful chime' (Wordsworth, 'Guilt and sorrow').